"An excellent description of perfectionism and its self-sabotaging disadvantages. Presents many efficient and effective cognitive-behavioral methods for dealing with and minimizing this affliction. Quite practical and thorough—but nicely flexible and unperfectionistic!"

—Albert Ellis, Ph.D., president of the Albert Ellis Institute in New York City and author of *A Guide to Rational Living*

"All of us know someone who is a perfectionist and most of us have joked about it at one time or another. For some it can be a useful trait that ensures some organization in a disorganized world. But for those individuals coping with too much perfectionism, it can be a curse that takes the pleasure out of life and in some cases can lead to severe anxiety disorders. Now two leading mental health practitioners and clinical scientists provide up-to-date, scientifically validated skills for overcoming perfectionism and regaining control of one's life. This long overdue book should relieve much suffering and enhance functioning for the millions of individuals dealing with excessive perfectionism."

—David H. Barlow, Ph.D., professor of psychology and director of the Center for Anxiety and Related Disorders at Boston University

"*When Perfect Isn't Good Enough* surpasses any of the other books on perfectionism in quality and scope. Antony and Swinson have synthesized what we know about perfectionism and used it to create the first well-integrated approach to reduce the suffering caused by it. The chapters clearly define perfectionism and provide concrete steps to master this demon. Final chapters focus on how perfectionism can manifest itself in other disorders, demonstrating how pernicious this phenomenon can be—and why such a book is so essential. This book will be invaluable to people suffering from perfectionism and to the therapists trying to help them."

—Randy O. Frost, Ph.D., professor of psychology at Smith College in Northampton, MA

"*When Perfect Isn't Good Enough* is an excellent source for people looking to adjust their standards and expectations and, by so doing, increase the joy in their lives. It is easy to read, filled with solid advice, and based on the best scientific research. Unlike most other self-help books, the many exercises suggested by the authors provide the reader with the tools to put these words into action. Antony and Swinson have produced a thorough and systemic manual to lead the perfectionist out of the misery of depression, anger, worry, and social anxiety, and into the promised land of realistic self-evaluation, self-esteem, and positive interpersonal relations. Bravo!"

—Richard Heimberg, Ph.D., Adult Anxiety Clinic in the department of psychology at Temple University in Philadelphia, PA

When Perfect Isn't Good Enough

— SECOND EDITION —

Strategies for Coping with Perfectionism

MARTIN M. ANTONY, PH.D.
RICHARD P. SWINSON, MD

New Harbinger Publications, Inc.

Publisher's Note

Distributed in Canada by Raincoast Books

Copyright © 2009 by Martin M. Antony and Richard P. Swinson
New Harbinger Publications, Inc.
5674 Shattuck Avenue
Oakland, CA 94609
www.newharbinger.com

Mixed Sources
Product group from well-managed
forests and other controlled sources
www.fsc.org Cert no. SW-COC-002283
© 1996 Forest Stewardship Council
FSC

Acquired by Tesilya Hanauer; Cover design by Amy Shoup;
Edited by Carole Honeychurch

Library of Congress Cataloging-in-Publication Data
Antony, Martin M.
  When perfect isn't good enough : strategies for coping with perfectionism / Martin
M. Antony and Richard P. Swinson. -- 2nd ed.
       p. cm.
Includes bibliographical references (p.   ).
ISBN-13: 978-1-57224-559-4 (pbk. : alk. paper)
ISBN-10: 1-57224-559-X (pbk. : alk. paper)
1. Perfectionism (Personality trait) I. Swinson, Richard P. II. Title.
BF698.35.P47A58 2009
158.1--dc22
                              2008039802

11 10 09

10 9 8 7 6 5 4 3 2 1   First printing

For Cynthia
—MMA

For Carolyn
—RPS

Contents

PART 1
Understanding Perfectionism

CHAPTER 1

CHAPTER 2

CHAPTER 3

CHAPTER 4

PART 2
Strategies for Overcoming Perfectionism

CHAPTER 5

CHAPTER 6

PART 3
Working with Specific Problems and Perfectionism

PART 4
What Next?

Acknowledgments

We are grateful to our editors at New Harbinger Publications for their invitation to revise the first edition of this book and for their support and help throughout the process of bringing the project to completion. Also, thanks to Valerie Vorstenbosch and Heather Hood for their assistance in researching some of the material that went into this revised addition. Finally, thank you to Lizabeth Roemer and Josh Bartok for their helpful comments on an early draft of chapter 9.

Introduction

THE PURPOSE OF THIS BOOK

When we began our work on the first edition of this book, we struggled to decide on exactly what the scope should be. It was difficult to choose which aspects of perfectionism to focus on, because the term "perfectionist" can be applied to many different types of people. Consider the following examples:

In an interview with Oprah Winfrey, Martha Stewart described herself as a "maniacal perfectionist" (Winfrey 2000). In fact, according to a 2004 article in *Forbes*, Ms. Stewart allegedly once threatened to fire her stockbroker because she didn't like his company's telephone "hold" music (Ackman 2004).

People who worked with director James Cameron on the blockbuster film *Titanic* often described him in interviews as being a perfectionist. They told stories of how he often lost his temper when things didn't go his way. In fact, Cameron's apparent temper, stemming from his insistence that his film crew meet his high standards, was the subject of many stories in the media around the time of the film's release.

In 2003, French chef Bernard Loiseau committed suicide shortly after his restaurant's rating in the *Michelin Red Guide* was reduced from 19/20 to 17/20. The story is chronicled in Rudolph Chelminski's 2005 book, "*The Perfectionist: Life and Death in Haute Cuisine.*"

In her 1995 biography, *Movement Never Lies: An Autobiography*, Canadian ballet dancer Karen Kain described herself as a perfectionist.

Although she had established herself as one of the most respected dancers in the world, she occasionally had bouts of depression, stemming from self-imposed standards that she felt she rarely met.

The character of Niles Crane from TV's *Frasier* can be described as a perfectionist. He sees everyone other than himself as inferior in some way, and he goes to great lengths to make sure that things are correct—even the graffiti in the Café Nervosa toilets (which he corrected with a red pen). Other TV perfectionists include Monica Gellar (*Friends*), Bree Van De Kamp (*Desperate Housewives*), and Felix Unger (*The Odd Couple*).

Although all of these individuals can be described as perfectionists, they are very different in the ways they express their perfectionism. In some of these examples, perfectionism is associated with anger; in others, perfectionism is associated with depression; and in some, perfectionism is associated with anxiety, inflexibility, or a lack of spontaneity. Despite these differences, the people in each of these examples share an important quality. In each case, there appears to be strict standards or expectations for oneself or others that either cannot be met or can only be met at a great cost.

Perfectionism is often associated with certain psychological problems, including excessive anger, depression, anxiety, body image problems, and obsessive-compulsive behaviors. In fact, it's hard to imagine a comprehensive book on perfectionism that doesn't touch on these areas. Therefore, in writing this book, we chose to focus on methods of dealing with perfectionistic thoughts and behaviors in general, as well as perfectionistic thoughts and behaviors that are associated with specific psychological problems.

In part 1 of this book, we discuss general aspects of perfectionism, including the nature and impact of perfectionism and the role of thoughts and behaviors in maintaining perfectionism. Part 2 provides specific instructions on how to conduct a self-assessment of your perfectionism and how to use specific strategies to overcome perfectionistic thinking and related behaviors. In part 2, we have added a new chapter on acceptance-based strategies. In part 3 we discuss the association between perfectionism and specific psychological problems (such as depression, anxiety, and so on). These chapters will be helpful if you experience some of these issues. Part 4 includes a new chapter on preventing your perfectionism from returning. The completely updated "Further Readings" list provides suggestions for those who want more in-depth information about the various topics covered in this book.

DO THE STRATEGIES IN THIS BOOK WORK?

When we wrote the first edition of this book (published in 1998), there was almost no research available on the treatment of perfectionism. There were well-established treatments available for the types of problems that are typically associated with perfectionism (like anxiety, depression, body-image issues, obsessive-compulsive problems, and so on), but not specifically for perfectionism. That has all changed in recent years. In 2007, we published a study showing that treating social anxiety using the types of strategies described in this book led to changes not only in anxiety about social situations, but also reductions in perfectionism (Ashbaugh et al. 2007). Following treatment for social anxiety, participants in our study reported being less concerned about making mistakes and were less likely to doubt whether their actions were correct. However, this study didn't include a treatment focused specifically on perfectionism—rather the treatment was focused on anxiety.

In another study, Riley et al. (2007) used strategies that were similar to those in this book to provide ten sessions of treatment designed to help people who suffer with high levels of perfectionism. In this study, the symptoms of 75 percent of the participants were significantly improved following treatment. In fact, scores on the main measure of perfectionism used in this study decreased by 46 percent for those who received the treatment, compared to only 7.6 percent for individuals who were on a wait-list but didn't actually receive any treatment.

In a third study, Australian researchers (Pleva and Wade 2007) compared a pure self-help treatment for perfectionism (the first edition of this book, actually) to a self-help treatment that included this book as well as brief contact with a therapist (eight fifty-minute sessions). Participants in both treatments experienced a reduction in perfectionism, though people did best when the book was combined with guidance from a therapist. For example, 40 percent of individuals in the pure self-help treatment and 46 percent of individuals in the guided self-help treatment reported a significant reduction in concern over making mistakes.

In summary, there is now emerging evidence that the strategies described in this book are helpful—both on their own and when combined with treatment by a professional therapist who has experience in using these methods.

HOW TO USE THIS BOOK

We recommend that you read all of the chapters in parts 1, 2, and 4. In part 3, you may wish to select chapters that are most relevant to you and read them thoroughly. It can also be helpful to read the other chapters, as you may recognize issues that you were not aware you had.

Many of the chapters include exercises designed to change perfectionistic beliefs and behaviors. On its own, just reading this book is unlikely to lead to a dramatic reduction in your perfectionistic thoughts and behaviors. To see real changes, it will be important to actually use the strategies described. This book isn't a replacement for obtaining help from a qualified mental health professional, and you may wish to seek professional help for your perfectionism and associated problems. The chapters in part 3 describe treatments that have been effective for the particular clinical problems that are sometimes related to perfectionism. In addition, chapter 6 includes ideas regarding how to find additional help, if necessary.

Obtaining a Journal

The exercises in this book require you to answer specific questions and record relevant information. Therefore, it will be important to pick up a notebook or journal to use as you work through this book. Be sure to have your journal ready before beginning chapter 1. Alternatively, you can complete the exercises on a computer.

HOW NOT TO USE THIS BOOK

A warning: don't try to do everything in this book *perfectly*. We describe many more techniques, strategies, and ideas than you could possibly use effectively. It is best to choose a relatively small number of techniques and practice them until you can use them well. If you try to do everything that this book suggests, you probably won't benefit much from any of the strategies. Instead, pick and choose techniques that seem most relevant to your problem.

However, many of the strategies described in this book require repeated practice to be beneficial. If you find that a particular method is not working for you, you will need to decide whether to continue practicing that technique or to move on to another strategy. If a particular suggestion is not working for you, try not to react like a perfectionist. It will take time to notice changes. Giving yourself permission to fall short of meeting your high expectations while trying to overcome your perfectionism is a good first step toward learning to have more flexible and realistic expectations.

PART 1

Understanding Perfectionism

CHAPTER 1

What Is Perfectionism?

Most of us are bombarded with demands to improve our performance. From the time we are born, we must endure being evaluated and corrected by different people in our lives. When we first learn to talk, our parents correct our pronunciation. When we are young, we are taught by others how to walk, dress ourselves, hold our forks properly, refrain from putting our elbows on the table, wash behind our ears, and make our beds.

As we grow up, our behavior continues to be evaluated, criticized, corrected, and rewarded. In school and at home, we learn that to attain the approval of others we must achieve specific standards. When we make mistakes, there are often practical negative consequences. For example, as children, if our grades fall below a particular level, we may be criticized by our teachers, parents, and friends. Sometimes, privileges (for example, permission to talk on the telephone, go out with friends, or receive an allowance) are taken away until the level of performance is back where it is expected to be.

The frequent demands to meet and surpass established standards continue into adulthood. Many workplaces expect employees to improve their performance by accomplishing more in less time. Sales people are expected to break the previous years' sales records. Companies strive to be more successful than their competitors.

In addition to pressures from the outside, many people feel pressure from within to succeed or perform at a certain level. When cooking a meal for friends, it feels good to have your guests enjoy their meal. When trying to maintain a level of physical fitness, you may feel a sense of personal satisfaction when you have reached some new goal, such as being able to run a mile in less time.

The desire to improve your performance or to meet high standards is not the same as being perfectionistic. It is this very desire to meet certain goals that often helps you perform effectively in your environment. For example, students who don't care about their performance in school probably don't study as hard and are likely to perform more poorly than students who have high personal standards. If this pattern of performance becomes a habit, there are often negative consequences. Their grades are lower, and they may not be accepted into their preferred college or university. People at the top of their field, such as elite athletes, must also set high standards to achieve what they do. Without standards, people generally achieve less.

DEFINITIONS OF PERFECTIONISM

So, what is perfectionism, and how is it different from a healthy desire to achieve high standards? As a starting point, let's consider a dictionary definition. The online version of the *Merriam Webster Dictionary* defines perfectionism as "a disposition to regard anything short of perfection as unacceptable." In contrast, professionals who study perfectionism tend to define the term in more detail. For example, in his frequently cited article in *Psychology Today*, psychiatrist David Burns (1980) defined perfectionists as people "whose standards are high beyond reach or reason" and "who strain compulsively and unremittingly toward impossible goals and who measure their own worth entirely in terms of productivity and accomplishment." Burns pointed out that for these individuals, the drive to do well can actually impair performance.

Multidimensional Definitions of Perfectionism

Recently, psychologists have begun to define perfectionism as a multidimensional concept (Flett and Hewitt 2002). In other words, researchers increasingly view perfectionism as consisting of several different components or aspects. For example, Canadian psychologists Gordon Flett and Paul Hewitt have identified three main types of perfectionism:

self-oriented perfectionism, other-oriented perfectionism, and socially prescribed perfectionism.

Self-oriented perfectionism is a tendency to have standards for yourself that are unrealistically high and impossible to attain. These standards are self-imposed and tend to be associated with self-criticism and an inability to accept your own mistakes and faults. When self-oriented perfectionism is combined with negative life events or perceived failure, it can lead to difficulties with depression.

Other-oriented perfectionism is a tendency to demand that others meet your unrealistically high standards. People who are other-oriented perfectionists are often unable to delegate tasks to others for fear of being disappointed by a less-than-perfect performance of the job. Other-oriented perfectionists may also have problems with excessive anger, relationship stress, and other difficulties related to their high expectations of others.

Socially prescribed perfectionism is a tendency to assume that others have expectations of you that are impossible to meet. Socially prescribed perfectionists also believe that to gain approval from others, these high standards must be met. Unlike self-oriented perfectionism, in which expectations are self-imposed, in socially prescribed perfectionism, the high standards are believed to be imposed by others. Socially prescribed perfectionism can lead to feelings of anger (at people who are perceived to have unrealistically high standards), depression (if high standards are not met), or social anxiety (fear of being judged by other people).

In addition to the three dimensions of perfectionism proposed by Hewitt and Flett, psychologist Randy Frost and his colleagues have also been influential with respect to increasing the understanding of the multidimensional aspects of perfectionism (Frost et al. 1990). However, unlike Hewitt and Flett, Frost and colleagues proposed six different dimensions of perfectionism, including tendencies to be overly concerned about making mistakes, to have overly high personal standards, to doubt whether one has done things correctly, to have an extreme need for organization, to have parents with unreasonably high expectations, and to have parents who are overly critical.

In summary, there are several different ways in which perfectionism can be defined. Some researchers define perfectionism as a single concept or dimension. Others view perfectionism as consisting of several related dimensions. Regardless of which view is taken, most definitions appear to share several features that can be summarized as follows:

- People who are perfectionistic tend to have standards and expectations that are very difficult or impossible to meet.

- Although having high standards is often helpful, perfectionism is associated with having standards that are so high that they actually interfere with performance.

- Perfectionism is often associated with other problems, such as anxiety and depression.

APPROPRIATELY HIGH STANDARDS VERSUS PERFECTIONISTIC BELIEFS

Most people have strong opinions about how they should perform and about how certain things should be done. Although some standards are helpful, other standards may not be. For example, a person who has to speak in front of groups may have the belief: "It is important to do an excellent job." Is this a perfectionistic belief or just an appropriate belief that leads to improved performance in public speaking situations? Unfortunately, people are often not very good at assessing the accuracy of their own beliefs about their standards, because most of us assume that our beliefs are correct.

The appropriateness of a belief about standards for performance depends on several factors: the excessiveness of the standard (for example, can this goal be met?), the accuracy of the belief (for instance, is it true that this standard must be met?), the costs and benefits of imposing the standard (for example, does it help me to have the belief or standard?), and the flexibility of the standard or belief (for instance, am I able to adjust my standards and change my beliefs when necessary?).

Consider an example. Most people believe that it's important to wash regularly and to keep clean. Is this a perfectionistic belief or realistic high standard? Well, for most people, the standards for cleanliness are defined in a way that can be met with little effort, and, for most people, keeping clean has more benefits than costs. For example, with minimal effort, keeping clean makes it more likely that others will want to spend time with you. Finally, most people are also able to be flexible regarding their standards for cleanliness. Surgeons may raise the standard and wash their hands more carefully before doing surgery, whereas people who are camping in the wilderness may lower their standards and tolerate being less clean.

In contrast, a person who has perfectionistic thoughts about cleanliness may have excessive beliefs that are inaccurate, inflexible, and cause more harm than good. For example, in our clinic we see some individuals with obsessive-compulsive disorder who wash their hands hundreds of times each day, to the point where their hands are red and sore from scrubbing. This repetitive washing may be triggered by perfectionistic beliefs about avoiding contamination from germs, toxins, and other substances. However, this level of washing doesn't reduce the risk of becoming ill (compared to a more moderate amount of washing), and the person may actually be more at risk for infections (from cracking skin on their hands, and so on). For these individuals, the excessive frequency of washing often takes up hours each day and can interfere with all aspects of functioning, including work and social relationships.

This may seem like an extreme example of perfectionistic behavior. For more subtle perfectionistic beliefs and behaviors, it may be difficult to decide whether the reactions are excessive, but the same principles apply. You must first determine whether the beliefs and standards are excessive, accurate, helpful, and flexible. We will return to the issue of how to determine whether beliefs are excessively perfectionistic in later chapters.

The main point to consider here is that the more inflexible your beliefs are and the more situations in which you have inflexible opinions, the more likely you are to run into problems. This is particularly true in situations where your beliefs are arbitrary and subjective rather than based on facts or hard evidence. For example, the belief that one should not drink and drive is consistent with statistics showing that more than half of automobile accidents involve alcohol. On the other hand, an inflexible belief that people should only listen to classical music and that all other types of music are inferior might cause problems if you are surrounded by other people who are not classical music lovers.

PERFECTIONISM AS A PERSONALITY TRAIT

Personality traits are stable characteristics that make people who they are. The term "stable" implies that personality traits affect your behavior across situations and over time. For years, psychologists have debated about the exact number of basic personality traits. Earlier, researchers tended to view personality as being comprised of many different personality traits. The exact number of traits differed from theory to theory, although in some cases, the number of traits specified was in the hundreds. These traits included such dimensions as perfectionism, happiness, honesty, aggressiveness, anxiety, creativity, ambition, and just about any other dimension imaginable.

More recently, many psychologists have come to believe that there are relatively few basic personality dimensions on which personality should be measured. One view of personality dimensions that has been supported by extensive research is that proposed by Robert McCrae and Paul Costa (2003), called the "Big Five Theory." According to this view, there are five main dimensions on which personality can be measured: *neuroticism* (the extent to which people are insecure and anxious versus the extent to which they are calm and secure), *extraversion* (the extent to which people are sociable and talkative versus the extent to which they are quiet and reserved), *openness* (the extent to which people are curious and imaginative versus the extent to which they are conventional and unimaginative), *agreeableness* (the extent to which people are good natured and trusting versus the extent to which they are rude, suspicious, and irritable), and *conscientiousness* (the extent to which people are organized, reliable, and scrupulous versus the extent to which they are unreliable and careless).

According to researchers who study personality theories such as the Big Five model, the specific ways in which people's behaviors can be described along the five basic personality dimensions determine the precise personality composition that makes each person unique. This is similar to the way in which three primary colors (red, blue, and yellow) can be combined in different ways to produce all the different colors that we see.

A number of the big five dimensions may contribute to perfectionism and related behaviors. For example, high levels of conscientiousness have been found to be associated with higher levels of self-oriented perfectionism (Hill, McIntire, and Bacharach 1997). However, there is a clear need for more research on the relationship between perfectionism and the big five dimensions. It's possible that high conscientiousness may lead a person to be overly concerned with organization, order, cleanliness, and following rules. Neuroticism may contribute to the anxiety and poor self-esteem that is sometimes seen in perfectionists. Not being open may make it difficult for perfectionistic individuals to view situations in new and flexible ways. Finally, perfectionistic individuals who aren't very agreeable may also be harder on others who do not meet their high standards.

Of course, personality traits alone don't determine our behavior. Behavior is the result of a complex interaction between personality traits and the situations in which we find ourselves. You may be a perfectionist in some situations and contexts but not others.

AREAS PRONE TO PERFECTIONISM

Below are some of the common areas in life in which unreasonably high standards can lead to problems:

Performance at Work or School

Some people tend to be particularly perfectionistic in their work, setting overly strict standards for their own performance or for the performance of their coworkers. For example, a construction worker who is very concerned about having every measurement perfect may spend too much time measuring and re-measuring, only to find that jobs are never completed on time. Similarly, supervisors who have very strict standards regarding the time their staff should arrive at work may frequently become angry and frustrated when employees arrive for work a few minutes late. Finally, a student who believes that any grade that is less than an A is unacceptable may feel depressed for a week or more after receiving a B on a test or a paper.

Neatness and Aesthetics

People who are perfectionistic with respect to neatness and cleaning often spend so much time cleaning that little time is left for other activities. Sometimes people can have very rigid beliefs about what looks good and may have difficulty allowing someone else to see things differently. Perfectionism can interfere with a person's ability to get along with roommates or partners who don't meet these standards for cleanliness or aesthetics. For example, individuals who believe that the house should be vacuumed twice daily may have difficulty convincing their housemates to share equally in the labor, especially if the housemates believe that vacuuming once every week or so is enough.

Organization and Ordering

Perfectionism can be associated with a need to have things organized or ordered in a particular way. For example, some people might need to have all their clothes folded and stored in a particular order (for instance, according to color), or they might spend hours each day making and revising lists of things that need to be done.

Writing

Writing can be difficult for some people who are perfectionistic. Individuals who fear making mistakes when writing may take a long time to fill out forms, write letters, finish term papers and exams, or complete other written work. They may procrastinate because the process of writing feels like torture.

Speaking

People who are perfectionistic with respect to speaking are often very self-conscious about how they speak and often worry about mispronouncing words or saying things incorrectly. Or, they may have overly rigid standards for others and feel compelled to correct people when they perceive that a mistake has been made, no matter how trivial.

Physical Appearance

For some people, perfectionism is focused on physical appearance. For example, people may hold perfectionistic standards about weight and body image, hair loss, and even their clothing. For example, one person who was seen in our clinic spent hours getting dressed in the morning. She would try on many different outfits, searching for the one that looked "just right." As a result, she was usually late for work.

People can also hold perfectionistic beliefs about the appearance of other individuals. On the TV show *Seinfeld*, the character of Jerry Seinfeld was never able to find a perfect partner with whom to settle down. Many of the women he dated had something "wrong" with them from his perspective, including hands that were too big, a voice that was too low, and a laugh that he perceived as unattractive. If his standards had been more flexible, Jerry might have found the "right" partner before the show finally ended in the spring of 1998.

Health and Personal Cleanliness

Sometimes health can be the focus of perfectionistic behavior. Some people become very rigid about what they do for fear of compromising their health. This may include being very particular about foods eaten (for example, never eating anything containing fat), compulsively exercising, or avoiding computer screens and other devices that give off radiation. Health-obsessed perfectionists may visit doctors frequently to check out unusual symptoms or to have unnecessary medical tests administered. Perfectionism can also cause some people to wash themselves excessively or to avoid touching anything that might be viewed as contaminated (for example, toilet seats, money, people's hands, and so on).

THE ORIGINS OF PERFECTIONISM

Where does perfectionism come from? Is it learned through your experiences? Is it genetically inherited, like eye or hair color? Very little research has been done in this area, so a definitive answer will have to await further study. Nevertheless, we can speculate about the causes of perfectionism based on what we know about the origins of other person-ality traits. It appears that both psychological factors (for instance, learn-ing) and biological factors (such as genetics) probably contribute to our personalities. This view has been supported by various studies examining the role of genetics and learning in the development of personality traits in general, and in the development of specific psychological problems like depression and anxiety. In this section, we discuss factors that may influence the development and maintenance of perfectionism, includ-ing biological influences, like genetics, and psychological influences, like reward and reinforcement, punishment, modeling, and information and instruction.

Genetic Influences

Numerous research studies have found that genetics plays a role in the development of various personality traits (Serretti et al. 2007), and recent evidence suggests that perfectionism is no exception (Tozzi et al. 2004). If perfectionism is partly inherited, does that mean that per-fectionism cannot be changed? Not at all. Genetics affects just about every aspect of who you are, including physical fitness, academic ability, depression, anxiety, and even your interests and hobbies. Yet exercise can have an enormous effect on fitness level. Likewise, specific types of psy-chological therapies can help people to overcome problems with anxiety and depression. So, while there may be a biological component to your perfectionism, you can still change the way you think or behave.

Reward and Reinforcement

As we discussed earlier, having high standards is often rewarded by society. For example, society reinforces your working hard at school. Doing well in high school generally leads to higher grades, praise from teachers and parents, and admission to better colleges and universities. Society also rewards physical attractiveness. Looking your best by dress-ing nicely and staying clean can result in others finding you more attrac-tive, which can, in turn, improve your chances of attracting a romantic partner and finding certain types of work.

You may frequently hear stories of successful artists (actors, painters, film directors, and so on) who are difficult to work with because they are perfectionists. Perhaps their perfectionism has been rewarded or reinforced by their success. Being rewarded for perfectionistic behavior may lead to the belief that if one isn't perfectionistic, one's work will be compromised and the final product will be inferior.

EXERCISE 1.1   How Reward and Reinforcement Have Contributed to Your Perfectionism

Are there ways in which you have been rewarded for being a perfectionist? Try to recall situations from your past as well as from your current life. Think back to when you were in school—were you rewarded for being a perfectionist (for example, did you do better in school when you set higher standards for yourself)? Think about your work—did you ever have a supervisor who was especially appreciative of the care and high standards that went into your job? What about when you were growing up at home—did your parents ever reward you with praise, gifts, or special privileges when you engaged in perfectionistic behavior? What about in your current life—do friends or family reinforce your perfectionistic behavior in subtle ways? As you recall ways in which you might have been rewarded or reinforced for perfectionistic behavior, record them in your journal.

Punishment

A second type of learning experience that can affect an individual's behavior is punishment. Punishment involves receiving some sort of negative consequence following a behavior. The overall effect of punishment is often to decrease the frequency of the punished behavior. Criticism from others is one form of punishment. For example, a child who is often criticized for doing things improperly (such as making a mess at the bathroom sink, not making the bed properly, mispronouncing words) may learn that it is always important to do things correctly.

Individuals who are in a relationship with a person who is never pleased with their partner's behavior (clothing, hairstyle, cooking, and so on), can develop a belief that it is very important to meet certain standards in order to please others. Other forms of punishment may include receiving low grades on a test, being laughed at by one's peers, losing money, getting reprimanded at work, or failing to be hired for a new job. In fact, any type of negative consequence that follows a behavior can be considered punishment. If individuals are punished excessively for making even small mistakes, they may be more likely to develop a rigid belief that it's very important not to make mistakes.

EXERCISE 1.2   How Punishment Has Contributed to Your Perfectionism

Can you recall times when you behaved in a particular way and were punished for your behavior? Did this tend to happen a lot when you were growing up? What about in your current life? Consider past and present situations at home, at school, and with friends. If you have frequently been punished for making mistakes, do some of these experiences appear to be responsible for triggering perfectionistic attitudes? Record your responses in your journal.

Modeling

Modeling involves learning to behave in certain ways by observing others. People can develop fears by watching other people who are afraid. People may start smoking, drinking alcohol, or using drugs after watching their peers use these substances. There also appears to be a relationship between watching violence on television and engaging in violent behavior, and that observing violent behavior can lead to more violence (Huesmann and Taylor 2006). All of these are examples of modeling. If people can learn these behaviors by observing others, it is possible that perfectionistic behaviors can develop in the same way. Many people who describe themselves as overly perfectionistic report that they grew up around others who had the same standards. As a result, there were opportunities to develop perfectionistic beliefs and behaviors by observing other family members, especially parents and older siblings.

> ## EXERCISE 1.3 How Modeling Has Contributed to Your Perfectionism
>
> Did you grow up with other people who are overly perfectionistic? If so, is it possible that modeling or observational learning contributed to your own perfectionistic attitudes? Can you think of ways in which your family members or other important people in your life are overly perfectionistic? Record your responses in your journal.

Information and Instruction

Another way in which people learn how to behave is through exposure to information in the media, talking to other people, or any other source of information. For example, people may learn to fear flying after hearing about various plane crashes in the news, even though flying is statistically one of the safest ways to travel.

How can information contribute to perfectionism? Consider the following case example. One individual who was seen in our clinic reported intense anxiety over completing her college term papers perfectly. She wanted to be accepted into graduate school, so it was very important that her grades be high. She worked endlessly on each paper and had prepared many rough drafts for each one. However, she was not quite able to complete her work and hand in the papers for fear that they would not be good enough. While exploring the origins of her perfectionistic behavior, it became clear that the client's parents may have had something to do with it. She was an only child, and her parents had very high expectations for her. From a very young age, the client's parents had told her that they expected her to attend medical school at a top university and to eventually win the Nobel prize in medicine. No other career paths were possible for her. The client was not even sure whether she wanted to attend medical school, but she didn't see herself as having any choice. Her parents were supporting her financially and had made their expectations clear since she was a child. In addition, the client truly believed that anything less than near-perfect performance in school was unacceptable. Of course, the price she was paying for this belief was not being able to complete her papers and not doing well in her courses.

Another patient from our clinic reported that her perfectionistic beliefs about physical attractiveness were related to constantly being bombarded by extremely attractive people in advertising, movies, magazines, and catalogs. This particular individual had very perfectionistic beliefs about the importance of being thin, having perfect hair, and dressing immaculately. Not only were her beliefs unrealistic, but they were also unhealthy, leading her to maintain a weight level lower than that recommended for her height and frame. Apparently, for this individual, constantly being confronted with models and actors that she perceived as looking "perfect" provided her with an unreachable and unrealistic standard. Not surprisingly, eating disorders such as anorexia nervosa are particularly common among models, dancers, and other professions where there is intense pressure to be thin.

EXERCISE 1.4 How Exposure to Information Has Contributed to Your Perfectionism

Being told repeatedly by parents, teachers, or partners, or even by society in general, that it is important that things are done in a particular way, or that it is essential that mistakes are not made, can contribute to perfectionism. Can you think of ways in which you were exposed to certain types of information or instruction that contributed to your perfectionistic beliefs and behaviors? Record your responses in your journal.

WHO IS TO BLAME FOR YOUR PERFECTIONISM?

Throughout this section, we have described negative experiences that may have contributed to your perfectionism. In many cases, the examples and illustrations may seem to imply that criticism from others (parents, teachers, and so on) plays a role. However, we are not suggesting that these other people are to blame for your problem. Nor are we suggesting that you are to blame for your perfectionism. Although your patterns of thinking and behaving, as well as the way others have behaved around you, may have contributed to the development of excessively high standards, there are many factors that interact to form a person's personality. In fact, it is preferable to completely sidestep the issue of who is to blame (because you will never know for sure exactly how the problem came to be) and focus instead on what can be done to change the problem.

IF YOU CAN'T FIGURE OUT WHERE YOUR PERFECTIONISM COMES FROM...

It's not a problem if you can't think of any particular experiences that may have contributed to your perfectionistic beliefs or behaviors. Although some people find it helpful to have an understanding of where their perfectionism may have come from, this understanding is not necessary for changing perfectionistic ways of thinking and doing things. In reality, the factors that may have initially caused you to become perfectionistic in certain situations may not be the same factors that maintain your perfectionism today.

CHAPTER 2

The Impact of Perfectionism

HOW PERFECTIONISM AFFECTS YOUR LIFE

Perfectionism is a problem when it leads to unhappiness or interferes with functioning. Having excessively high standards can affect almost any area of life, including health, diet, work, relationships, and interests. In this section, we focus on some of the main areas that are often impaired by perfectionism: work, home and school, relationships, and recreation.

Work, Home, and School

Many people define themselves, at least in part, by the work they do. Therefore, it is generally important to them to do a good job. A salesperson experiences a sense of satisfaction after making a large sale. A student feels good after receiving an outstanding grade on an exam or assignment. However, perfectionism may get in the way of your performance at work, home, or school. Even if your performance is not affected directly, perfectionism may still reduce your ability to enjoy your work or may influence the ways in which you treat others at work. Consider these examples.

Ronak is a high school history teacher who was overly concerned about doing a perfect job when the principal observed his class. He was so focused on how he was coming across that he was unable to focus on the content of his lecture. As a result, he actually made more mistakes than he might have if he was willing to settle for doing an "average" job on that particular day.

Heather was so concerned about doing well at her job as a government clerk that she felt very uncomfortable doing just about anything else. Although her workload was not especially heavy, she tended to avoid coworkers who wanted to talk during work hours, and she avoided taking breaks (including lunch). She was also the first person to arrive at work and the last person to leave. Although it was her intention to make a good impression at work, her behavior had the effect of alienating her coworkers, including her supervisor. In her case, excessively high standards for herself affected the impression that she made on others at work.

Frank was overly concerned about keeping the house clean, though you would never know it by looking at his house, which was extremely dirty and filled with clutter. He had grown up with parents who were extremely neat and tidy and expected the same of their children. His mother did not work outside of the home, and as far back as he could remember, she spent all of her day cleaning and re-cleaning the house. When he had moved into his own apartment after starting college, he had also cleaned excessively. Every room had to be spotless, and everything had to be put away at all times. After a few months, he began falling behind in his school work because of the time he spent cleaning. One day, after realizing that he could never keep the house clean enough to meet his standards, he stopped cleaning almost entirely. When he first came to our clinic, Frank hadn't done any cleaning for over six months. He feared that if he started, he would be unable to stop.

Valerie is a hospital administrator who had very high standards for her staff. She was completely intolerant of anyone arriving late for work, making small mistakes, or completing their work after a deadline—with no exceptions. She tended to respond to these behaviors with anger, and she had a reputation for being overly critical when completing performance evaluations of her staff. As a result, her staff stayed away from her as much as possible. They neither trusted her nor especially liked her. Staff turnover was significantly higher in her department, compared to similar departments in other hospitals. Her staff was unmotivated in their work because they knew that Valerie could never be satisfied, no matter how well they performed.

Ben, a student, was terrified of getting anything less than an A on his midterm history exam. He started studying two weeks before the exam. He put everything else aside, including friends, family, sleep, and even food. He ate irregularly and stayed up all night studying for three days before the exam. Although he knew the material well, he was very tired the day of the exam. He drank several cups of coffee to stay alert, but the caffeine only made him more anxious. Although he passed the exam, he did more poorly than he would have if he had studied a bit less and had enough sleep.

EXERCISE 2.1   The Effects of Perfectionism on Your Career, Studies, and Home Life

Are there ways in which perfectionism affects your work? Does it take you forever to get your home looking just right? Are you sometimes so focused on doing a good job that you actually perform more poorly? Does your perfectionism affect your enjoyment of work or school? Does perfectionism affect the people who work with you? Do small tasks take too long because you spend too much time trying to do them perfectly? Record your responses in your journal.

Relationships, Friendships, and Family Life

For many people, relationships have an all-important role in maintaining their sense of well-being. Important relationships may include those with romantic partners, friends, family members, coworkers, and even acquaintances and strangers. Perfectionism can have an enormous impact on relationships, sometimes even contributing to the end of a relationship.

Sometimes perfectionists are intolerant of people who do things differently than they do. This may be especially problematic in close relationships with family members or partners, and it can lead to any number of consequences. For example, if you are perfectionistic toward the people in your family, they may learn that the best way to please you is to not tell you things. They may assume (perhaps correctly) that what you don't know won't hurt them. An inability to communicate honestly in a relationship can compromise the quality of that relationship.

Perfectionistic standards for others may also lead to arguments and disagreements with those around you, who may believe that you are being unreasonable or have expectations that are impossible to meet. If you continually criticize others who wash dishes differently than you do, choose to drive in a different lane than you would, or enjoy different types of movies than you do, these people are likely to become angry or hurt in response to your criticism.

Perfectionistic standards toward others can affect the self-esteem and sense of worth of those around you. If your children are constantly led to believe that they are not living up to your expectations, they may feel worse about themselves and may even stop trying in school or other activities in which they are involved. Perfectionistic standards can also contribute to anxiety problems among those who are close to you.

Being overly perfectionistic toward oneself can also lead to problems in relationships and friendships. For example, complaining excessively whenever you get less than an A on an exam may be insulting to friends who have to struggle to get a B or C. They might wonder what you think of them, given that their grades are so much lower than what you expect.

People who have excessively high standards for themselves may also have problems with social anxiety that impairs their ability to make friends easily and develop close relationships. They may be overly concerned that others also have high standards and are likely to be critical. By avoiding contact with others, they never get to learn that others may be less critical than expected. Therefore, for people who are anxious in social situations, avoidance helps to maintain perfectionistic beliefs about the self. The relationship between perfectionism and social anxiety is discussed in more detail later in this chapter, as well as in chapter 12.

Leisure and Recreation

Does perfectionism sometimes make it difficult for you to enjoy yourself? Stephen was a business executive who complained that it was difficult for him to have fun. Upon further questioning, he reported that when he tried to have fun, his perfectionism got in the way. Leisure activities usually ended up feeling like work. One year, Stephen decided to learn to play the guitar, thinking that it would help him to relax. He enrolled in private lessons with one of the best-known (and most expensive) teachers in the city and made a commitment to practice playing for two hours each evening. He set an alarm to ring after two hours and would not take a break until the whole time had elapsed. He never missed a practice, even on days when he didn't arrive home from work until late in the evening. After three weeks, he felt very discouraged because he was not enjoying practicing guitar and didn't like the way his playing sounded (he expected to sound more like a pro than he did—even though he had only been playing for a few weeks). He quit playing a few days later and never picked up the guitar again. This experience was typical for him. In fact, he had tried to learn a number of musical instruments over the years and always gave up after not meeting his own high standards.

Jean-Paul reported that his high standards made it very difficult to enjoy playing sports. Although he thought he should be involved in a sport, his perfectionism typically led him to take the game too seriously. For example, when playing baseball with friends, he tended to become very angry when a teammate dropped the ball or made some other mistake that cost the team a run. Usually, at the end of a game that didn't go well, he would leave feeling frustrated about losing and guilty for becoming angry with his friends. Although he got involved with baseball to get his mind off other stresses, the game itself ended up being another source of stress.

As seen in all of these examples, perfectionism can affect a person's ability to enjoy leisure activities and recreation. However, it can also make it almost impossible for some people to even get involved in these activities. For people who have very high standards in other areas (such as work), it may be very difficult to make the time to do something enjoyable that is not work related. If this is a problem for you, you may find that you spend almost no time getting involved in hobbies, sports, pleasure reading, or other forms of recreation.

EXERCISE 2.3 The Effects of Perfectionism on Your Leisure Time

Does perfectionism affect your ability to enjoy leisure time? Is it hard for you to take a break from work or other obligations? When you're engaged in some hobby or sport, does it feel like work? Do you feel compelled to do things perfectly, even when you are trying to relax and enjoy yourself? In your journal, record examples of the ways in which perfectionism impacts upon your leisure time.

PERFECTIONISM AND PSYCHOLOGICAL FUNCTIONING

Perfectionism is associated with a range of psychological problems, including depression, generalized anxiety and worry, social anxiety and shyness, obsessive-compulsive problems, anger difficulties, and issues related to body image and eating. This section discusses each of these potential problems that can arise from being overly perfectionistic.

Depression

Perfectionism is often a feature of depression. Depressed mood can vary in intensity from the normal periods of sadness that everyone experiences on occasion to a much more severe level of depression (such as clinical depression) that interferes with functioning. The course of depression also varies from individual to individual. For some people, depressed mood may last a few hours or a day at a time. Other people may experience depression for longer periods of time. In addition to depressed mood, symptoms of major depression may include lack of interest in one's normal activities, overeating or loss of appetite, changes in sleep, feeling restless and agitated (or very slowed down), feeling worthless or guilty, poor concentration or difficulty making decisions, feeling tired, or thoughts about death or suicide. People who suffer from clinical depression may find it difficult to socialize with others, to be productive at work, or to keep on top of housework.

Clinical forms of depression appear to be related to a variety of factors. Biological factors that may play a role include genetic inheritance, changes in levels of chemicals in the brain called *neurotransmitters* (for example, serotonin and norepinephrine), and changes in hormonal levels (for example, variation in the phase of the menstrual cycle, hormonal changes associated with pregnancy and childbirth). Other biological factors such as sleep, the amount of available sunlight, and diet can also play a role in depression for some individuals. Psychological factors in depression include a person's learning history (for example, growing up in a home where you are frequently told you are inadequate or worthless), history of uncontrollable, stressful life events (for instance, the death of a close friend or family member, the loss of a job), and negative thinking patterns (thoughts like "things never seem to work out right").

Perfectionistic thoughts and behaviors are often important in the maintenance of depression. People who are perfectionistic often set very high standards for themselves in their work, interpersonal relationships, or other areas. If these standards are continually not met, such an individual may start to feel inadequate, disappointed, or even hopeless or worthless. If depression is a problem for you, it might feel like there is something wrong with you that interferes with your ability to reach your goals and meet your expectations. However, the truth may be that the goals are unrealistic or that you place too much importance on reaching them. Finding ways to increase flexibility and become more willing to make mistakes and risk being average can help to decrease feelings of depression.

Generalized Anxiety and Worry

Are you a worrywart? Excessive anxiety and worry can be both unpleasant and unproductive. Anxiety is an emotion that we experience when we believe we are vulnerable to some sort of threat in the future, such as failing an exam, missing a flight, losing our luggage, having harm come to a loved one, or upsetting the boss. Though it would be natural to experience intense anxiety over learning about a parent who was just diagnosed with cancer, most people would agree that worrying to the same degree about a relative who has a common cold is excessive. Often, anxiety is very helpful in that it helps you plan for the future. If people didn't worry at all, no one would bother studying for exams or getting to work on time when they wanted to sleep in. Some anxiety is essential for getting things done. However, when anxiety occurs too often or too intensely, it can begin to interfere with a person's sleep, concentration, and enjoyment of life.

Perfectionism is often associated with generalized anxiety and worry. When you set very high standards for yourself or others, there is always a risk of those standards not being met, which can lead to anxiety. For example, if you believe that your children should be performing at the highest level in all of their activities, including school, sports, piano practice, and anything else they do, you may always be worried that their performance may slip in one of these areas. You may also worry excessively about your abilities as a parent if your child does poorly.

Social Anxiety and Shyness

One particular type of anxiety that has a particularly strong association with perfectionism is *social anxiety*. By social anxiety, we mean anxiety, fear, or discomfort around other people, usually associated with a fear of being embarrassed or humiliated (extreme shyness and stage fright are examples). Typical social situations that are often feared by people who are socially anxious include those involving interaction with others (for instance, talking to strangers, having friends over for dinner, going to parties, being assertive) as well as performance situations in which others might be focused on your behavior (things like public speaking, talking in a meeting, exercising in front of others, and so on).

When confronted with a feared situation, people who are socially anxious may experience a whole range of symptoms that may include elevated heart rate, breathlessness, dizziness, and other symptoms of arousal. The most frightening of these symptoms are often those that might be noticed by other people, including blushing, sweating, shaking, and losing one's train of thought. People who are anxious in social situations often are particularly nervous that others will find them to be strange, incompetent, stupid, or unattractive. They may be fearful of saying the wrong thing or of seeming overly anxious. People with high levels of social anxiety tend to believe that others are likely to judge them negatively. Social anxiety is associated with a tendency to be overly concerned about making mistakes, as well as a tendency to have very high standards for oneself. Socially anxious individuals may hold beliefs like, "I should be liked by everyone," "I should never make mistakes," or "I should never allow my anxiety to show."

Anger

Like anxiety, anger is a normal emotion that sometimes occurs when we are prevented from achieving some goal or are faced with some threat. For example, a person who undeservingly receives a poor performance appraisal at work might become angry at his or her supervisor. Anger can be helpful when it motivates us to correct a situation (for example, by confronting the supervisor and requesting that the performance appraisal be changed) or to meet a threat head on. However, like other emotions, anger can lead to problems when it occurs too frequently, too intensely, or in situations where it is not warranted.

Although everyone gets angry from time to time, excessive anger and irritability are commonly associated with other negative feelings such as anxiety and depression. The tendency to experience excessive anger is believed to stem from a complex interaction among biological processes (for example, genetics, hormones, and so on) and psychological processes (for instance, our learning and our beliefs). Inflexible beliefs about the way things "should be" can easily lead to disappointment and anger when expectations are not met. Therefore, people who are perfectionistic are often more prone to experience difficulties with anger, frustration, and irritability when compared to individuals who are less perfectionistic. Because perfectionistic standards are often unattainable, rigid, and inflexible, they often are not met. As a result, you may be very frustrated when your hair is not cut exactly the way you expected or when your children leave a book or toy in the wrong place. Perfectionism can also lead other people to become angry if you tend to correct them over and over again. Trying too hard to make others see or do things your way can lead to bickering and arguments. One strategy for decreasing anger and irritability is learning to change unreasonable expectations of yourself and others.

Obsessive-Compulsive Behavior

Up to 80 percent of people in the general population experience obsessions and compulsions from time to time (Antony, Downie, and Swinson 1998). *Obsessions* are unwanted thoughts, images, or urges that occur repeatedly, despite efforts to resist them. Examples may include thoughts about being contaminated by germs; images of hurting other people, even though you have no desire to hurt anyone; and recurrent doubts about whether tasks have been completed correctly. *Compulsions* are repetitive behaviors that occur in response to obsessions or according to rigidly applied rules. Compulsions typically decrease the discomfort and anxiety created by the obsessions, or they are used to prevent some dreaded event. For example, people who have obsessions about cleanliness and germs may engage in compulsive rituals involving cleaning and washing. People with doubts about their actions may check their work excessively, to the point of not getting anything done.

Obsessive-compulsive disorder (OCD) is a problem in which people experience obsessions and compulsions frequently and there is impairment in functioning as a result. For example, whereas many people may feel compelled to check their appliances once or twice before leaving the house, an individual with OCD may check many times over the course of an hour or more. In the 1997 film *As Good as it Gets*, Jack Nicholson portrayed a man who suffers from OCD. In the film, his character has a fear of contamination (he only eats with wrapped plastic utensils) and engages in compulsive washing rituals. He also tends to be quite rigid about a range of activities. He insists on eating at the same table each time he visits his favorite restaurant and will only be served by a particular server. Also, he cannot step on sidewalk cracks and has to complete the same tasks each day, in the same order. Although Jack Nicholson's character has other problems that are not related to OCD (a tendency to offend everyone who interacted with him), the film does a nice job demonstrating some of the features of the disorder.

Todd had obsessions about making mistakes when talking to other people, and he engaged in compulsions involving repeating sentences and asking for reassurance that he was understood correctly. For example, he feared that he might give someone incorrect directions or that some detail might be misunderstood when he told his coworkers about what he did on the weekend. As a result, he often avoided talking to people in case he said something wrong, and he usually repeated everything he said to other people to be sure that he was not misunderstood. Occasionally, he recorded conversations he had over the telephone and even in person so he could check them later for possible misunderstandings.

Like the other problems discussed in this chapter, there is evidence that both biological and psychological factors contribute to OCD. Genetics appears to play a role. In addition, there is evidence that the neurotransmitter serotonin may be important in the development of the problem. From a psychological perspective, learning may play a role for some individuals. In addition, the types of beliefs and behaviors engaged in by individuals with OCD probably help to maintain the problem. For example, whereas most people have unpleasant intrusive thoughts from time to time, people with OCD are much more afraid of these thoughts compared to the average person. They may feel overly responsible for preventing negative things from happening. People with OCD are also more likely than others to suppress or to resist having their unpleasant intrusive thoughts. Unfortunately, one consequence of trying to resist unpleasant thoughts is that they tend to come back more strongly later.

Perfectionism plays a role in OCD, in that compulsive behaviors often need to be repeated over and over until they "feel right." Also, the order in which activities are completed is sometimes inflexible. For example, for some people who wash compulsively, the order in which various parts of the body are washed is very important. People with OCD may also doubt whether they have completed tasks or said things to others correctly, even though their definition of "correct" may be very different from that of another person.

In addition to OCD, there is a related problem called obsessive-compulsive-personality disorder (OCPD). OCPD is a personality style in which an individual is extremely perfectionistic and inflexible and is preoccupied with being orderly and organized. People with this problem tend to be so preoccupied with rules, lists, details, order, and organization that they actually get very little done. They tend to be overly devoted to work and productivity, leaving little time for recreation. Because of rigid views regarding how things should be done, people with OCPD typically have difficulty letting others do things for them. In many ways, the criteria for OCPD correspond directly with the defining features of perfectionism.

Although OCD and OCPD have similar names, they differ in a number of important ways. In OCD, compulsive behaviors are designed to decrease anxiety created by very specific obsessions (such as washing in response to thoughts about contamination or checking in response to thoughts about losing things). In contrast, OCPD reflects a general personality style that cuts across many different activities and situations. Furthermore, OCPD is generally not considered to be anxiety based, and the people with this problem may be unaware that their perfectionistic thoughts and behaviors are excessive. In chapter 14, we discuss the relationship between perfectionism and obsessive-compulsive behavior in more detail.

Body-Image Problems and Eating Disorders

Another domain in which some people are perfectionistic is their physical appearance. Especially in North American and Western European cultures, there has been an increasing emphasis on being thin, particularly among women. Consider some of the trends over the past few decades. Women who work as models, actors, and dancers continue to get thinner, as the average woman living in North America has become heavier. In fact, 77.5 percent of recent Playboy centerfolds weighed at least 15 percent below that expected for their age and height—thin enough to meet the weight criterion for anorexia nervosa (Katzmarzky and Davis 2001).

The standards for thinness reflected by the media are becoming increasingly impossible to meet. One study found that body dissatisfaction is increasing and occurring at younger ages (Cramer and Steinwert 1998). By school age, girls report more fear of looking fat than they do of losing their parents, getting cancer, or experiencing a nuclear war. There has also been a steady increase in the number of individuals suffering from eating disorders. Perfectionism tends to be a feature of disordered eating, particularly for people suffering from anorexia nervosa and bulimia nervosa.

Anorexia nervosa is an eating disorder in which an individual engages in self-starvation in order to maintain a very low body weight (at least 15 percent below a minimally normal weight for a person's age and height). In addition, there is an intense fear of becoming fat and often a denial that one is underweight. In addition to having unhealthy standards for what one's weight should be, people with anorexia nervosa may be perfectionistic in other areas as well. *Bulimia nervosa* is an eating disorder in which the individual engages in frequent episodes of binge eating (that is, eating large amounts of food in a very short time and feeling a lack of control over eating). In addition, the individual uses various strategies to "undo" the effects of having overeaten, including self-induced vomiting, laxative abuse, the use of diuretics, and/or excessive exercise. Like anorexia nervosa, bulimia nervosa is associated with a tendency to put too much of an emphasis on body shape and weight when evaluating oneself.

People with eating disorders often have very rigid and inflexible rules about eating and food. We once saw two individuals with eating disorders who ended up having an argument about which part of their bread had more calories. One person insisted that the crust had more calories and would only eat the inside of the bread. The other person believed the inside of the bread was more fattening and would only eat the crust. Of course, both the inside and outside of a loaf of bread have similar amounts of fat, yet both women were very resistant to changing their views. Both had very strict views about what foods could be eaten and which were to be avoided. This rigidity is a characteristic of perfectionism.

Sometimes, individuals can have perfectionistic beliefs focused on some aspect of physical appearance other than weight. Such people may become very focused on a particular body part that they view as imperfect. For example, a person may become overly concerned with his or her hair, spending hours per day styling it and even trimming it themselves so that it is perfect. Some men may become overly focused on losing their hair, imagining their hair loss to be extremely unattractive. Others may be unhappy with their nose, or the shape of their legs or other body part. Although many people are occasionally unhappy with some aspect of the way they look (the cosmetic surgery industry depends on this!), some people may be so preoccupied with some aspect of their appearance that they have trouble thinking about anything else. Typically, they imagine themselves to be extremely ugly, even though most people would disagree. When this imagined ugliness begins to interfere with functioning, it may meet criteria for a condition known as *body dysmorphic disorder*. Like the eating disorders, body dysmorphic disorder is associated with extremely rigid and perfectionistic thinking regarding physical appearance. Chapter 15 discusses further the relationship between perfectionism and problems related to body image.

CHAPTER 3

Perfectionism and Thoughts

Research from around the world has consistently found a relationship between people's emotions and their beliefs, thoughts, expectations, and interpretations. Negative thinking seems to be related to experiences of anxiety, anger, and sadness. Perfectionism, which is often part of these emotional states, is also associated with these negative styles of thinking. In this chapter, we will explain the styles of thinking that contribute to perfectionism; in later chapters, we will discuss how changing these styles of thinking can have a dramatic effect on the tendency to engage in perfectionistic behaviors.

HOW BELIEFS AFFECT EMOTIONS

Here is an exercise to illustrate how beliefs can affect emotions:

EXERCISE 3.1 The Link Between Your Beliefs and Emotions

Imagine that you have arranged to have a close friend pick you up at home and drive you to dinner at a restaurant where you have made a reservation for 7:00 p.m. Because you live about fifteen minutes from the restaurant, your friend was scheduled to pick you up at 6:45 p.m. Imagine that your clock says 6:45, and your friend has not yet arrived. How might you feel at this point? What emotion do you think you might be experiencing, if any? What thoughts would be running through your head? In your journal, record (1) any emotions that you think you might be experiencing at 6:45 p.m., and (2) any specific thoughts that might be going through your head at that time.

Now, imagine that you continue to wait for your friend for another twenty minutes. It's 7:05, you are late for your reservation, and your friend has still not arrived. You try calling your friend's cell phone, but there is no response. What emotion would you be feeling at this point? What thoughts might be going through your head? In your journal, record (1) any emotions that you think you might be experiencing at 7:05 p.m., and (2) any specific thoughts that might be going through your head at that time.

Imagine that another forty minutes go by. It's now 7:45, and you are very hungry. Still no friend at your door. You phone your friend's home and there is no answer. What would you be feeling and thinking now? Would your feelings or thoughts have changed from earlier? In your journal, record (1) any emotions that you think you might be experiencing at 7:45 p.m., and (2) any specific thoughts that might be going through your head at that time.

Finally, at 7:55 p.m., your friend shows up covered in grease from having to change a flat tire on the highway, which, as it turns out, is the reason your friend was late. He had forgotten to pick up his cell phone when he left in a hurry to meet you and couldn't get in touch with you. Your friend apologizes for the delay and clearly seems quite frazzled about the whole situation. You agree to stay home and order in food. How would you be feeling now that your friend has arrived? Would your feelings or thoughts be different than they were ten minutes earlier? In your journal, record (1) any emotions that you think you might be experiencing at 8:00 p.m., shortly after your friend arrives and explains why he or she is late, and (2) any specific thoughts that might be going through your head at that time.

Interpretation and Emotions

When working with people who experience problems with anxiety, depression, and related difficulties, we ask them to imagine scenarios such as this one to help illustrate the relationship between thoughts and emotions. Although the scenario we describe is often the same, the responses we get from people to these questions differ dramatically from person to person. Some individuals tell us that they would be unlikely to react negatively to their friend's lateness. Rather, they might simply have a small snack to tide them over and keep busy with various chores around the house until the friend shows up. Other individuals tell us that they would become increasingly angry with the friend as they waited. These feelings might be associated with thoughts that the friend was being inconsiderate. This behavior might be seen as contradicting a particular value or attitude, such as the belief that "people should not be late." When the friend arrives and it becomes clear that the delay was beyond his or her control, these feelings of anger might be replaced by feelings of guilt for assuming the worst about the friend.

Other people tell us that they would probably feel very worried if their friend hadn't arrived on time. As the evening progressed, they would be having increasingly frequent thoughts that something terrible had happened to their friend. When the friend finally arrives, these feelings of anxiety and worry might be replaced by feelings of relief.

Still other people tell us that they would feel sad if their friend did not show up on time. They might believe that the friend doesn't care enough about them to show up on time, and as a result, they might question their own self-worth as they waited for their friend. As with people who respond to this scenario with anxiety and worry, individuals who predict that they would feel sad often report that they would likely feel relieved when the person finally showed up and the reason for the friend's lateness became clear.

This scenario illustrates how the same situation can lead to a full range of emotions depending on an individual's interpretation of the events. Despite all the possible interpretations of this scenario, the actual situation is the same in all cases: a friend is late for dinner because of a flat tire. Yet, the reaction of the person waiting for the friend may be anger, anxiety, sadness, or any of a range of emotions, depending on how the situation is interpreted.

The key idea here is that, in general, people do not respond to *events* in their lives, but rather to their *interpretations* of events. The same event can lead to very different reactions from different people, depending on the meaning the event holds for them. It is your beliefs, thoughts, interpretations, predictions, assumptions, and other cognitive patterns that determine how you react to situations and events.

People who are perfectionistic tend to have specific patterns of beliefs that help to maintain their perfectionism. For example, someone who tends to be perfectionistic might believe that there is only one correct way to wash the dishes. Most people believe that they know how to wash the dishes properly. But if you actually take the time to watch how different people wash dishes, it quickly becomes apparent that there are many different ways to get the job done—all of which work pretty well. For example, some people fill the sink with water and let the dishes soak. Other people let the water run continuously and wash each dish separately under the tap. People may use various kinds of scrubbers and sponges, or they may use only their hands. Some people insist on a particular brand of soap, whereas other people will use any kind of dish soap, and still others may not use any soap at all. Some people will only use very hot water to ensure that all germs are killed; others prefer to use warm or cold water. Some people don't even bother with water and just wipe off the dishes. Some people wash their dishes right after they are used, and others let them sit for a few hours, days, or weeks before washing them.

You get the idea—there are many different ways to wash dishes. If a person adheres too rigidly to beliefs about how tasks should be completed, he or she is likely to run into problems with other people who also have strong opinions about how things should be done. Perfectionism can affect your interpretations ("That's the wrong way to wash dishes") which, in turn, affects your emotions ("Now I'm irritated").

AUTOMATIC AND UNCONSCIOUS PERFECTIONISTIC THOUGHTS

People are often unaware of the thoughts and interpretations that lead to their intense reactions to situations. Often, these thoughts occur so quickly and automatically that they are outside of your conscious awareness. In fact, there are many situations in which you process information outside of your awareness. When you walk, you don't have to think, "Right foot … left foot … right foot … left foot." Rather, you walk without thinking about it. If there is a pole in the way, you automatically walk around it. In fact, a minute later, you might forget that there was a pole to be walked around.

In situations that are very familiar, such as walking, you are able to process information with limited cognitive resources or attention. You even process information while you sleep. For example, people are more likely to wake up to the sound of their own name than to other sounds. Many parents with a new baby report that they are more likely to wake up to the sound of their own baby's crying than to other sounds.

Given that you often process information outside of your awareness, many of the beliefs that are associated with perfectionistic thinking may be hard to identify. With practice, identifying perfectionistic beliefs will become easier. One way of doing this is to notice situations in which you experience a negative emotion such as anxiety, sadness, anger, frustration, or a feeling that something is not "right." Once the emotion has been identified and labeled, it is sometimes easier to identify the thoughts and interpretations that might be contributing to the negative feeling. There may even be contradictory beliefs leading to a mixture of emotions. For example, if a supervisor feels frustrated because an employee is not doing a job "properly," the supervisor might notice frustration-producing thoughts such as, "It's very important that my employees do the job my way." At the same time, the supervisor may still recognize on some level that there are different ways of doing the job and that it might be okay to have employees do the job their own way.

Before you can learn to change perfectionistic patterns of thinking, it is important to identify these thoughts, interpretations, and beliefs. Using a thought monitoring form, such as the example provided here, can help you monitor such thoughts. The next time you find yourself feeling inadequate because you think you haven't performed well enough on a task or are frustrated by the behavior of someone around you, try completing this form. You will probably want to create your own form on a full-sized sheet of paper because there isn't much space on the sample provided in this book. After reading the completed example, use the first column of your blank form to record the situation that triggers your perfectionistic thoughts or brings these thoughts to your awareness. In the second column, record the emotion that you are experiencing (for example, fear, anxiety, anger, sadness, frustration, and so on). Also, record the intensity of the emotion using a scale ranging from 0 to 100, where 0 means nonexistent and 100 equals emotion as intense as you can imagine. Finally, in the third column, record your perfectionistic beliefs and thoughts. By stepping back and observing your reactions in situations, perfectionistic thoughts are likely to become more evident. Becoming more aware of your perfectionistic thoughts is the first step toward changing them—a topic that will be discussed in more detail in chapter 7.

Thought Monitoring Form – Completed Sample

Situation	Emotion and Intensity (0-100)	Perfectionistic Thoughts, Beliefs, and Interpretations
I keep writing and rewriting each sentence in this letter to my boss.	Frustrated (70) Anxious (50)	If I don't get each sentence just right, my boss will think I am stupid and incompetent. If I continue to rewrite this letter, eventually I will get it right. There is a right way and a wrong way to word things.
My wife arrived home from work one hour late and had not called me.	Anger (90) Worried (70)	I am never late, and neither should other people be late. If my wife continues to be late for things, she will never get anywhere in life.
I gained two pounds last week.	Sad (80)	It is important that my weight does not fluctuate. I am less attractive now. I am going to continue to gain weight.
My roommate left his coat on my favorite chair.	Anger (50)	My roommate is inconsiderate. The smell of smoke from my roommate's coat will get all over my chair.

Thought Monitoring Form – Blank Sample

Situation	Emotion and Intensity (0-100)	Perfectionistic Thoughts, Beliefs, and Interpretations

TRYING TO CONFIRM PERFECTIONISTIC BELIEFS

Everyone likes to be correct. Therefore, people tend to seek out experiences that confirm their beliefs. In other words, people seek information in a biased way, in an effort to support their assumptions, interpretations, and thoughts. They prefer to spend time with people who think the way they do. If they are politically active, they may go to rallies for their own side—to hear what they already believe. If they are active in their religion, they may seek out experiences that bolster their religious beliefs (for instance, attending services at a church or some other place of worship) rather than seeking out experiences that challenge their beliefs.

Unfortunately, this tendency to seek out information that confirms one's beliefs can sometimes get people into trouble. For example, a person who has a fear of flying is likely to pay extra attention to stories in the media about airline crashes, compared to the attention paid to all the airplanes that take off and land safely. People who are feeling depressed are more likely to remember all the mistakes that they have made in the past, rather than their successes. People who are socially anxious and believe that others are judging them negatively are more likely to interpret ambiguous social information (something like being given an ambiguous look from another person) as confirming their feelings of inadequacy.

People who are particularly perfectionistic are in danger of paying more attention to events that confirm their perfectionistic beliefs than to information that contradicts these beliefs. For example, students who are afraid to hand in term papers without checking them over repeatedly might remember stories they have heard about students who handed in exams without checking them over and happened to forget to answer an entire page of questions. They might ignore the fact that there are also many people who hand things in after rechecking their work once, twice, or not at all—without any negative consequences.

PERFECTIONISTIC THINKING STYLES

People do not think like computers. Computers use complex mathematical formulas to process information and solve problems. In contrast, people often interpret their environments using what psychologists call *heuristics*. A heuristic is a rule that people use to make a decision or interpret an event. For example, if an individual sees an unleashed dog while walking on the sidewalk, he or she might rely on various stereotypes about various dog breeds to help guide the decision of whether to cross the road and get away from the dog. If the dog is from a large breed known for biting, the individual might be more likely to avoid the dog than if it's a smaller breed that is unlikely to do any serious damage. This rule of thumb (that is, "Avoid big, unleashed dogs that have a reputation for biting, but not dogs that are not known for biting") is an example of a heuristic. Following this rule may improve one's chances of not being bitten. However, it's not always going to lead to a correct decision. Many large dogs with reputations for biting are perfectly safe, and some small dogs bite. Heuristics are quick ways of interpreting the environment and making decisions, and they often lead to correct decisions, which is why the human mind continues to rely on these strategies for processing information.

However, sometimes people process information incorrectly or in ways that are biased. Psychologists sometimes refer to styles of thinking as *cognitive distortions*, particularly when they are biased in a negative direction. Proponents of cognitive therapy have identified a number of cognitive distortions that make people more likely to experience feelings of anxiety, depression, anger, and other negative emotional states.

In this section, we will highlight some of these cognitive distortions and other styles of thinking that are especially relevant to perfectionistic thinking. We are indebted to people such as Aaron T. Beck, Albert Ellis, and David Burns for identifying these distortions. Note that these categories of negative thinking styles are not necessarily as distinct as they might seem on the surface. They overlap considerably, and a particular perfectionistic thought may fit into several of these categories.

All-or-Nothing Thinking and Excessively High Standards

All-or-nothing thinking (also known as "black-and-white thinking," "categorical thinking," or "polarized thinking") is a tendency to see things as either right or wrong, without recognizing that situations are often complex and that there are often many points on the continuum between the extremes of "right" and "wrong." This is one of the most common cognitive distortions among people who are perfectionistic. All-or-nothing thoughts focused on the behavior of others (for example, "People can do things my way or the wrong way") may be associated with anger, whereas all-or-nothing thoughts focused on one's own behavior (for instance, "If I lose my temper with my children, I am a bad parent") are more often associated with feelings of anxiety, depression, or inadequacy.

Here are some examples of statements reflecting all-or-nothing thinking:

- Anything less than sticking to my diet perfectly is a failure. If I eat one cookie, I may as well have eaten ten cookies.

- I always need to look perfect in front of other people.

- If I don't get an A+ in this course, I don't deserve to be in this program.

- My reports are never good enough.

- I seem to be the only person in this house who knows how to clean things properly.

- There is a right way and a wrong way to do everything.

All-or-nothing thinking may also be thought of as being related to having excessively high standards. People who are perfectionistic often have standards, either for themselves or for others, that are unrealistic or excessively high. Although it is sometimes helpful to have standards that are slightly higher than your current level of performance (this gives you a goal that you have a good chance of reaching), perfectionism is often associated with having standards that are extremely difficult, if not impossible, to attain. Consider the following examples.

Deborah feels inadequate if she is not able to manage all the demands in her life, which include working full time, taking a night course two evenings a week, being attentive to her partner, cooking for her family, spending several hours a day with her children, visiting her parents weekly, spending time with several of her close friends, and finding time to nurture herself.

All of his life, Mark has wanted to be an attorney. In fact, there is nothing else that he can imagine doing. Unfortunately, he is a senior in college, his average is a C, and he is very unlikely to be accepted into law school.

Louis is constantly correcting his seven-year-old son's use of language, to the point that his son is sometimes afraid to speak in front of him. The son cannot understand why he is always being corrected by his father, since his grades are among the highest in his class and he is often told by his teachers, friends, and other family members that he speaks very well.

Alexis weighs 130 pounds and is five feet, four inches in height. Although her doctor insists that she is not overweight, and her friends tell her she looks great, Alexis feels guilty because she cannot seem to reach her goal weight of 110 pounds.

EXERCISE 3.3 All-or-Nothing Thinking

In your journal, record examples of all-or-nothing thinking that you engage in from time to time, as well as standards you hold that others might consider excessively high.

Filtering

Filtering is a tendency to selectively focus on and magnify negative details at the expense of positive information, which is dismissed as less important. Here are some examples of filtering:

Ella receives a two-page performance evaluation at work that is very positive overall, emphasizing that she is among the most valued employees in the company. However, she feels angry and hurt over one criticism suggesting that she try to participate more in meetings.

When people tell Rico that he looks good, he assumes that they are being insincere and that they actually feel sorry for him or are trying to manipulate him in some way. In contrast, when someone tells Rico that he looks tired, he assumes that they find him unattractive, and he feels extremely self-conscious.

Carrie is a tenth-grade student who has gained five pounds. She is sure that everyone at school finds her unattractive now, despite the fact that she is often asked out on dates and her friends tell her that she looks great.

Mia's daughter has become much better at putting away her toys in recent months. However, on one occasion when she left a toy on the steps, Mia became very angry.

EXERCISE 3.4   Filtering

Do you engage in filtering from time to time? In your journal, record examples of filtering from your own life.

Mind Reading

Mind reading involves assuming that you know what other people are thinking and that their thoughts about you are negative. This style of thinking is common in people who are perfectionistic and may contribute to feelings of depression and anxiety. Examples of mind reading include the following:

When Evelyn's supervisor does not give Evelyn feedback on her report for over a week, Evelyn assumes this is because her supervisor thought that the report was not good enough.

After cooking dinner for several friends, Jack is convinced that his guests are not enjoying their food when one of them excuses himself from the table to visit the bathroom.

Ricardo is hurt and angry when a woman he is attracted to fails to return his phone call. He is certain that she is either irresponsible or uninterested in him, and he wonders if he'll ever find a partner who meets his high standards.

EXERCISE 3.5 Mind Reading

Do you engage in mind reading from time to time? In your journal, record examples of mind reading from your own life.

Probability Overestimations

Perfectionism is often associated with a tendency to predict that negative events are more likely to occur than they really are. We call these predictions *probability overestimations*. Here are some examples:

Alex is a straight-A student, yet before every exam, he believes that he is definitely not going to pass.

Francesca is sure that she is going to come across as unprepared and dull during her presentation, even though she is well-prepared and her coworkers usually enjoy her talks.

Mary rarely misses work and is highly regarded by her supervisors. Yet, when she must take off a few days due to illness, she believes that her boss will not believe she is sick and that she will receive a negative performance appraisal.

EXERCISE 3.6 Probability Overestimation

Do you engage in probability overestimation from time to time? In your journal, record examples of probability overestimation from your own life.

Tunnel Vision

Tunnel vision is a cognitive style in which people pay too much attention to detail and therefore miss the big picture. This can also be thought of as "missing the forest for the trees." Tunnel vision can slow people down and get in the way of task completion. Following are a few examples of tunnel vision:

Peter spent many hours reading and taking hundreds of pages of notes in preparation to complete his ten-page paper on World War II.

Before making any new purchase, no matter how small, David spends many hours reading past issues of *Consumer Reports*, talking to sales people, and discussing his options with friends.

When taking multiple-choice exams at school, Amy obsesses about the meaning of each question and often does not finish the exam before she runs out of time.

Susan spends so much time organizing (making lists, filing, putting things in order) that she is often not able to finish her work.

EXERCISE 3.7   Tunnel Vision

Do you have tunnel vision from time to time? In your journal, record examples of tunnel vision from your own life.

Interpersonal Sensitivity

People who are perfectionistic are often overly concerned about the opinions of others. Most people prefer to be liked by others. However, perfectionism may be associated with an extreme need for approval from others. Examples of beliefs reflecting exaggerated interpersonal sensitivity include:

■ It is very important that everyone likes me.

■ If others think I am incompetent, then I am incompetent.

■ If someone doesn't love me, then I am unlovable.

■ It is very important not to make mistakes so that others will approve of me.

EXERCISE 3.8 Interpersonal Sensitivity

Is interpersonal sensitivity a problem for you? In your journal, record examples of interpersonal sensitivity in your own life.

Catastrophic Thinking

Catastrophic thinking (also known as *catastrophizing*) involves incorrectly assuming that one could not cope with a negative outcome if it were to occur. This style of thinking also includes predictions that particular events would be unmanageable if they were to occur. Catastrophic thinking is common in people who are prone to experiencing problems with anxiety, depression, and anger. Examples of catastrophic thinking include:

- I couldn't handle making a mistake in front of the class.

- It would be absolutely terrible if I missed a deadline.

- If this deal doesn't go through, I don't know how I will manage.

- If I do not stay thin, nobody will ever be attracted to me.

- If I back down or change my mind, I will be perceived as weak.

- It would be unmanageable to develop an illness that caused me to miss even a day of work.

EXERCISE 3.9 Catastrophic Thinking

Do you engage in catastrophic thinking from time to time? In your journal, record examples of catastrophic thinking from your own life.

Excessively Rigid Standards and Inflexibility

Everyone has standards that not only influence their own behavior, but also help them to decide whether to attempt to influence the behavior of others (for example, providing constructive feedback to coworkers to improve their performance on a project). When people cannot achieve a particular goal or are unable to influence someone else, they may either keep trying or lower their standards or expectations. Perfectionistic people sometimes view a decision to lower their standards as giving up or settling for less than they should. This view may make it difficult to be flexible with respect to one's standards for oneself or for others. It may be very hard for people who have developed an inflexible style or are critical of themselves or others to know when it is okay to break rules. Following are some examples of excessively rigid standards:

Laura always arrives home before her midnight curfew. On the weekend of her high school prom, Laura asked her parents for permission to come home at 1:00 a.m., since the prom ended at midnight. Her parents refused to allow her to come home later, explaining that her curfew was midnight and that there could be no exceptions.

Graham was used to winning when he played squash. When he lost to a friend from work, he was quite angry and found it difficult to accept that he had lost the game.

Jonathan had just made a very nice dinner for his girlfriend. However, she refused to eat the dinner because she noticed that he had forgotten to wash his hands before cooking it.

Paul is accustomed to running five miles each day to keep fit. One week, he comes down with a bad case of the flu and ends up feeling like a failure because he was unable to run for three days.

Angela gets very upset whenever plans are changed. For example, if she and her husband decide to see a movie and the movie ends up being sold out, Angela becomes very angry and disappointed at the prospect of having to find something else to do.

EXERCISE 3.10 Rigid Standards and Inflexibility

Are rigid and inflexible standards sometimes a problem for you? In your journal, record examples of times when you were unwilling or unable to settle for less.

Over-Responsibility and an Excessive Need for Control

Often, people who are perfectionistic believe that they have more control over events in their life than they actually do. This may lead people to feel overly responsible for events that, in reality, they cannot control. Feelings of over-responsibility can lead people to spend too much time on tasks, to engage in excessive checking and rechecking, or to go to great lengths to protect themselves from making a mistake or from being harmed. Perfectionistic individuals may also believe that it is important to control the behavior or thoughts of other people in their lives in order to prevent them from making mistakes or encountering harm. These beliefs can lead to relationship problems if individuals are frequently critical of the behavior of their loved ones. Some example statements reflecting a sense of over-responsibility or an exaggerated need for control include:

- If I spend a long time double checking the content of my letter before I send it, I can make sure that there is nothing in there that might be offensive.

- If I practice this talk enough times, I can ensure that everyone in the audience will like it.

- I can prevent my daughter from getting sick if I constantly remind her to dress warmly, eat her vegetables, wash her hands, get enough sleep, and so on.

- I can control whether others like me by being very careful about how I phrase things when I speak.

- It's important for me to be able to convince people to do things my way at work.

- I need to correct other people when they make mistakes, no matter how small.

EXERCISE 3.11 Over-Responsibility and Need for Control

Do you have an inflated sense of responsibility or a high need for control? If so, record some examples in your journal.

Should Statements

Should statements are arbitrary rules for how things ought to be. If others break these rules, a person may feel angry or resentful. If individuals break their own rules, feelings of guilt, sadness, inadequacy, or anxiety often occur. Statements containing the words "should" or "must" are often a sign that one is engaging in this style of thinking. Following are a few examples of "should" statements:

- My children should always do what I tell them to do.

- My coworkers should never be late for work.

- I should never make mistakes at work.

- I should never come across as nervous or anxious.

- I should be able to anticipate problems before they occur.

- I should be assertive and, at the same time, never upset other people.

- I must never get a grade lower than an A.

Do you have a lot of shoulds in your life? In your journal, record examples of your shoulds.

Difficulty Trusting Others

Perfectionism is often associated with a difficulty in trusting others to complete tasks. People who are perfectionistic might have difficulty delegating tasks to others or may feel the need to watch people closely when they are completing tasks at work or in other situations. Examples of statements reflecting difficulty trusting others include:

- If I let my partner cook dinner for me, I will not enjoy my food.

- I have to do everything myself because other people just don't know how to get the job done properly.

- If I send my husband to pick up a new telephone, he will probably get the wrong one.

- I don't like other people to buy me gifts because they couldn't possibly know what I want.

Do you find it difficult to trust others? In your journal, record some examples.

Inappropriate Social Comparisons

One strategy that we all use to evaluate our performance is to compare ourselves to other people. Everyone engages in social comparisons from time to time in order to see how they measure up compared to others whom they perceive as similar to them. For example, if you receive a raise at work, you might be interested in knowing whether other individuals doing similar jobs received comparable raises. Following a test in school, students often try to find out how other people in the class performed on the exam. Usually, people compare themselves to others whom they perceive to be similar or slightly better than them in the dimension being compared. So, following a term test, average students are likely to compare themselves to other average students. This would tell them more about their own performance than making comparisons to the top student or the weakest student in the class.

People who are particularly perfectionistic might find themselves making social comparisons more frequently than other people and may be more likely to experience negative emotions following these comparisons. Perfectionistic individuals may also compare themselves to others in a manner that serves to maintain their perfectionistic attitudes. Thus, they may compare themselves to others who are much stronger in a particular dimension, thereby strengthening their beliefs that they have to meet an almost impossibly high standard. In fact, in any particular dimension you choose to measure (for instance, intelligence, sense of humor, creativity, athletic ability, physical appearance, and so on), there will likely always be someone else who you perceive as being "better." Comparing yourself to others whom you perceive as much better in a specific dimension may help to maintain perfectionistic beliefs and foster a negative self-image or feelings of inadequacy. Following are examples of inappropriate social comparisons:

Neil compares his athletic ability to that of a professional athlete and feels pressure to meet that standard.

Sheila feels inadequate after reading a new fashion magazine and thinking that she will never be as thin or attractive as the models in the magazine.

Danielle feels like a failure after finding out that her friend received a higher exam grade than she, even though her friend usually receives the highest grades in all her classes.

EXERCISE 3.14   Inappropriate Social Comparisons

Do you tend to compare yourself to others in a way that makes you feel worse? In your journal, record some examples.

LOOKING AHEAD

In summary, identifying your perfectionistic thoughts and understanding the relationship between thinking and perfectionism are important steps in overcoming excessively high standards. Later in the book, we will discuss strategies for changing your perfectionistic thoughts. First, however, we will provide an overview of the ways in which certain types of behaviors can help to maintain your perfectionism. As we explain in the next chapter, perfectionistic thoughts and behaviors are closely related in that perfectionistic beliefs can lead to perfectionistic behaviors and perfectionistic behaviors can help to maintain perfectionistic beliefs. It is difficult to overcome perfectionism without addressing both the thoughts and behaviors that contribute to the problem.

CHAPTER 4

Perfectionism and Behavior

THE PARADOX OF PERFECTIONISM

Joanne has great difficulty making choices when shopping for clothes or other items. She fears that if she only buys one item, she'll get home and feel that she's purchased the wrong one. As a result, when faced with several options, she tends to buy one of each. For example, if she can't decide between six colors of a blouse, she buys one in each color. Only by purchasing one of each can she guarantee that she has the correct item.

Unfortunately, she does this with everything she buys. Her home is cluttered with things she doesn't need or use, including several hundred pairs of shoes, closets full of clothing, shelves filled with unread books and magazines, and cupboards overstocked with food. Joanne's difficulty making decisions when shopping is one manifestation of her belief that it's important not to make mistakes and that mistakes should always be prevented. Ironically, Joanne's struggle to avoid making mistakes leads to many different problems, including considerable credit card debt, no time to do things other than shop, and very little empty space in her home. Joanne recognizes that her compulsive shopping is controlling her life.

Reid cannot resist the temptation to correct other people when he believes they have made an error. For example, whenever someone mispronounces a word, he's quick to let the person know how the word should be pronounced. If his girlfriend is telling a story to a group of friends and leaves out details that Reid believes are important, Reid feels compelled to fill in those details so their friends do not misinterpret any of the information they are hearing. Most of the people in Reid's life (including his girlfriend, friends, family members, and coworkers) find him difficult to be around. They interpret his behavior to mean that he always needs to show people how smart he is and that he enjoys putting others down. People feel as though they need to be careful about what they say in front of Reid. In reality, his tendency to correct others has more to do with the intense discomfort that he feels when a mistake has been made, leading to a feeling of intense internal pressure to set things right. Reid understands that his need to correct others has caused problems in his relationships, but he has trouble stopping himself.

These case examples illustrate the paradox of perfectionism. People who are perfectionistic often believe that, in order to maintain order and control in their lives, they must engage in various perfectionistic behaviors. Perfectionistic behaviors can be divided into two main types: behaviors designed to help an individual meet his or her unreasonably high standards and behaviors that involve *avoidance* of situations that trigger the need to be perfect. Behaviors aimed at meeting perfectionistic standards include checking and reassurance seeking (for example, to make sure that a goal is being met), correcting others, repeating actions, and dwelling too long before making decisions. Both Reid and Joanne engage in these types of behaviors. Examples of avoidance behaviors include procrastination (putting off starting a task because one's desire for perfection is likely to make the task difficult and unpleasant) and giving up on tasks prematurely (because perfectionistic standards are unlikely to be met).

Unfortunately, when performed excessively, perfectionistic behaviors can have an effect that is the exact opposite of what is desired. Instead of adding order and control to a person's life, they actually lead to disorder and a lack of control. Perfectionistic behaviors can increase the time needed to get things done and can make others feel uncomfortable. For example, individuals who constantly correct the work of their coworkers are likely to find that others either get angry or eventually learn to stay away. People who check and recheck their reports in order to avoid making mistakes are likely to get less done than people who are able to submit a report with minimal checking.

HOW BEHAVIOR MAINTAINS PERFECTIONISTIC BELIEFS

The relationship between behavior and thoughts is complex. Your beliefs, expectations, and interpretations all influence your behavior. For example, if you believe that being late for an appointment is unforgivable and that you should be able to plan ahead for all possible delays, you would likely leave the house earlier than necessary in order to guarantee a prompt arrival. People who believe that there is only one way to get a particular job done may be inclined to do the work themselves rather than allow others to help with the task. Students who believe that a term paper must be perfect may be inclined to procrastinate and put off starting their papers because they know that they cannot possibly meet the impossible standards that they have set for themselves.

The relationship between thoughts and behavior can also work in the opposite direction—there are ways in which behaviors can affect thoughts. Behaviors often have the function of maintaining beliefs. For example, certain behaviors can maintain perfectionistic beliefs by preventing the individual from learning that the belief is not true. People who believe that the only way to avoid making mistakes is to check and recheck their work may never learn that they could probably get by with being somewhat less careful.

Here's another example of how perfectionistic behavior can maintain perfectionistic beliefs: some people who go into too much unnecessary detail when giving other people instructions (about how to bake a cake, how to get to the mall, and so on) may believe that such detailed information is necessary to ensure that the task is carried out correctly. By continuing to go overboard when giving other people instructions, the perfectionist never learns that these beliefs are untrue. To test out the validity of the perfectionistic beliefs, it would be necessary to leave out some of the detail and see whether the instructions are still carried out correctly.

APPROPRIATE STANDARDS VS. PERFECTIONISTIC BEHAVIORS

In order to perform effectively in the world, it is important that people set standards and work toward meeting them. For example, most of us would take the time to straighten a picture that was hanging crooked on the living room wall. For many people, straightening the picture would make spending time in the living room more pleasant than would leaving it crooked. Similarly, most students check over their exams and proofread their papers before handing them in. Checking over one's schoolwork is likely to reduce the number of errors, ultimately leading to higher grades. It's not unusual for people to ask others for feedback or reassurance when unsure about whether they have performed well during a presentation. Asking for feedback allows people to find out how they perform and provides them with suggestions for improvement.

These are examples of methods that people use to ensure that their behavior meets certain standards. If people didn't adhere to their standards, the quality of their work would decrease, their relationships would suffer, their work would suffer, and there would likely be other negative consequences. In moderation, behaviors such as checking your work and fixing things that aren't quite right can be useful.

Perfectionistic behaviors are similar in content to the types of behaviors that most people engage in to maintain their standards. However, they differ in frequency and intensity. As an example, consider behavior aimed at being organized. You may know people whom you perceive as disorganized. These people are chronically late, are always losing things, and have trouble getting things done. This lack of organization affects all aspects of their functioning. Friends may be reluctant to lend money (or other items) to people who appear to be disorganized, for fear of never seeing their money again. They may also avoid making plans with people whom they perceive as disorganized, for fear that the person will not follow through with his or her part of the plan (for example, showing up on time for a dinner reservation).

Most people appreciate the importance of being organized. However, if a person's level of organization is perfectionistic, it no longer has a useful function because the person may be overly concerned about organization—to the point of not being able to get things done. This type of organization can be associated with procrastination or with a tendency to spend so much time organizing and generating lists of things to do that the actual work never gets done.

Consider the following examples of behaviors that might be considered either helpful or overly perfectionistic, depending on the context, frequency, and intensity of the behavior.

Potentially Helpful Behaviors	Perfectionistic Behaviors
Skimming a credit card application once before handing it in at the bank.	Reading every word on the credit card application four or five times and having a friend read it over as well, just to make sure there are no mistakes.
Correcting a coworker when he or she mispronounces your name.	Correcting everyone (including strangers) when they mispronounce any word at all.
Straightening up the house for an hour before guests arrive for dinner.	Taking two days off work to clean the house before guests arrive for dinner.
Changing your shirt when you realize it doesn't match your pants.	Trying on five or six different outfits each morning until you find the one that is "just right."

PERFECTIONISTIC STYLES OF BEHAVING

As we discussed before, the term "perfectionism" means different things to different people. No one person is a perfectionist in every situation or engages in every perfectionistic behavior listed in this section. On the other hand, many people do behave like a perfectionist from time to time, and it can be helpful to identify the types of perfectionistic behaviors that may be a problem for you. As you read through the following pages, identify examples from your own experience of any perfectionistic behaviors that are problematic in your life. Keep in mind that these categories of behavior overlap considerably. A particular perfectionistic behavior may fit equally well in two or more of these categories.

Overcompensating

Because perfectionism is often associated with anxiety or discomfort about the possibility of not meeting their high standards, people who are perfectionistic often overcompensate in their behavior. *Overcompensation* involves overdoing some behavior to make absolutely sure that everything is "just right." Examples of overcompensation include the following:

Natasha lives about twenty minutes from work. However, she leaves ninety minutes before having to arrive at work—just in case there are unanticipated delays.

To ensure that his tax return was completed correctly, Danny hired the most expensive accountant in town, even though his return was very straightforward.

To make sure that his client received his communication, Thomas left the message by telephone, e-mail, fax, and regular mail. He then telephoned the client a week later to make sure that the messages were received.

Oliver tends to tell stories in excruciating detail to make sure that nothing is left out.

Miles believes that by keeping perfectly clean, he can avoid becoming ill. He is especially concerned about avoiding possible contamination from germs and other agents that may cause him to get sick. To be sure that he stays germ-free, he washes his hands more than thirty times a day and frequently asks his family members to wash their hands.

Barry worries excessively about losing documents on his computer. Therefore, he tends to back up each document that he writes—on five separate CDs.

EXERCISE 4.1 Overcompensating

Do you sometimes overcompensate to make sure everything is perfect? If so, record some examples of your own overcompensating in your journal.

Excessive Checking and Reassurance Seeking

People who tend to be perfectionistic often engage in frequent or excessive checking to make sure that they have done things correctly, that no one else has made a mistake, or that some standard has been met by themselves or another person. A specific form of checking involves repeatedly seeking reassurance from others that a particular task was done well enough or that some other standard has been met. Examples of excessive checking and reassurance seeking include the following experiences:

Before submitting a completed form (for instance, a credit card or job application), Dana spends hours looking it over for errors. If he is unable to check an important form to his satisfaction, he sometimes is up all night worrying about it.

Patrick cannot leave the house without checking over and over again to make sure that all the appliances have been turned off and unplugged. Because of his excessive checking, he is usually late for work and sometimes doesn't make it in to work at all.

Although she is often told she looks attractive, Louise is convinced that her nose is too large for her face. She spends several hours each day looking in the mirror to evaluate whether her nose looks too big.

Ken makes a point of watching his fellow coworkers each day to see who arrives on time and who is late.

Karyn, a pharmacist, feels compelled to check the amounts and names of all medications that she dispenses ten to twelve times each before giving them to a customer.

Although she rarely makes mistakes, Jennifer asks her supervisor and coworkers many times daily to check over her work. She does this so that she can be reassured that she has done it correctly.

Even though Gus is an excellent cook, he constantly doubts his ability to cook well and, as a result, rarely cooks for other people. When he does, he requires excessive reassurance from everyone in his family that they enjoyed the meal.

Do you check excessively to make sure that everything is perfect? In your journal, list some examples of excessive checking and reassurance seeking from your own life.

Repeating and Correcting

If a behavior is perceived as incorrect or a situation doesn't "feel" right, it may seem overly important to correct the behavior or situation. At times, perfectionism can be associated with a tendency to go overboard with respect to correcting one's own behavior or that of another person, even if the consequences of not correcting the behavior are, in reality, minimal. In fact, the consequences of repeating and correcting one's actions are often greater than the consequences of not engaging in these behaviors.

For example, an individual who constantly points out every time anyone makes a mistake—even if the "mistake" is minor (for example, how the other person chooses to complete a task)—can lead others to become angry or hurt. Furthermore, no matter how consistently people are corrected, they are going to continue making mistakes. Here are some examples of repeating actions and correcting situations:

If Candace notices that a book on her shelf has a creased cover, she feels compelled to replace the book with a new copy. She spends several hundred dollars per year replacing things because of defects that most people would not even notice.

If Nathan's laundry is not folded perfectly, he tends to refold it many times until he is satisfied.

When talking to people, Phyllis tends to repeat herself to make absolutely sure that she is being understood. Unfortunately, people often become bored with the conversation and listen less and less as time goes on.

Do you tend to repeat actions and correct information to make sure that everything is perfect? In your journal, list some examples of repeating and correcting from your own life.

Excessive Organizing and List Making

People who are perfectionistic may spend too much time on organizational details, such as making lists of things to do, making lists of possessions, or putting belongings in a particular order. Although some level of organization is helpful (for example, it makes it easier to find things that you're looking for), excessive organization can get in the way of completing tasks. Following are some examples of excessive organization and list making:

Bruce spends several hours each week organizing his family's music, books, movies, and computer software. In addition, he keeps a detailed inventory on his computer of all his music, books, and software. Each week, he checks to make sure that all of his CDs, DVDs, books, and software are stored in alphabetical order. If items have been misplaced or filed out of order, he becomes frustrated with his family for not being able to put things back where they belong.

Each morning, Maya spends more than an hour making a list of all the chores and tasks that she needs to accomplish for the day. She spends additional time making sure that the items are listed in the most efficient order, so that no unnecessary time is lost between tasks. If she misses a task or has to complete the list out of order, she feels compelled to rewrite her list so that it accurately reflects what she is doing. She keeps her lists of things to do for years, just in case she needs them.

Jeffrey cannot get any work done until his office is completely tidy and organized. As a result, he often spends more time making his office tidy and organized than he actually spends working.

Dar is a student who spends many hours each week planning her strategy for studying (for example, calculating exactly how much time she should spend studying for each subject). As a result, she is left with little time to actually study.

EXERCISE 4.4   Excessive Organizing and List Making

Do you tend to spend too much time organizing and making lists? If so, list some examples of excessive organizing and list making in your journal.

Difficulty Making Decisions

People who are perfectionistic sometimes have a hard time making decisions. Faced with many different alternatives, perfectionistic individuals may be anxious about making a mistake that might be irreversible and potentially catastrophic. Difficulty making decisions can affect almost any area of an individual's functioning by making it hard to do one's work, complete tasks, and even respond to questions. Below are some examples of difficulty in making decisions:

Ray finds it very difficult to make decisions about everyday activities (for example, deciding what movie to watch or deciding what to wear in the morning) because he fears making a wrong choice. As a result, it takes him longer to get things done compared to other people. His friends and family often become frustrated while waiting for him to make decisions.

Because of his difficulty making decisions, Miguel changes his mind frequently. For example, after ordering a meal in a restaurant, it is not unusual for him to change his order several times before actually receiving his food.

Linda prefers to have others make decisions for her so that she cannot be blamed for making a wrong choice.

EXERCISE 4.5   Difficulty Making Decisions

Do you find it hard to make decisions? Does it take you a long time to choose among several options? If so, record in your journal some examples of the types of decisions you find it difficult to make.

Procrastination

Because perfection can almost never be achieved, people who are constantly aiming for perfection may put off doing things for fear that they will never meet their targets or goals. By not starting things, perfectionists don't need to deal with the possibility of doing a less-than-perfect job. In some cases, perfectionism may lead to complete avoidance of situations in which an individual may not measure up. Following are examples of procrastination:

Because Michelle feels such intense pressure to do well in all her classes, she tends to take her schoolwork very seriously. With each paper that she hands in, it is very important to her that she impresses her professor. She tends to put off starting her work because she fears that the task of writing the perfect paper will be too overwhelming.

In order to lose weight, Michael has come up with a very complex list of rules for what he can and cannot eat, as well as a detailed exercise plan. However, he has serious doubts about whether he is going to be able to stick to his plan. To minimize the chances of failing, he has delayed starting his new weight loss plan until the time feels "right." So far, it's been two years and the time has not yet felt right.

Jason has been interested in getting to know a new coworker for several weeks. However, rather than just saying hello, he has been dwelling on trying to come up with the best way to introduce himself.

EXERCISE 4.6   Procrastination

Are you a procrastinator? In your journal, list some examples of procrastination from your own life.

Not Knowing When to Quit

In order to reach a particular goal or target, people who are perfectionistic will sometimes continue to work on a task for too long. This can interfere with their ability to complete projects and can also frustrate other people. Here are some examples of not knowing when to quit:

Despite being very bright, Anne rarely finishes her exams on time. When she encounters a question for which she doesn't know the answer, she becomes determined to get it right. As a result of her determination, she often spends too much time on these difficult items and doesn't have time to complete later questions on the test.

Alice finds it very difficult to accept others who don't see things the way she does. When she disagrees with another person about a matter, she usually continues trying to convince the other person of her point of view, often to the point of getting into arguments and compromising her relationships with others.

In preparation for his wedding, Rashad had a very difficult time deciding whom to invite. In preparing his list (which was to be no more than one hundred people), he began with his immediate family, close friends, and coworkers. However, as he continued to add names, he had great difficulty stopping. He worried that people might be offended if they were not invited. He ended up with a list of over three hundred people that included distant relatives, people at work that he hardly knew, and many friends with whom he had lost touch.

Do you sometimes spend so much time on tasks that you don't get your other work done? In your journal, list some examples of not knowing when to quit from your own life.

Giving Up Too Soon

This particular behavioral style is the opposite of not knowing when to quit. People who tend to be perfectionistic sometimes give up trying because of their anxiety over not being able to reach a particular goal or standard. Examples of giving up too soon include the following:

Despite being told by his guitar teacher that his playing was coming along very well, Hans quit taking guitar lessons because he felt that it was taking too long to achieve the level of competence that he desired.

Phyllis believed that she wasn't living up to her supervisor's expectations, even though her supervisor was very happy with her job performance. Phyllis decided to quit her job, rather than wait to be fired for making a mistake.

Danny quit his job as an interior designer because he believed that he would never be among the top designers in the country.

Because she thought that she could never find a partner that met all her needs, Keisha gave up trying and decided to stay single.

EXERCISE 4.8   Giving Up Too Soon

In your journal, list some examples of giving up too soon from your own life.

Excessive Slowness

Perfectionism can sometimes lead people to do things more slowly than they would otherwise. Slowness is often related to some of the other behaviors discussed earlier. For example, procrastination can cause people to take longer before starting a particular project or activity. Also, people who have difficulty making decisions often take a long time to choose among several options (things like choosing what color to paint the living room). Finally, people who check excessively sometimes take longer to complete tasks, particularly if they continually check their performance as they go along. Perfectionism can even lead to slower performance beyond these other behaviors. Some individuals who are perfectionistic have a slower style of getting things done. By doing things more slowly and carefully, they may feel less likely to make an error. Examples of excessive slowness follow:

Jed tends to read very slowly so that he doesn't miss any important information.

Tia speaks more slowly than other people do so that she can think very carefully about what she says and avoid saying the wrong thing.

Danielle spends much more time than most people do when she showers, washes her hands, or brushes her teeth. While cleaning herself, she wants to be absolutely sure that she has done it properly.

Luke is very handy with tools. He finished his basement on his own and loves building and fixing things. He would like to have his own renovation company; however, his perfectionism slows him down. He does an excellent job, but he works much more slowly than other contractors and therefore would have a hard time earning enough money working as a contractor.

EXERCISE 4.9   Excessive Slowness

Does it take you a long time to get things done? If so, list some examples of your own excessive slowness in your journal.

Failure to Delegate

Perfectionism is sometimes associated with a tendency to mistrust that others can do things properly. Individuals who have trouble trusting others may avoid delegating tasks to people unless they are sure that the other person will complete them perfectly. Here are a few examples illustrating a failure to delegate.

Louis insists on doing all of the cooking and cleaning at home, despite the fact that his wife and children often offer to help. Although Louis doesn't enjoy these chores, he has very strict beliefs about how things should be done. He is therefore reluctant to let others help him, for fear that the tasks won't be done correctly and his standards will not be met.

Phil has just been promoted to a new managerial position, which includes a new, full-time secretary. Although his new secretary is very experienced and competent, Phil has trouble asking him to do any of Phil's clerical work (typing, filing, and so on), for fear that he will not do things the way Phil likes them done.

Hilary refused to leave her children with a babysitter because she was convinced that the babysitter would not enforce the household rules (things like bedtime and so on) and that her children would learn bad habits.

EXERCISE 4.10   Failure to Delegate

Do you need to do everything yourself to make sure that it's all done correctly? If so, list in your journal some examples of your own failures to delegate.

Hoarding

For some people, perfectionism can be associated with difficulty throwing things away. For example, people may hold on to old newspapers, magazines, or pamphlets. Other people may keep empty jars, packages, letters, broken appliances, or other trivial items. In fact, people can hoard almost anything. Hoarding is not the same as having a collection of some kind. Nor is it the same as keeping things for sentimental value. People who have problems with hoarding often have their homes filled with various things that they don't need or enjoy. Hoarding can lead to problems in relationships (for instance, if an individual's partner wants to throw something away) and can make it difficult to keep one's home clean. The most common reasons why people keep things they don't need include the belief that the item may be needed one day, as well as a more general discomfort with the thought of throwing the item away. Examples of hoarding include these experiences:

Donald has kept every bill, bank statement, and receipt that he has received in the past fifteen years. All of his papers are neatly filed in filing cabinets that fill nearly an entire room. Although he has only had to refer to an old bill or receipt a few times over the years, he keeps everything, just in case he needs them.

Karla hates the thought of running out of things she needs. Therefore, she always has extra stores of food, tissues, toothpaste, cleaning products, office supplies, and other items that she uses regularly. However, whereas most people might have an extra tube of toothpaste in the house, Karla feels very uncomfortable unless she has many extras of each item she might require. For example, at any one time, she tends to have twenty tubes of toothpaste, fifty rolls of toilet paper, fifteen bottles of dish soap, and many extras of most other household items.

EXERCISE 4.11   Hoarding

Are you a pack rat? If so, describe briefly your own hoarding tendencies in your journal.

Avoidance

Because perfectionistic standards are often so difficult to meet, people who strive to be perfect will sometimes avoid situations in which they might feel compelled to meet these impossible standards. We described some specific examples of avoidance earlier. These include failing to delegate tasks to others, procrastinating, and giving up on tasks too quickly. Following are some additional examples of avoidance:

Julie avoids weighing herself because she knows that if she has gained even one pound, it will ruin her day.

Although he is very bright and competent, Darcy decided not to attend college because he believes that he could never be satisfied with his performance.

Pierre, a chef, is rarely able to enjoy other people's cooking. To avoid being disappointed, he tends not to have his partner or friends cook for him, and he rarely eats in restaurants.

Lois never asks for help or advice from anyone. She worries that if she asks for help other people would notice that she is not perfect, and it is very important to Lois that others think she is flawless.

Naomi tends to avoid spending time around other people at work or socially because she believes that others perceive her as not being particularly entertaining, interesting, witty, or bright. Even when other people invite her to a party or gathering, she assumes that they would not enjoy her company if she did show up.

EXERCISE 4.12   Avoidance

Do you avoid any situations because of your perfectionism? In your journal, list some examples of avoidance from your own life.

Attempts to Change the Behavior of Others

When people are too concerned about how things are done, they may be overly critical of the behavior of others and may frequently try to change that behavior. Examples of attempts to change the behavior of others include the following:

On a daily basis, Amelia feels compelled to correct the way her boyfriend washes dishes. Despite her frequent reminders for him to use warmer water, use more detergent, and let the dishes soak, he continues to wash the dishes the way he has always washed them.

Gary is uncomfortable with the fact that not everyone at work shares his religious beliefs. In hopes of converting his coworkers to his way of seeing things, he frequently brings in religious literature and invites people to attend religious services with him, even after they have declined his offer several times and haven't expressed any interest.

Lately, Jane finds that almost every little thing her fourteen-year-old daughter does gets on her nerves. She constantly reminds her daughter to hold her fork properly, sit up straight, take off her shoes in the house, and behave more or less the way Jane does whenever possible.

EXERCISE 4.13 Attempts to Change
the Behavior of Others

Do you find yourself always trying to change the behavior of those around you? If so, list some examples in your journal.

PART 2

Strategies for Overcoming Perfectionism

CHAPTER 5

Measuring Your Perfectionism

THE PURPOSE OF CONDUCTING AN ASSESSMENT

Before a psychologist, psychiatrist, or other professional begins to help an individual to deal with a particular problem, there is typically a period of assessment. Assessment involves collecting information to better understand the nature and severity of a problem and to help develop the best possible treatment plan. For example, if a client visits a therapist seeking help for problems with anxiety, the therapist is likely to begin the first session (or even the first few sessions) by simply asking questions about the main problem, other difficulties the client may be experiencing, and the client's background. The client may be asked to complete a series of questionnaires that measure anxiety and related problems. In addition, diaries may be completed to measure anxiety and other reactions throughout the week, when the person actually encounters particular anxiety-provoking situations. The assessment process helps the clinician to get to know the client and is essential for identifying and understanding the problem. In addition, the findings from the assessment are often important for choosing and recommending a course of treatment.

In the same way, a detailed self-assessment will help you to understand and change your difficulties with perfectionism. Before you begin to work on changing your own perfectionism, this chapter will guide you through a detailed self-assessment with three main components:

identifying key problem areas, measuring the severity of the problem, and measuring changes that may result from using the strategies described in this book.

IDENTIFYING PROBLEM AREAS

An important function of the initial assessment phase is to describe the features of your perfectionism and to identify the main problem areas. These include identification of perfectionistic thoughts and behaviors as well as situations that trigger perfectionistic responses.

Isolating Your Perfectionistic Thoughts and Behaviors

In chapters 3 and 4, you identified your perfectionistic thoughts and behaviors. Because perfectionistic beliefs and behaviors vary across people, it is important to identify the unique ways in which your perfectionism is manifested. Reviewing the beliefs and behaviors that you identified in chapters 3 and 4 will be helpful.

EXERCISE 5.1   Perfectionism Diary

Here is an example of a diary to record episodes during which perfectionism comes up in your everyday life. You may want to photocopy this sample or develop your own. Each time you find yourself having a perfectionistic thought (such as those you listed in your journal while reading chapter 3) or engaging in a perfectionistic behavior (such as those you listed while reading chapter 4), record the information requested on your perfectionism diary. The first step to changing perfectionistic thinking is to catch yourself in the act. Completing the perfectionism diary will help you to identify times when you are thinking or behaving in a perfectionistic manner.

Perfectionism Diary

Date _____   Time _____

Situation _____

_____

Perfectionistic Thoughts

_____

_____

Perfectionistic Behaviors

_____

_____

Mood (anxiety, sadness, anger, and so on)

_____

_____

Isolating Situations and Triggers for Your Perfectionism

For many perfectionists, their overly high standards are more problematic in some situations than in others. For example, they may be very perfectionistic in their work, but fairly laid-back at home. Therefore, as part of your self-assessment, it's important to identify the specific situations that trigger your perfectionism. For example, do your perfectionistic thoughts and behaviors occur more often with certain people, during particular activities, or in certain places?

EXERCISE 5.2 Identifying Your Perfectionism Triggers

Below is a list of people (part 1) and activities (part 2) that sometimes trigger perfectionistic beliefs and behaviors. For each item that reflects an area in which you tend to be perfectionistic, list some examples of the ways in which your perfectionism is manifested. Next, for each item in the list, estimate the degree to which perfectionism is a problem for you. You may need to think carefully about this task and to take some time to complete it. Use a scale ranging from 0 (perfectionism is not at all a problem) to 100 (perfectionism is very much a problem). For example, a score of 50 would reflect a moderate level of perfectionism. Later, these numbers will help you to choose specific areas to work on. Areas in which perfectionism is more of a problem may be those that you will choose to focus on first.

Part 1: People with Whom You Tend to Be Overly Perfectionistic

Person	Examples	Intensity (0-100)
Partner	I tend to be overly concerned about what clothes my boyfriend wears when we go out.	65
	I get very angry if my wife arrives home even five minutes later than she said she would arrive.	70

Person	Examples	Intensity (0-100)
Spouse or partner	_____	
	_____	_____
Children	_____	
	_____	_____
Parents	_____	
	_____	_____
Siblings	_____	
	_____	_____
Friends	_____	
	_____	_____
Coworkers	_____	
	_____	_____
Strangers	_____	
	_____	_____
Service people	_____	
	_____	_____
Other	_____	
	_____	_____

Part 2: Activities in Which You Tend to Be Overly Perfectionistic

Activity	Examples	Intensity (0-100)
Cleaning	I spend many more hours cleaning than most people in an effort to makes sure that everything is perfectly clean.	80
	I get overly angry with my children when they leave toys lying around.	80
Work	I get irritated when my employees are even ten minutes late to work.	45

Activity	Examples	Intensity (0-100)
Work/School	_____ _____	_____
Art or Music	_____ _____	_____
Housework	_____ _____	_____
Organizing things	_____ _____	_____
Relationships	_____ _____	_____

Small
decisions   _____

             _____   _____

Eating   _____

             _____   _____

Sports/
Fitness   _____

             _____   _____

Grooming/
Washing   _____

             _____   _____

Driving   _____

             _____   _____

Other   _____

             _____   _____

Other   _____

             _____   _____

MEASURING THE SEVERITY OF THE PROBLEM

Your self-assessment should include an analysis of how severe or impairing your perfectionism is. In examining the severity of the problem, you will need to take several different steps, including: deciding whether your high standards are helpful or unhelpful, identifying the areas of functioning that are impaired as a result of the perfectionism (work, relationships, emotional well-being, and so on), estimating the impact of your perfectionism on others, identifying the effects of perfectionism on your emotional functioning, and identifying the extent to which your perfectionistic beliefs are flexible versus rigid.

Helpful vs. Unhelpful Standards

Perfectionistic standards, as opposed to beneficial high standards, are so high that they either can't be met or they can only be met at an enormous cost to yourself or others. Making the distinction between helpful and unhelpful standards can often be difficult for people who are perfectionists. One reason for this is that a standard that is helpful for one person may be overly perfectionistic for another person. For example, a professional squash player must meet very high standards in order to make a living at the game, while an individual who plays squash in their leisure time can afford to have lower standards. In fact, having overly high standards can lead to unnecessary anger and disappointment when a mistake is made or a game is lost. For such a person, overly high standards might be considered perfectionistic and, therefore, not especially helpful.

EXERCISE 5.3 Reevaluating Your Standards

The best way to identify whether your own standards are overly perfectionistic is to look at the impact of having these standards. For each of the following questions, record your responses in your journal:

- Are your standards higher than those of other people?

- Are you able to meet your standards?

- Are other people able to meet your standards?

- Do your standards help you to achieve your goals or do they get in the way (for example, by making you overly disappointed or angry when your standards are not met or causing you to get less work done)?

- What would the costs be of relaxing a particular standard or ignoring a rule?

- What would the benefits be of relaxing a particular standard or ignoring a rule?

Sometimes, when you are too close to an issue, it's hard to have a realistic perspective. For example, if you have been behaving in a perfectionistic way for a long time, it may be hard to imagine thinking differently about a certain issue. If you're unsure about how to answer any or all of the above questions, try to get some distance from the issue by imagining how someone else might look at the particular problem. You may even want to consider asking people whom you trust about their beliefs regarding the standard or rule in question. For example, if you are overly concerned about making a mistake when giving a presentation, you could try to imagine how another person might feel about the consequences of making mistakes during presentations. You might even ask a coworker what he or she thinks when a presenter makes a mistake while talking. This will help you to determine whether your concern about doing a perfect presentation is exaggerated.

If you determine that a particular standard cannot be met or that the costs of having a particular standard or rule outweigh the benefits, you may want to consider loosening your standards for that particular issue. For example, during times when you are very busy at work, maybe it's okay if your home is a bit messier than usual.

If you still feel unsure about whether your standards are exaggerated or perfectionistic, or if others continue to complain about behaviors that you feel reflect appropriately high standards and your relationships are suffering as a result, it may be helpful to visit a therapist and get a professional opinion from an unbiased third party.

In your journal, make a list of (1) standards held by you that are helpful
and worth holding on to, and (2) standards held by you that are unhelpful (that is, standards that sometimes get in the way, slow you down, or
disturb people who are close to you).

PERFECTIONISM AND AREAS OF FUNCTIONING

One measure of the severity of a problem is the extent to which it interferes with a person's functioning. In chapter 2, you identified ways in
which particular areas of your life are affected by perfectionistic beliefs
and behaviors. On the next page is a list of areas that are often affected
by perfectionism. For each relevant area, list some examples of ways
in which your perfectionism interferes. Next, for each item in the list,
estimate the degree to which perfectionism interferes with that specific
area. Use a scale ranging from 0 (perfectionism causes no interference)
to 100 (perfectionism is completely impairing). For example, a score of
50 would reflect a moderate level of interference in that domain. You
may wish to refer back to the notes you made in your journal while
reading chapter 2 for examples of how perfectionism affects these areas
of your life.

Assessing the Degree of Impairment Caused by Perfectionism in Your Life

Domain	Examples	Intensity (0-100)
Work	I am unable to get all my work done because I tend to check my work excessively.	70
	My coworkers tend to avoid me because I often correct everything they do—even when the issue doesn't affect me directly.	55
Work/School	_____ _____	____
Housework	_____ _____	____
Recreation/ Hobbies	_____ _____	____
Close Relationships	_____ _____	____
Other Relationships	_____ _____	____
Diet	_____ _____	____

Domain	Examples	Intensity (0-100)
Self-care	_____	
	_____	_____
Other	_____	
	_____	_____
Other	_____	
	_____	_____

THE EFFECT OF PERFECTIONISM ON OTHERS

It is important to assess the impact of your perfectionism on those around you. By doing this, you can improve your interpersonal relationships by reducing the strain that can be caused by perfectionistic criticizing and directing, as well as reducing your own irritation and anger about the actions of others that you would perform differently.

EXERCISE 5.6   How Your Perfectionism Affects Those Around You

In your journal, answer the following questions to the best of your ability:

- How do people react to you when you impose your standards on them?

- How do others respond when they observe you imposing inappropriately high standards on yourself?

- Are there times when others become frustrated with your perfectionistic behaviors?

- Are some people anxious around you for fear of making a mistake in your presence?

- How do *you* respond to other people who tend to be perfectionistic with themselves or with other people?

If you are not sure how your perfectionism affects other people, it might be worth asking one or two people how they are affected by your perfectionistic behaviors. Choose people who are close to you and who you can trust. Here are some questions that you might ask the other individual:

- Have you noticed ways (for instance, situations, behaviors, and so on) in which I am overly perfectionistic or rigid?

- How are you affected when I do _____?

- In what areas would you like to see me become less perfectionistic?

- What impact would it have on our relationship if I were to become less perfectionistic?

After you have obtained more information about the effect of your perfectionism on other people, try to process the information in a way that is helpful. Here are some questions to ask yourself (record your responses in your journal):

- How do you feel after hearing about the effects of your perfectionism on others?

- Does your perfectionism affect your relationships?

- Do you want to become less perfectionistic in your relationships?

- Which specific behaviors or standards do you want to decrease or end completely?

- Which specific behaviors or standards do you want to keep the same?

PERFECTIONISM AND EMOTIONAL FUNCTIONING

Your self-assessment should include an examination of the ways in which perfectionism affects you *emotionally*. Sometimes perfectionism can lead to feelings of depression if a person finds that his or her high standards are never met (for example, a student who feels depressed because his grades are not high enough to be accepted into graduate school).

For other individuals, perfectionism can be associated with intense anxiety, nervousness, or fear. For example, some people with unreasonably high standards for themselves report intense anxiety about being judged negatively by others if they make a mistake or do not meet their own unrealistically high standards. Finally, for some people, perfectionism is associated with feelings of frequent anger, irritability, and frustration. This is often the case for individuals who hold unreasonably high standards for those around them.

EXERCISE 5.7 How Your Perfectionism Affects Your Emotional Functioning

Take a few moments to consider the ways in which perfectionism contributes to your emotional states. Can you think of times when your perfectionistic beliefs or standards led to feelings of depression, anxiety, or anger?

Part 1: Think about times when your perfectionism has caused you to feel sad or depressed. In your diary, record all relevant details, including (1) the situation or trigger, (2) your reaction in the situation (your perfectionistic thoughts and behaviors), and (3) the intensity of the sadness or depression (using a scale from 0 to 100).

Part 2: Think about times when your perfectionism has caused you to feel anxious. In your diary, record all relevant details, including (1) the situation or trigger, (2) your reaction in the situation (your perfectionistic thoughts and behaviors), and (3) the intensity of your anxiety (using a scale from 0 to 100).

Part 3: Think about times when your perfectionism has caused you to feel angry, irritable, or frustrated. In your diary, record all relevant details, including (1) the situation or trigger, (2) your reaction in the situation (your perfectionistic thoughts and behaviors), and (3) the intensity of your angry feelings (using a scale from 0 to 100).

FLEXIBLE VS. RIGID PERFECTIONISTIC BELIEFS

Another important aspect of your perfectionism to consider is the extent to which your perfectionistic attitudes are flexible and therefore easily changed. Your self-assessment should include an evaluation of how rigid your perfectionistic beliefs are. The less rigid you are with yourself and your beliefs, the easier it will be to change. Just recognizing your rigidity in particular areas may motivate you to become more flexible.

EXERCISE 5.8   Assessing the Flexibility of Your Perfectionistic Beliefs

The extent to which you answer yes to the following questions may be an indication that your perfectionistic beliefs are relatively inflexible. If this is the case, you will need to work especially hard at changing these beliefs and behaviors. You may also need to remind yourself from time to time about the costs and benefits of changing your standards (chapter 6 discusses this issue in more detail). If you answer no to most of these questions, you will likely find it easier to change your beliefs and behaviors using the exercises described in upcoming chapters. Record your responses to each of the following questions in your journal:

- Is it difficult for you to recognize when you are being overly perfectionistic? If so, list examples.

- Do you find it difficult to relax your standards? If so, list examples.

- Typically, are you unwilling to consider the possibility that you are being overly perfectionistic (even when your relationships are suffering and others blame your perfectionism)? If so, list examples.

- Do you often find yourself disagreeing with other people when they tell you that your standards are too high or too rigid? If so, list examples.

- Do you become very upset when you are unable to meet your own standards? If so, list examples.

- Do you become very upset when others are unable to meet your standards? If so, list examples.

EXERCISE 5.9   Putting It All Together

Throughout this chapter (as well as chapters 3 and 4), you have recorded a large amount of information about your perfectionism. Now it's time to compile the information into one handy summary. You may wish to refer to your responses throughout chapters 3, 4, and 5 when completing this summary. Record your responses to the following items in your journal:

Styles of Perfectionistic Thinking

List (from chapter 3) the styles of perfectionistic thinking (all-or-nothing thinking, filtering, and so on) that are most problematic for you. Give an example of each from your own life.

Styles of Perfectionistic Behavior

List (from chapter 4) the styles of perfectionistic behavior (overcompensating, excessive checking, and so on) that are most problematic for you. Give an example of each from your own life.

People with Whom You Tend to Be Overly Perfectionistic

List (from this chapter) the people with whom you tend to be overly perfectionistic (partner, coworkers, and so on).

Activities That Tend to Trigger Your Perfectionism

List (from this chapter) the activities that are most likely to trigger your perfectionistic thoughts and behaviors (work, relationships, and so on) and are the most problematic for you.

Helpful and Unhelpful Standards

List the most important helpful standards, rules, or preferences that you recorded earlier in this chapter, which you may wish to maintain. Then list the most unhelpful (perfectionistic) standards that are problematic for you and that you may wish to change.

Areas of Functioning That Are Most Impaired Because of Your Perfectionism

List (from this chapter) the areas of functioning that are most impaired because of your perfectionism (relationships, hobbies, and so on). Note that these areas are likely to overlap somewhat with the activities that trigger your perfectionism.

The Effect of Your Perfectionism on Others

List examples of how your perfectionism affects other people.

Perfectionism and Emotional Functioning

List examples (see earlier section in this chapter) of how your perfectionism causes you to feel depressed, anxious, or angry from time to time.

MEASURING IMPROVEMENT AND CHANGE

In addition to helping you understand the origins and nature of your perfectionistic beliefs and behaviors, another function of assessment is to measure changes in perfectionism over time. Therapists sometimes ask their clients to repeat the initial measures (for example, questionnaires, diaries, and so on) periodically during their treatment. This is a helpful way to assess whether a person's problem is improving.

By continuing to use the assessment strategies discussed in this chapter throughout the process of changing your thoughts and behaviors, you will be able to determine whether you are in fact making progress. Here are some specific recommendations for how to continue to assess your perfectionism as you work through this book. Note that these are only suggestions. You can pick and choose among these recommendations based on your own needs:

- Examine the responses in your perfectionism summary (exercise 5.9) from time to time to assess whether there have been changes in the types of perfectionistic thoughts and behaviors you experience, the intensity of your perfectionism, and the ways it impacts your day-to-day functioning. When you examine the summary, you may add items if you notice new triggers for your perfectionism, or perfectionistic thoughts or behaviors, that were not recorded initially.

- Note any items on the summary that no longer belong on the list (in fact, you can complete a new summary periodically, to assess how things have changed).

- Initially, you should reexamine the summary weekly. After six to eight weeks, when things have begun to improve, you may decrease the frequency of looking at the form to once every two weeks. When your perfectionism has decreased even further, you may reduce the frequency further (for example, monthly). When you are no longer working on your perfectionism, you can stop the formal assessments. You may still want to conduct an informal assessment from time to time, by just asking yourself how things are going with respect to your perfectionistic thoughts and behaviors.

- Continue using the perfectionism diary, described in this chapter, as long as you are working on changing your perfectionistic beliefs and behaviors.

CHAPTER 6

Developing a Plan for Change

Before beginning to use the strategies for overcoming perfectionism, there are several steps that should be taken to prepare for change. In this chapter, we will help you examine the costs and benefits of becoming less perfect so you can assess whether you really are motivated to work on your perfectionism at this time. We will also help you identify specific goals for change, so you can choose exercises that will help you to reach those goals, and so you can judge whether you are making the improvements that you had hoped to make.

In preparation for the process of change, we also discuss ways of choosing among the various treatment strategies in this book, as well as strategies for finding additional help if the techniques described in the book are difficult to implement on your own. The chapter concludes with a discussion of some possible obstacles to overcoming perfectionism and how to deal with them.

COSTS AND BENEFITS OF LOWERING YOUR STANDARDS

If perfectionism is a problem for you, chances are that the high standards you hold for yourself or others are long-standing and deeply ingrained. The thought of giving up these standards may be very frightening for a number of reasons. First, although you may be aware of your tendency to be perfectionistic, it may be difficult for you to determine which beliefs are overly perfectionistic and which standards are appropriate. If overcoming perfectionism involves lowering certain standards, you may be fearful of lowering the "wrong" standards.

Second, you may be reluctant to relax your standards if you believe that your performance will suffer. For example, if you believe that it is very important to be on time for appointments and therefore you always allow an extra hour to get anywhere, you may be fearful of giving up this practice in case you end up being late for appointments in the future. If you tend to be very detailed in everything you do (for example, when giving people directions, writing memos, cleaning), you may be fearful that performing tasks in a less detailed way will lead to problems. People often believe that their perfectionistic standards keep everything in their life from falling apart. They fear that giving up perfectionistic standards will lead to chaos.

A third reason why people are reluctant to become less perfectionistic is because they don't want to seem inconsistent or wishy-washy to others. If you have spent a lot of time and energy trying to have others do things your way or trying to create a certain image of yourself, the thought of changing your expectations or image may feel threatening to you. It may be very difficult to admit that you may have been too strict, or even worse, that you may have been wrong. It's ironic that most people admire others who can admit when they have made a mistake, yet it is often very difficult for us to admit our own mistakes.

Before making the decision to become less perfectionistic, you should consider the possible costs and benefits of changing. For some standards and rules that you hold, the costs of changing may outweigh the benefits. For other standards, the benefits will outweigh the costs. Examining the costs and benefits of becoming less perfectionistic can help you to decide which standards to relax.

EXERCISE 6.1 Determining Benefits and Negative Consequences of Loosening Perfectionistic Standards

In your journal, list all the possible costs of becoming less perfectionistic. Examples may include: I will make more mistakes at work; I will be more anxious while I get used to the idea of being less rigid and perfectionistic; my level of performance at school may decrease; the level of performance of others around me may decrease; others may think I am incompetent; my home won't be as clean and organized; I won't be able to find anything; I will gain weight; and so on.

Many of the possible costs that you list will be fairly unlikely to occur. So, in addition to listing these costs, you should estimate just how likely that outcome is. To estimate the likelihood of a particular negative consequence happening, use a scale ranging from 0 (definitely will not occur) to 100 (definitely will occur). An estimate of 50 means that a consequence is equally likely to occur as it is to not occur. Go back over your list and add a number estimating the likelihood that each consequence might come true.

Now, list all the possible benefits of becoming less perfectionistic. Examples may include: I will be less hurtful and critical of the people in my family; people will enjoy spending time with me; I will have time to do more things; I will be less anxious about making mistakes; work will be more enjoyable; I will be less concerned about what other people think of me; my depression will decrease; and so on. As in the earlier section on costs of becoming less perfectionistic, you should also estimate the likelihood that each positive outcome or benefit will occur if you are able to decrease your perfectionistic thinking and behavior. Use a scale ranging from 0 (definitely will not occur) to 100 (definitely will occur). An estimate of 50 means that a benefit is equally likely to occur as it is to not occur.

IDENTIFYING GOALS

Before starting to overcome any problem, it's important to define the problem and to identify goals. It's not enough to say that you want to "become less perfectionistic." The only way to evaluate whether your perfectionism has improved is to set specific goals. Remember—your goals should not be too perfectionistic! They should be realistic and achievable. Also, you should think about both long-term and short-term goals. Long-term goals may include changes that you want to make over the next year or even longer. Short-term goals may involve changes that you want to make over the next few days, weeks, or months.

Although it is helpful to think of a few general goals, you should also try to come up with goals that are as specific as possible. For example, the goal, "I will be less critical of my children" is not as specific as the goal, "I will not criticize the clothes that my children wear to school." The more specific the goal, the easier it will be to come up with strategies for reaching the goal. Below are some examples of general and specific goals.

Examples of Goals

General Goals	Specific Goals
Be less perfectionistic about physical appearance.	Be willing to gain five pounds without getting upset. Be able to tolerate missing a workout at the gym. Take no more than thirty minutes to get ready in the morning.
Be less detail oriented.	Tell stories to other people without including every detail. Hand in papers that are no longer than they're supposed to be. Submit monthly reports without checking them over more than once.
Be less concerned about being judged by others.	Mispronounce words when talking to people without becoming anxious. Be more comfortable when telling other people about what I do for a living. Be comfortable around people I perceive as smarter or more attractive than me. Be less concerned about showing signs of anxiety, such as shaking and blushing.

Become more tolerant of others.	Stop complaining about how my house-mate washes the dishes.
	Learn to tolerate my spouse arriving home thirty minutes late without phoning.
	Allow my children to make a mess when playing, as long as they clean it up by the end of each day.
Be less concerned about being clean.	Wash my hands only if visibly dirty, after bathroom breaks, and when handling food.
	Spend no more than one hour per day cleaning.
	Shake hands with others comfortably.
	Be willing to use public rest rooms.

EXERCISE 6.2   Making Your Own General and Specific Goals

Now, think about what types of changes you would like to make. Specifically, think about perfectionistic ways of thinking or behaving that you would like to decrease or stop all together. In your journal, make a list of short-term goals and long-term goals. For example, you can include goals for the next month, as well as goals for the next year. Of course, you may choose other time periods if you prefer. The main point to remember is that you may have different goals for the short term and the long term. Although some goals may be realistic targets for a year or two from now, they may not be realistic goals for one week or one month from now. In your lists, include general goals, as well as examples of specific goals that fall under each general goal.

WHAT TO CHANGE FIRST: SETTING PRIORITIES

Now that you have identified thoughts and behaviors that you would like to change, the next step is figuring out where to start. There are two general principles to keep in mind when deciding which aspects of your perfectionism to work on first: which thoughts and behaviors cause the most interference in your life, and which thoughts and behaviors are likely to be the easiest to change.

In most cases, it's best to start with the problem that interferes the most in your life or causes the most problems with other people. By choosing to work on the most important goals first, your efforts will have the largest possible impact on your life in the shortest amount of time. This will likely have the effect of motivating you to continue to work on other aspects of your perfectionism. In addition, you should also consider which goals are easiest to meet. By choosing to work on goals that are very difficult to meet, you may end up becoming discouraged and give up before making any significant changes.

Review the short-term and long-term goals that you listed earlier. Put them in order with respect to how important each goal is, as well as how attainable. We recommend beginning with the most impairing problem, but try to choose goals that you feel are manageable and realistic. If a problem seems too big and overwhelming, it will be necessary to break it up into smaller steps.

EXERCISE 6.3   Choosing Your Priorities for Change

In your journal, list the most important goals on which you plan to work. Ten or so goals is probably a good number to start with. List the goals in the order that you want to work on them. Note that the list may change as you begin working on these issues. You may decide that a particular goal is too difficult to work on right away. Or, a goal from the bottom of your list may become more important, depending on what else is happening in your life.

HOW TO CHOOSE AMONG SPECIFIC STRATEGIES

Chapters 7 and 8 describe many different techniques and exercises for overcoming perfectionistic styles of thinking and behaving. It is unlikely that you will want to use each of the methods listed. Because perfectionism affects different people in different ways, this book includes a broad range of strategies that are designed to be helpful for different people. When reading the next two chapters, it's better to choose a relatively small number of techniques and to practice them frequently. Overcoming perfectionism requires learning new skills. If you attempt to use all of the techniques described in this book, you will probably not learn any of them well enough to use them effectively. On the other hand, if you choose a small number of strategies and practice them regularly, you are more likely to notice change.

We recommend that you read through chapters 7 and 8 once, taking note of the techniques that seem most relevant to you and then rereading those sections. Also, you should choose strategies that are practical, given your lifestyle and your available resources. After trying several of the strategies described in these chapters, you will quickly discover which ones are likely to help you overcome your perfectionistic thoughts and behaviors. The main point to keep in mind as you begin to implement the strategies is that it's better to do a few things thoroughly than to attempt to do everything suggested in this book.

THE IMPORTANCE OF REGULAR PRACTICE

The strategies and exercises described in the remainder of this book will require regular practice. Ideally, you should expect to conduct some sort of practice almost every day. Although some of these practices may be quite brief, others may last up to several hours. Exercises will include such activities as completing diaries each time you experience perfectionistic thoughts, purposely making small mistakes until the thought of doing things imperfectly is less anxiety provoking, and eliminating perfectionistic behaviors such as excessive checking.

In many cases, these practices will be exercises that you can integrate into your normal activities (for example, when talking to people, working, and so on), so they need not take up much time. For other exercises, you will need to set aside blocks of time to practice. To be most effective, practices should be regular, structured, and planned in advance. You should plan to practice regardless of whether you are in the mood when the scheduled time actually comes. Also, you should have a backup plan, in case a particular practice falls through.

INVOLVING OTHERS IN YOUR PRACTICES

Because perfectionism involves other people, it may be important to include other people in your efforts to overcome perfectionistic thoughts and behaviors. There are several ways in which involving others can be helpful. First, by reading relevant sections of this book, people who are close to you will develop a better understanding of the causes of perfectionism and the methods for changing perfectionistic habits. This should help the people in your life to be more patient and understanding with you while you work on becoming less perfectionistic.

Second, some of the exercises described in the remaining chapters of the book may be difficult to do alone and may depend on the cooperation of those around you. For example, if you want to become more comfortable with people in your family doing things differently than you do, you may want to make sure that your family members understand the purpose of the exercises and ask them if they are willing to assist the process by purposely doing things that you view as imperfect.

Finally, it is likely that family, friends, and coworkers have found ways of working around your perfectionism or compensating for difficulties that you may have. For example, people who fear that you will be overly critical may avoid telling you about things that they have done. If you tend to be overly critical of your own behavior, people may avoid giving you feedback for fear of offending you. If you tend to avoid certain activities (such as cooking, paying bills, certain projects at work, and so on), for fear of making mistakes, other people in your life may be doing more than their share of these activities. If the people around you have changed their behavior because of your perfectionism, you may want to have them stop behaviors that make it easy for you to continue your perfectionistic habits, such as doing things for you or purposely trying to avoid saying anything that might trigger a perfectionistic response from you.

WHEN AND HOW TO SEEK PROFESSIONAL HELP

You may find that it is too difficult to overcome your perfectionism alone or with the help of your family or friends. It may be that your perfectionistic beliefs are too rigid and difficult to change on your own, or it may be that your anxiety is too intense to conduct the practices described in this book by yourself. Perhaps you have other difficulties such as depression or significant anxiety that interfere with your ability or motivation to work on your perfectionism. Or, perhaps you would benefit from working with another person, such as a therapist, to discuss problems that arise during treatment or to check on your progress. For many people, a trained professional can help in ways that go beyond what a book such as this can offer.

There are several advantages of seeking help from a psychologist, psychiatrist, social worker, or other mental health professional. A trained professional can help to explain various concepts, explore the causes of a problem, be involved in practices, generate appropriate exercises and practices, help solve problems that arise, and help to improve motivation. In addition, a therapist may be qualified to treat the problems that often go together with perfectionism, including anxiety disorders, eating disorders, anger, and depression. A psychiatrist, family doctor, and some psychologists can also prescribe medications that may be helpful for problems with anxiety and depression, as well as the perfectionism that can accompany these problems.

If you are interested in seeking professional help, there are several places to look for a therapist or doctor. A good place to start is with your family physician. He or she may know of other professionals who can help. Most therapists who are experienced with problems such as anxiety and depression are likely to be able to help with your perfectionism.

If you suffer from a particular anxiety disorder, depression, or another specific problem, there may also be clinics in your area that specialize in your problem. Some specialty clinics (particularly research and training clinics associated with universities) offer services at reduced costs. In the third section of this book, the chapters describe the types of treatments that have been shown to be effective for particular problems. Because there are so many different types of therapies available, it will be helpful for you to have an idea of the type of treatment that you are seeking.

Another place to get information on treatment options is through national organizations that offer referrals to consumers. An example is the Anxiety Disorders Association of America in Silver Spring, Maryland, which has a comprehensive Web site, including referrals to professionals who can help. Additional information on where to obtain treatment is available on the Web site for the National Alliance on Mental Illness (www.nami.org).

OBSTACLES TO BECOMING LESS PERFECTIONISTIC

In order to maximize your chances of making positive changes as you start the process of overcoming your perfectionism, it will be helpful to anticipate any obstacles that might get in the way of your success. By preparing for possible roadblocks in advance, you will be less likely to be affected by these potential difficulties.

If You're Unable or Unwilling to Consider Alternative Ways of Thinking

As we discussed previously, there are three reasons why it's often difficult to change ways of thinking, even when your beliefs get in the way of life. First, the natural tendency is to assume that your thoughts are true. In other words, if you are like most people, your beliefs may be ingrained and difficult to change. Second, if you come across information that disproves your beliefs, you probably tend to view it as an exception, or even worse, you ignore the information. Instead, people tend to pay more attention to information that confirms their beliefs. Finally, even when you do begin to doubt whether a belief is true, you may still do everything you can to avoid admitting that you have made a mistake. Perfectionistic thinking is especially prone to being rigid and difficult to change. In order to become less perfectionistic, you will need to be able to make a commitment to consider the possibility that particular beliefs are not true and that particular standards are not helpful. The fact that you are reading this book suggests that you're aware that perfectionism is a problem for you, and this awareness is the first step toward being willing to consider the possibility of changing your perfectionistic thoughts.

If You Feel That Perfectionism Isn't Causing Significant Problems for You

You may feel that perfectionism is not a big enough problem to warrant spending all the time and energy needed to change your perfectionistic thoughts and behaviors. In fact, the benefits of having high standards may outweigh the costs. If this is the case, you may not want to invest too much in the strategies described in this book. Even if you feel this way, it is also possible that your high standards do cause problems of which you are unaware. For example, perhaps your perfectionism has negative effects on those who are close to you. Before assuming that your perfectionism is not a problem, you may want to get a second opinion from someone who knows you well.

Even if perfectionism is currently a problem, you may find that as you practice the exercises in this book, your perfectionism gradually interferes less and less. As the problem starts to be less impairing, your motivation to work on it may decrease. You may start to think, "Why bother spending all that time and effort on the problem if it isn't bothering me anymore?" It is important to continue to work on your perfectionism even when it starts to improve. This perseverance will help to build on the gains that you have made. Also, continuing to use the strategies in this book will help to prevent the problem from getting worse again in the future (for example, during a stressful time in your life).

If You Don't Believe That You Can Change

Because perfectionism is part of your personality, you may feel as though becoming less perfectionistic is beyond the realm of possibility. You may believe that it is impossible to change a person's personality. If you hold this belief, it may be helpful to remember that your personality is really just the sum of your beliefs, attitudes, and behaviors. Breaking perfectionism down into its parts will make it easier to make changes. On a cautionary note, remember that just having the belief that you cannot change may have a negative impact on your likelihood of making changes. Researchers have shown consistently that people's expectations have an effect on whether they respond positively to therapy, medication, and other medical interventions. Therefore, it will be helpful if you can be open-minded and optimistic until you have had a chance to see whether the strategies described in this book are likely to be effective for you.

If You Feel There Are Too Many Other Things Going On in Your Life

You may find that there are other stresses or demands on your time that interfere with your ability to put forth the necessary effort for overcoming your perfectionism. Perhaps you are dealing with extreme stress at work or a serious problem in your relationship. Or perhaps you are suffering from another difficulty (for instance, excessive alcohol use, severe depression, or a serious medical problem). Or maybe you are just too busy with work, school, or taking care of your family. If this is the case, now may not be the best time to begin working on your perfectionism. If your effort is only halfhearted, you may only see a modest improvement. You may need to decide whether it's worth beginning to overcome your perfectionism now or if it would be best to wait until you can devote more time and energy to the problem. On the other hand, if your life is always stressful and busy, now may be as good a time as any.

If You Are Too Anxious to Practice

Many of the exercises described in this book are anxiety provoking. They involve purposely relaxing rules and standards for how things "should" be. For example, if you are overly concerned with being neat and clean, you may need to purposely leave things messy and purposely come into contact with things that are "dirty." The thought of allowing your standards to be lowered may be terrifying. You may fear making mistakes or having things fall apart. This fear is common among people who are using cognitive and behavioral strategies to overcome a problem. To deal with the anxiety, you need to remember that it will pass. With repeated practices, the strategies described in this book will be less scary. In fact, you will become more and more comfortable letting go of your perfectionistic thoughts and behaviors as you work.

CHAPTER 7

Changing Perfectionistic Thoughts

In chapter 3, we discussed the ways in which beliefs, interpretations, and predictions contribute to negative emotions such as anxiety, depression, and anger. We also discussed how negative thoughts contribute to perfectionism. You may recall from earlier chapters that people don't respond to what is actually occurring around them. Rather, they respond to their interpretations of what is happening around them. For example, if you fear making mistakes at work, it's not the possibility of making mistakes that makes you anxious. Instead, it's your beliefs about the meaning of making mistakes that cause you to feel upset or nervous. Perhaps you assume that making mistakes will lead to some terrible consequence that can't be corrected or undone (such as being fired or ridiculed by others). Or you may believe that making mistakes is a sign of weakness or incompetence.

Sometimes your thoughts are correct, and at other times they are incorrect. Sometimes standards are appropriate, and sometimes they are too strict. Most people's standards are not universal, and therefore, other people may not share them. In other words, everyone creates their own standards for performance based on their upbringing, past experiences, and beliefs about what kinds of behavior are appropriate. Beliefs and standards vary among individuals and across groups, including people from different cultures, ages, sexes, occupations, education levels, geographical locations, and so on.

Although standards and beliefs are subjective, people usually take for granted that their interpretations, beliefs, predictions, and standards are true. In other words, people assume that their beliefs are facts. They may also believe that other people share their beliefs and high standards. Even if they recognize that others have lower standards, they may believe that it is important to keep their own standards from slipping. Becoming less perfectionistic will involve relaxing your standards and changing your perfectionistic beliefs. It will involve treating your standards and beliefs as *possibilities* or *guesses* about the way the world should be—rather than as hard facts.

Of course, you don't need to change all beliefs and standards. Some expectations are appropriately high, and there can be costs to letting go of all standards that you have for yourself or others. The task will be trying to identify which beliefs are unrealistic or excessive and to work on changing those beliefs.

USING THOUGHT RECORDS TO CHANGE PERFECTIONISTIC THINKING

Learning to change your perfectionistic thoughts and standards is usually easier if you work through the process on paper, at least at the beginning. You can use your journal for this purpose, or you can develop a form to record and change your thoughts (we provide an example of such a form later in this chapter). With practice, the process of changing your thoughts will become more automatic, and you will no longer need to use diaries or forms.

STEPS FOR CHANGING PERFECTIONISTIC THOUGHTS

Changing thoughts involves four basic steps: identifying perfectionistic thoughts, listing possible alternative thoughts, considering the advantages and disadvantages of the original perfectionistic thoughts and the alternative thoughts, and choosing a more realistic or helpful way to view the situation. Although the process may seem easy as we describe it here, it is often more difficult in practice. Mastering these strategies will require perseverance and repetition.

Identifying Perfectionistic Thoughts

Before your perfectionistic thoughts can be changed, you must first identify them. This can be difficult for two reasons. First, you may incorrectly view your perfectionistic thoughts as appropriate and accurate. Second, you may be completely unaware of your perfectionistic assumptions—these thoughts may be so familiar and automatic that you don't even notice them.

It may be easier to identify times when you are engaging in perfectionistic thinking if you pay attention to three particular situations. First, notice when you feel that you are not living up to your own expectations (for instance, you're not performing well at work or school; other people are judging you to be unattractive, incompetent, or overly anxious; you are unhappy about some aspect of your body, such as your weight; you are anxious about saying the wrong thing, and so on). Second, notice when you feel that other people are not living up to your expectations (for example, people at work make too many careless mistakes, your children's grades never seem to live up to your expectations, people don't know how to drive properly, and so on). Finally, take note when you find yourself engaging in perfectionistic behaviors (such as checking and rechecking your work, apologizing too much for minor mistakes, exercising excessively to stay thin, spending too much time cleaning, and so on). If you find yourself engaging in perfectionistic behaviors or holding on to standards that are not being met, you may need to ask yourself, "Am I thinking like a perfectionist?" If you aren't sure, ask someone you trust for their opinion.

If you have difficulty identifying your perfectionistic thoughts, we recommend that you read chapter 3 again. That chapter lists types of perfectionistic thinking styles and provides several examples of each.

Listing Possible Alternative Thoughts

Once you have identified a particular perfectionistic belief, the next step is to consider possible alternative beliefs or thoughts. This can be difficult because perfectionistic thoughts and standards are often ingrained and automatic, and it can feel almost impossible to even consider other ways of viewing a situation. One way of helping with this process is to ask yourself the question, "How might someone else view this situation?" You can even think about particular people in your life (for instance, your spouse, best friend, boss, daughter, father, and so on) and ask yourself how they might view the situation. This strategy, which involves taking another person's perspective, is discussed in more detail later in this chapter.

Considering the Advantages and Disadvantages of the Original and Alternative Thoughts

The next step involves identifying the advantages and disadvantages of holding on to your original perfectionistic thoughts and standards versus adopting the alternative thoughts and standards. Strategies to use here include evaluating the evidence for and against particular beliefs or standards and testing out the accuracy of your beliefs using mini-experiments (also known as *hypothesis testing*). These and other techniques are described later in this chapter.

Choosing More Realistic or Helpful Ways to View the Situation

After you have evaluated the advantages and disadvantages of changing your beliefs and standards, you will be in a position to choose a more realistic and helpful way of thinking about the situation. Changing your thoughts will lead to a reduction in anxiety, depression, anger, or other negative feelings associated with perfectionism.

EXERCISE 7.1 A Diary for Changing Your Perfectionistic Thoughts

Here is a diary that you can use to help you work through the four steps for changing perfectionistic thoughts. We include two examples of completed diaries as well as a blank diary that you can complete whenever you find yourself thinking or behaving in a perfectionistic way. You can either develop a similar form to complete whenever you experience perfectionistic thinking, or you can record your responses in your journal. If you are unable to complete the diary at the time that you notice your perfectionism getting the best of you, you may complete it later.

Perfectionism Diary (Example 1)

Date: __July 17__   *Time:* __2:00 P.M.__

Situation: __My husband is fifteen minutes late picking me up__

__from work.__

Emotions: __Anger, impatience, frustration__

Perfectionistic Thoughts

- My husband should never be late to pick me up.

- I should not be kept waiting, even for a few minutes.

- My husband cannot be counted on for anything.

- My husband is always late with everything I ask him to do for me.

Alternative Thoughts

- It's okay for my husband to be late sometimes.

- It's okay to be kept waiting sometimes.

- My husband can be counted on most of the time.

- Sometimes he does do things when I would like him to.

Evaluating Perfectionistic Thoughts and Alternative Thoughts

- My expectation that my husband *always* pick me up on time only causes me to get angry and frustrated. It doesn't seem to change the situation at all.

- If I were more willing to be picked up a bit late from time to time, I would probably be less upset when it happens. The time I waste arguing and being angry is much more than the time I spend waiting for my husband when he is late.

- If I plan ahead, I can deal with his being late by using the time to relax, read a book, or make a telephone call.

- Even though my husband is sometimes ten or fifteen minutes late when he picks me up from work, he tends to be very responsible and considerate in most areas of our relationship.

- Just because I am early for everything I do, that doesn't mean that everyone else should always be early.

- The worst thing that will happen if I am kept waiting is that I will arrive home a few minutes later.

Choosing a More Realistic and Helpful Perspective

- Perhaps being picked up late from work is more manageable than I originally thought.

Perfectionism Diary (Example 2)

Date: ___December 29_____ *Time:* ___8:00 P.M._____

Situation: ___I told a joke at a party and nobody found it funny. In_____

___fact, my friends seemed to ignore me and they changed___

___the focus of the conversation to a different topic._____

Emotions: ___Embarrassment, sadness, anxiety_____

Perfectionistic Thoughts

- I should always be entertaining and funny.

- If I am not entertaining, people won't like me.

- People find me to be awkward, anxious, and boring.

Alternative Thoughts

- It's okay not to be entertaining all the time.

- People won't judge me on the basis of one uncomfortable interaction.

- People find me interesting to be with.

Evaluating Perfectionistic Thoughts and Alternative Thoughts

- Nobody is entertaining all the time. Everyone has awkward moments from time to time.

- My friends know me well and are unlikely to judge me based on one conversation. In fact, some of my friends are not terribly good at telling jokes, and I still enjoy being with them.

- For the rest of the evening, people seemed to talk to me normally, suggesting that they found me interesting and enjoyed my company.

- People probably find me interesting because they continue to invite me to spend time with them.

Choosing a More Realistic and Helpful Perspective

- Perhaps I need to give myself permission to make mistakes when I am talking to other people. I don't judge other people when they say something unusual or awkward. Perhaps they are not judging me when I make mistakes.

Your Perfectionism Diary (blank example)

Date: _____ *Time:* _____

Situation: _____

_____

Emotions: _____

Perfectionistic Thoughts

- ◼ _____
- ◼ _____
- ◼ _____

Alternative Thoughts

- ◼ _____
- ◼ _____
- ◼ _____

Evaluating Perfectionistic Thoughts and Alternative Thoughts

- ◼ _____
- ◼ _____
- ◼ _____

Choosing a More Realistic and Helpful Perspective

- ◼ _____
- ◼ _____
- ◼ _____

STRATEGIES FOR CHANGING THOUGHTS

There are many different ways to change thoughts. In this section, we describe methods that are often helpful. As you will see, these methods overlap with one another to some extent and aren't completely separate or distinct. Ideally, you should practice using strategies such as these each time you find yourself engaging in perfectionistic thinking. You may even use these strategies before the thought occurs. For example, if you are about to enter a situation or get involved in some activity (for example, a hobby, sport, or task at work) that usually leads to perfectionistic thinking, you can anticipate the thoughts and challenge them before they even occur. If you forget to use these strategies, or if it's not practical to use these techniques before or during the episode of perfectionistic thinking, they may be used later.

Examining the Evidence

One of the most useful methods of challenging perfectionistic beliefs is to examine the evidence that confirms and contradicts your beliefs. This process may involve examining your previous experiences in a given situation. For example, if you are a student who believes that it would be terrible to receive less than an A on a paper, you could try to recall what happened in the past when you received a lower grade on a paper or exam. Did you survive the experience? What happens when other people receive grades that are lower than an A? Do terrible things necessarily occur as a result? The following conversation between a therapist and Maureen illustrates how examining evidence for and against perfectionistic beliefs can be a helpful way of changing them.

Maureen: It really bothers me when my children lie. Yesterday at dinner, my four-year-old son fed his broccoli to the dog. When I asked him what happened to his broccoli, he said that he ate it. I was up all night worrying that my son was going to grow up to be a pathological liar.

Therapist: Rather than automatically assuming that your prediction is true, let's look at the evidence. Can you think of any

	evidence to support your prediction that your son is going to become a pathological liar?
Maureen:	Well, I imagine that most people who lie a lot begin their lying in childhood.
Therapist:	Are there reasons to think that your prediction may not come true?
Maureen:	I guess my son doesn't lie that often. In fact, sometimes when he does lie, he feels so guilty that he admits his lie a day or two later.
Therapist:	Can you think of times when you lied to your parents?
Maureen:	I remember when I got into a minor accident in my father's car. I told him that the car was hit in a shopping-mall parking lot, while I was shopping.
Therapist:	Did you grow up to become a pathological liar?
Maureen:	No, I guess I didn't.
Therapist:	No one likes to be lied to, but most people do hide the truth from time to time. Perhaps we can find ways of helping you to be more accepting of others when they tell small lies.
Maureen:	But isn't it wrong to lie?
Therapist:	Being lied to can lead others to feel hurt and lose trust in the person who lies. Nevertheless, the severity of the lying can be looked at on a continuum. For example, there is a big difference between telling a small lie to avoid hurting a person's feelings (like when you tell someone you like their new haircut even when you don't) versus cheating on your partner and then lying about the affair.
Maureen:	I guess I have been treating all lying as the same. I was thinking that if someone told a small lie, they were likely to lie about anything and everything. I can see how that isn't very realistic.

Examining the evidence for your beliefs can combat many of the perfectionistic thinking styles that are described in chapter 3. For example, examining the evidence for and against a particular thought can be used to combat filtering (paying attention only to information that confirms or supports a perfectionistic thought). Similarly, catastrophic thinking (the tendency to assume that things would be terrible if a particular event were to occur) can be combated by asking questions such as, "What if that event did occur?" and "How could I cope with that if it were to happen?"

Education

One reason why people sometimes maintain perfectionistic beliefs is a lack of accurate information. Seeking accurate information on a given topic can help change perfectionistic or rigid beliefs. Becoming educated is one way of examining the evidence that supports and refutes perfectionistic beliefs.

For example, education can be a helpful method of changing unrealistic standards with respect to weight and physical appearance. Many people are overly concerned about maintaining a weight that is actually below what is normally considered to be healthy. In Western cultures, this tends to be a more frequent issue for women than men. These unrealistic standards are probably related in part to constant exposure to models and celebrities who themselves are underweight. To help people change their overly stringent beliefs about how much body fat is acceptable, health professionals often educate their patients and clients about their ideal weight range—that is, the weight range that has been shown to be predictive of living longer and having fewer health problems.

Taking Another Perspective

Taking the perspective of someone else is a powerful way of changing perfectionistic beliefs. This can be achieved by asking the question, "How do other people view this situation?" Allowing yourself to view the situation as other people might can help to change unrealistic beliefs. Consider the following conversation between a therapist and Enrico.

Enrico:	If people notice how anxious I am during my presentation, they will surely think I'm a complete idiot.
Therapist:	How would they know you're anxious?
Enrico:	I tend to blush when I'm nervous. Also, they would notice me losing my train of thought and forgetting words.
Therapist:	Put yourself in the shoes of the audience members for a moment. Can you think of a time when you have seen other people blush or lose their train of thought?
Enrico:	I have a good friend who often blushes.
Therapist:	What do you think of this person when you notice them blushing?
Enrico:	Actually, I rarely notice. If I do notice, I don't really give it much thought. I suppose that I might think he's embarrassed.
Therapist:	Do you think he is an idiot?:
Enrico:	No, but that may be because he's my friend.
Therapist:	When you see another presenter blushing, forgetting words, or looking anxious, do you think he or she is an idiot?
Enrico:	No.
Therapist:	Do you think others would view the presenter as an idiot?
Enrico:	I suppose it is possible, but probably not.
Therapist:	Then how likely is it that you will be viewed as an idiot if you blush or forget a few words during your presentation?
Enrico:	I guess it's pretty unlikely. But, it's still a possibility. That's what bothers me.
Therapist:	What if one or more people in the audience actually did think you were an idiot? Would there be any real consequences?

Enrico:	I always assumed that it would be terrible, but as I think about it now, I can't think of any real consequences. I guess nothing would happen.
Therapist:	Is it okay for some people not to like you?
Enrico:	I would prefer to always make a good impression, but I imagine that it wouldn't be the end of the world if I made a less-than-perfect impression sometimes.

One way of making it easier to take the perspective of other people is to actually ask other people how they think about a particular situation. For example, Katie believed that it was essential that her house be completely dusted, cleaned, and vacuumed daily. Her parents kept a very clean home, and she intended to do the same. This belief led Katie to spend several hours a day cleaning, at the expense of being able to look for work or enjoy other hobbies or activities. It also led to frequent arguments with her family because they refused to help. From their perspective, it was enough to vacuum and dust once a week. As a homework assignment, Katie was instructed to ask several friends and neighbors how often they dusted and vacuumed. She was surprised to discover that nobody—not even people whose homes she considered to be spotless—cleaned as often as she did. After surveying her friends' cleaning habits, she was willing to try cleaning less often and her family began to help more frequently.

Compromising with Yourself and Others

Rather than being unwilling to accept anything less than perfection, try asking the question, "What level of imperfection is acceptable?" You may believe that if you lower your standards regarding a particular dimension or issue, chaos will ensue. If the thought of lowering your standards too much is frightening, perhaps you can consider lowering them somewhat. This is a good technique for dealing with all-or-nothing thinking. If you tend to view situations in terms of black and white or right and wrong, it can be helpful to compromise by viewing situations in shades of gray and realizing that there are different ways of doing things. Viewing situations as either right or wrong can lead you to miss out on important complexities that are inherent in most situations.

You can also compromise with others when your standards are different than those of people around you. For example, if you have difficulty discarding or giving away old objects (things like clothing, magazines, household items, and so on) and your family asks you to reduce the clutter, perhaps you could agree to throw out items that you haven't looked at or used for a certain length of time (one year, five years, and so on). This might be a good compromise between keeping everything (which is what your perfectionism may be telling you to do) and throwing out everything (which is what your family may be telling you to do).

Hypothesis Testing

An excellent way to test the accuracy of your perfectionistic thoughts and predictions is to carry out small experiments, a process also known as hypothesis testing. Carefully designed experiments will provide an opportunity to disprove your perfectionistic beliefs. For example, if you tend to write papers that are too detailed, try leaving out some of the detail and seeing what happens. Regardless of the outcome, you will obtain valuable information. If there is no consequence, you will learn that your beliefs about the importance of including all of the details are not true. On the other hand, if your boss tells you that your most recent report was not detailed enough, you will learn that the amount of detail you had in your earlier reports was appropriate and you can behave accordingly in the future.

Hypothesis testing can be used to test the validity of most perfectionistic predictions. By behaving in ways that do not meet your own high standards (for instance, purposely making small mistakes in your work, saying things incorrectly, leaving the house dirty, and so on), you will learn whether the standards are in fact necessary. Of course, you want to choose exercises that are relevant to your perfectionistic thoughts. If you are not overly concerned about the cleanliness of your house, there is no reason for you to purposely leave the house messy. Also, you should use good judgment when designing hypothesis-testing experiments. Don't plan experiments that have a very good chance of backfiring and leading to serious negative consequences. For example, if you are a nurse who checks medications dozens of times because you worry about giving a patient an incorrect drug, don't purposely give a patient the wrong medication just to see what happens! Instead, a good exercise might be to find out how often most nurses check medications before dispensing them to a patient and do what they do. In other words, check once or twice, but not dozens of times.

EXERCISE 7.2 Hypothesis Testing to Change Your Perfectionistic Beliefs

Evaluate the accuracy of your perfectionistic beliefs by designing and carrying out experiments to test out your hypotheses. In your journal, record the day and time, as well as a description of the experiment you've decided to conduct. Before conducting the experiment, record any specific predictions about what you think will happen. Then, conduct the experiment and record what actually happens. You may be surprised at how often your predictions don't come true. Here is an example of what you might write in your journal for a particular experiment.

Hypothesis Testing Example

Date: May 3   *Time:*   4:00 P.M.

Description of Experiment:	Arrive five minutes late for a doctor's appointment instead of thirty minutes early.
Predicted Outcome:	The receptionist and doctor will be angry with me.
Actual Outcome:	Neither the receptionist nor the doctor seemed angry at all. In fact, the doctor talked to me for quite a while about my new puppy and ended up being ten minutes late for her next appointment.

Changing Your Social-Comparison Habits

As mentioned in chapter 3, everyone compares themselves to other people as a way of evaluating their standing or performance in a particular area. Most people compare themselves to their peers. For example, if they want to evaluate whether they are doing a good job at work, they might compare themselves to their coworkers.

People who are perfectionists may be more likely to compare themselves to people who are much more experienced and skilled in that particular area. For example, perfectionistic amateur musicians might compare themselves to professional musicians who have already achieved great success (as measured by their ability to play music, their income, or their popularity). The tendency to compare oneself to people who are perceived as significantly more skilled, attractive, intelligent, physically fit, or "better" in some other way can make an individual feel more depressed or anxious about not meeting his or her own high standards. Therefore, it may be helpful to try to limit your social comparisons to people who are more similar to you in a particular dimension.

Looking at the Big Picture

Perfectionism is sometimes associated with a tendency to focus on unimportant details rather than looking at the big picture. Looking at the big picture involves assessing the overall impact of a particular event, situation, or outcome on your life. Situations that seem so important in the moment rarely end up being particularly important, even a short time later. Below are some examples of perfectionistic statements followed by alternative statements that illustrate how to look at the big picture.

Perfectionistic and Alternative Statements

Perfectionistic Statement	What am I going to do? I didn't do well on my English exam.
Alternative Statement	It's unlikely that my grade on this exam will have any impact on what I am doing a year from now (my career, income, relationships, and so on).
Perfectionistic Statement	I feel terrible that the cake I made for my daughter's birthday party did not turn out the way I hoped it would.
Alternative Statement	The children will probably still enjoy the cake, and even if they don't, it won't matter a week from now.
Perfectionistic Statement	My haircut looks terrible, and I am terrified of being seen in public.
Alternative Statement	People on the street are much less interested in my hair than I am, and they probably won't even notice. Besides, my hair will grow back eventually.
Perfectionistic Statement	It drives me crazy when my partner leaves her jacket lying on the floor.
Alternative Statement	I guess she only leaves her jacket lying around once a week or so. It's a small price to pay for an otherwise wonderful relationship.
Perfectionistic Statement	I'm so upset that my new car has a small scratch on the fender.
Alternative Statement	It is normal for cars to have small scratches. If it didn't happen today, it would have happened sooner or later.

Using Coping Statements

The process of changing perfectionistic thoughts and beliefs is complex. It involves using any of a number of techniques to identify your negative thoughts and replace them with more realistic alternative thoughts. Sometimes, you may not have the time to challenge your perfectionistic thoughts using some of the strategies already described in this chapter. Other times, you may feel so anxious, depressed, or angry that it is difficult to think clearly about the situation. Coping statements may be helpful in cases where it is difficult to use some of the other strategies discussed in this chapter. Coping statements are simple phrases that you can memorize and say to yourself when you find yourself thinking like a perfectionist. For example, saying to yourself, "It's okay to make mistakes," can make it easier to get through a stressful or difficult task. Similarly, the phrase, "It's okay if some people don't like me," can make it easier to deal with social situations that are anxiety provoking. Reminding yourself that there are many different right ways to fold laundry can help decrease the frustration that occurs when your family members fold the laundry differently than you like it.

Coping statements involve more than just "positive thinking." In fact, coping statements should reflect thoughts that you actually can believe, and they should be realistic—not just positive. For example, if you typically find yourself becoming anxious when giving a presentation, it wouldn't be helpful to prepare for a talk by saying to yourself, "I will not be anxious during this presentation." On the other hand, it might help to remind yourself that even if you do become anxious, there will be no real consequences, other than the temporary discomfort that you feel. If you decide to use coping statements, we recommend that you record them on an index card and carry them with you. This will help prompt your memory until these statements become second nature.

Tolerating Uncertainty and Ambiguity

Perfectionists go to great pains to control many different aspects of their lives, including their own behavior, the behavior of other people, and the environment in which they live. Although most people feel more comfortable when they can predict and control events that occur (particularly negative events), the need to know about and control events is often much stronger for people who have rigid, perfectionistic beliefs. For example, a person who is applying for a job may find it very difficult to wait until she finds out whether the job materializes. Similarly, arriving home to find a note from your partner saying that he or she will be home "later" may be frustrating if there is no specific time mentioned in the note. Because you often cannot control or predict things that occur, it can be helpful to find ways to tolerate some degree of uncertainty and ambiguity in your life.

One way of dealing with uncertainty involves mentally preparing for several possible outcomes. To return to the examples described earlier, the person who is waiting to find out about the job can make some decisions about what she might do if she gets the job and what she might do if she doesn't. Similarly, if you are impatiently waiting for your partner to come home but have no idea when to expect him or her, you can prepare for the possibility that he or she will return in the next few minutes, in an hour, or in several hours. By preparing for different possible outcomes, the uncertainty is likely to be less frustrating or anxiety provoking.

Another way of combating the need for certainty and control is to ask yourself questions such as, "Why do I need to know what will happen?", "Can I cope with not knowing?", "Is it really as important as it feels for me to control this situation or to be able to predict exactly how it will turn out?"

DIFFICULTY BELIEVING YOUR ALTERNATIVE THOUGHTS

One of the most common complaints of individuals who try to use the strategies described in this chapter is what is sometimes called the "head/heart problem." The head/heart problem occurs when an individual knows rationally that a particular style of thinking is incorrect or inappropriate, but nevertheless feels that the negative way of thinking is correct. In other words, the head is able to think about the situation in a realistic way, but the "heart" continues to react to the situation in a perfectionistic way. For example, you may realize rationally that there is generally very little to lose by making small mistakes. Nevertheless, you may continue to feel awful every time you do certain things incorrectly.

As you think about the head/heart problem, remember two things. First, realize that your perfectionistic beliefs have probably been around for a long time. The techniques described in this chapter are skills that need to be built through practice. It will take a while for your perfectionistic beliefs to change. With practice, it should become easier to believe the new, more flexible ways of thinking. Second, it is possible that trying to think rationally about situations that trigger your perfectionism may not be enough. You may actually need to do something differently rather than just trying to think differently. The techniques described in the next chapter involve changing perfectionistic behaviors. Behavioral strategies are among the most powerful ways to change thoughts, because they create new learning experiences that directly disprove your perfectionistic thoughts.

CHAPTER 8

Changing Perfectionistic Behaviors

WHY CHANGE PERFECTIONISTIC BEHAVIORS?

Perhaps the most effective method of overcoming perfectionism is to change the behaviors that help to keep your perfectionistic beliefs, attitudes, and predictions alive. If you have a tendency to set very high standards for yourself or others, you probably use some of the behaviors discussed in chapter 4, either to ensure that your standards are met or to avoid situations that force you to confront your high standards. Examples of perfectionistic behaviors include overcompensating by doing much more than is necessary to deal with a situation, unnecessary checking and reassurance seeking, repeating behaviors, excessive organizing and list making, procrastination, failure to delegate tasks to others, and avoidance of anxiety-provoking situations.

Behaviors associated with perfectionism help to maintain the problem. By engaging in these behaviors, you prevent yourself from testing out and disproving your perfectionistic thoughts. In other words, continuing to behave like a perfectionist makes it difficult to stop thinking like a perfectionist. For example, if you believe that only by checking and rechecking your work can you maintain your high standards, the act of repeatedly checking your work will prevent you from ever finding out whether that belief is true.

Similarly, procrastinating on a project because you are worried about not being able to do an adequate job prevents you from ever finding out whether that prediction is true. In fact, procrastination often makes it more difficult to perform well because, in the end, you have less time and are under more pressure. Therefore, procrastination can end up confirming your anxiety-provoking beliefs about not being able to do a job well.

In small amounts, the behaviors we are describing as perfectionistic can be helpful. For example, proofreading an important report *once or twice* is likely to improve the quality of your work. Putting off an unpleasant task *for a short time* may give you the necessary break you need to tackle the job later. On the other hand, overdoing these behaviors is likely to cause problems. For example, excessive checking gives you less time to do other things and may even increase your anxiety. Correcting other people too often may lead them to feel inadequate or angry with you for not trusting them. Including too much detail in your conversations with other people can lead the other person to become bored and to start daydreaming—therefore missing much of what you are trying to say.

Changing the behavior patterns that are associated with your perfectionism is a key step toward overcoming the problem. The strategies described in this chapter are especially important for people who have difficulty identifying or changing specific thoughts using the cognitive strategies discussed in chapter 7. The techniques in chapter 7 involve trying to change thoughts by examining the evidence for and against them and by trying to replace negative thinking patterns with more realistic beliefs. In contrast, the behavioral strategies discussed in this chapter change beliefs directly by providing new learning experiences that disprove the thoughts. Therefore, changing perfectionistic behaviors leads to automatic changes in perfectionistic thoughts.

STRATEGIES FOR CHANGING PERFECTIONISTIC BEHAVIORS

In this section, we discuss a range of strategies that are effective for changing your perfectionistic behaviors. We'll begin with exposure, which involves directly confronting the situations that make you uncomfortable.

Exposure-Based Strategies

For the past few decades, therapies based on exposure have been used to treat anxiety problems such as social anxiety and obsessive-compulsive disorder and, to some extent, other problems such as depression and eating disorders. Basically, *exposure* involves confronting a feared object or situation over and over again until the fear decreases. For people who fear driving, we encourage them to practice driving initially in safe settings until the discomfort subsides. For people who fear heights, we have them encounter increasingly high places until they no longer experience significant fear. Exposure is the best strategy to use for dealing with situations that trigger intense negative reactions, such as fear or anger. Similarly, exposure can be especially helpful for people who avoid situations because of their perfectionism.

Exposure is a very powerful strategy for dealing with unrealistic fears. In the case of certain phobias, such as animal phobias, most individuals are able to overcome their fear in a matter of hours (Antony et al. 2001; Rowa, McCabe and Antony 2006). For other fears, changes often take longer, but still a considerable percentage of people benefit from exposure-based treatments (Moscovitch, Antony, and Swinson, 2009). In our experience, exposure is also very useful for dealing with perfectionism, which is often associated with a fear of being imperfect or failing to meet some goal or standard. In dealing with perfectionism, exposure involves purposely allowing oneself to repeatedly encounter "imperfect" situations that cause anxiety, frustration, or discomfort, until they are no longer a problem.

The effects of exposure on fear and anxiety are universal. Even animals appear to become less anxious after repeated exposure to a frightening situation. For example, a new puppy may be fearful of strangers or of walking near busy streets. With repeated exposure, however, these situations become easier. In our experience, even spiders respond to exposure. When we work with people who are phobic of spiders, we encourage them to confront spiders by being near them and eventually touching them. Not only do our clients become less fearful of the spiders, but the spiders seem to become less fearful of our clients. By the end of the treatment session, the spider is much less likely to run away, compared to the beginning of the session.

In order to use exposure as a treatment for perfectionism, you must first identify situations that make you uncomfortable and then create exposure practices to target those particular situations. Later in this chapter, we describe exactly how to conduct exposure practices for particular situations that may occur.

Why Exposure Works

Exposure is based on the premise that people can get used to almost anything if they are given enough time. For example, people who go camping in the wilderness (as well as contestants on the TV show, *Survivor*) get used to being dirty if they don't have access to running water for a shower or bath. During war, people may even get used to the sound of bombs going off in nearby neighborhoods.

There are several different explanations for why exposure works. One of the most compelling theories is based on a cognitive model. From a cognitive view, exposure works by changing a person's beliefs about the feared situation. In other words, after repeated experiences in the feared situation, the person gradually learns that nothing bad is going to happen and eventually comes to see the situation as nonthreatening and safe. In the case of perfectionism, exposure works in part by teaching a person that even if mistakes are made, the consequences are usually not terrible. Even if your performance is not to someone else's liking, the situation is likely to be manageable. The same rule applies when someone else's behavior doesn't meet your high standards. It's bound to happen, and when it does, it's unlikely to be the end of the world. Exposure to situations where your standards are unlikely to be met is an excellent way to learn that these situations need not be threatening or that you may benefit from adjusting your standards.

Types of Exposure

There are different ways in which exposure can be implemented. For example, exposure can be conducted live (also called *in vivo exposure*) or in the imagination. Although we recommend live exposure whenever possible, exposure in imagination may be appropriate in cases where live exposure is impractical, impossible, or too frightening. For example, if you tend to be very frightened of making mistakes during presentations, we recommend first that you try live exposure by giving presentations and even making minor mistakes that are unlikely to cause any real harm (for example, purposely pausing for a few moments, as if you've lost your train of thought). However, if the thought of giving a real presentation is too overwhelming, you could start by imagining that you are giving a presentation and work up to the real thing.

A second way in which exposure practices can vary is in terms of how gradually steps are taken. We don't recommend that you start by practicing in the most upsetting situation that you can imagine. Rather, we recommend that you start with easier situations and gradually work up to more difficult situations. The rate at which you take steps toward more and more difficult situations is up to you. The faster you take steps, the quicker you will learn to tolerate more difficult situations. However, taking steps more quickly may also lead to more intense discomfort during the practices.

How to Conduct Exposure

You may be thinking to yourself, "I'm already exposed to the situation that I fear from time to time, but it doesn't seem to help." In fact, you may even have had experiences when your fear became worse after exposure to a situation you fear. For exposure to be effective, it has to be done in a particular way. In everyday life, exposure to feared situations tends to be unpredictable, brief, and infrequent. For example, when individuals with a spider phobia encounter a spider, it is usually a surprise (unpredictable exposure). In addition, they usually leave the situation quickly (brief exposure) and make sure it doesn't happen again (infrequent exposure). Also, people who are anxious or uncomfortable in a particular situation tend to use subtle ways of avoiding the full impact of the situation (such as distraction, excessive checking, or other overprotective behaviors), so they don't really benefit from the exposure.

To maximize the benefits of exposure practices, there are several steps you can take. First, in preparing to conduct exposure practices, develop an exposure hierarchy. An exposure hierarchy is a list of anxiety-provoking situations that are ranked in terms of difficulty. This list can be used to help guide your practices. The items in the hierarchy should be as specific as possible and should include items that are practical and easy to set up when you are ready. In other words, you should not choose items that would be impossible to try even if you wanted to. Following are some examples of exposure practices that can be conducted to change particular types of perfectionistic concerns.

Examples of Exposure Practices

Perfectionistic Concern	Sample Exposure Practice
I cannot handle my house being a mess.	Leave particular areas in the house messy.
I spend hours trying to get my hair perfect.	Spend no more than five minutes on my hair.
I feel compelled to correct my wife when she mispronounces words.	Ask my wife to purposely mispronounce words in a way that happens to bother me.
It would be terrible to have someone else notice my hands shaking.	Carry a glass of water and let my hand shake.
There is only one right way to fold socks.	Fold socks in various "wrong" ways.
I must never eat any high-calorie foods or I will get fat.	Eat dessert from time to time.
I avoid asking my secretary to do my typing because I am very particular about the way I like it done.	Ask my secretary to type my letters.

Once you have identified specific exercises that may help to challenge your high standards, the next step is to develop your exposure hierarchy. First, generate a list of ten to twenty exposure exercises. They should include items that range in difficulty from mildly difficult to extremely difficult. Next, estimate (using a scale from 0 to 100) how uncomfortable you will be conducting each practice. The final step is to rank the items in the hierarchy from hardest to easiest.

After developing your exposure hierarchy, you will be ready to start your exposure practices. Start with easier items, and work your way up to those that are more difficult. As you go along, you will find that some items become easy, and you may want to delete those from the hierarchy. Some steps may be too difficult, in which case you can add some in-between steps to make the process more gradual. It is okay to skip steps as you go along. The quicker you take steps, the quicker the situations will become easier. On the other hand, quicker steps will likely lead to more discomfort during your practices. Choose a pace that provides a balance between exercises that are manageable but also challenging.

If you have several different areas of perfectionism, you can develop separate exposure hierarchies for each area. For example, if you have very high standards with respect to cleanliness and school work, you can develop a hierarchy of situations for each of these areas. Or, if you prefer, you may combine them into one hierarchy and work on them together. Deciding between these two approaches is a matter of preference. However, you should keep in mind that trying to do too many things at once may compromise your success. Here is a sample hierarchy for someone with social anxiety who is afraid of making mistakes in front of other people.

Sample Exposure Hierarchy: Fear of Making Mistakes in Front of Others

Item	Fear (0-100)
Give a formal presentation about unfamiliar material in front of people who I don't know well (for instance, at work).	99
Throw a party for people from work and prepare a difficult dish that I have never made before.	85
Purposely forget my wallet when in line at the supermarket.	85
Ask someone to repeat themselves at my weekly staff meeting.	75
Show up for an appointment (like a haircut) on the wrong day.	60
Have lunch with a coworker, and allow uncomfortable silences.	50
Answer a question in my night-school class.	45
Forget my ticket when I pick up my dry cleaning.	40

EXERCISE 8.1 Developing Your Own Exposure Hierarchy

In your journal, make a list of items that you might include in your exposure hierarchy. Next, rate your fear level for each item, using a scale ranging from 0 (no fear or anxiety) to 100 (maximum fear or anxiety). Finally, rewrite your list in order of difficulty, with the most difficult items at the top, and the easier items at the bottom. Use the sample hierarchy as a guide to help you develop your own list.

Design Practices That Are Predictable, Structured, and Planned in Advance

Exposure works best when it is predictable and under your control. Whenever possible, plan your practices carefully and ensure that they have predictable outcomes. For example, if you are working on becoming less perfectionistic about your physical appearance, decide in advance how you will practice breaking your standards for appearance (for example, spending less time on your hair, wearing clothes that don't match, and so on). Ensuring the practices are predictable is most important when you first begin to practice. Later, you can purposely build more unpredictable practices into your program.

For many practices, you can't possibly know the outcome. For example, if you decide to practice arriving a few minutes late for appointments (to compensate for your belief that you always need to be early for everything), you may not be able to predict what will happen. Some people may not care, whereas others may be annoyed at having to wait for you. To deal with this situation, you can imagine several possible outcomes and think about how you can deal with them if they occur. Of course, you don't want to choose practices that are likely to get you into big trouble, like not showing up for work at all or completely missing a final exam. If you're not sure whether a practice is appropriate and safe, ask a few people whom you trust for their opinion.

Continue the Practice Long Enough to Learn the Situation is Safe

The goal of exposure is to learn that you can be in a situation and eventually feel comfortable. Exposure works best when the practice is prolonged. So, if you are nervous about being around people you don't know because you may say something "stupid," try spending an extended period with someone who makes you anxious (perhaps having a long lunch) until your anxiety decreases or until you learn that you can manage the situation. If you are uncomfortable leaving a mess in your house, try leaving things messy until you get used to it. Although prolonged exposure works best, some exposures are necessarily brief (things like asking a question in a meeting). In other situations, you may feel too overwhelmed to stay in the situation until the fear decreases. That's okay.

However, the best way to compensate for brief exposures is to repeat them often. If you absolutely must stop an exposure practice early, the best thing you can do is to repeat the practice as soon as possible.

Practice Frequently and Schedule Your Practices Close Together

Exposure works best if the practices are spaced closely together. For example, if you are afraid of speaking in front of groups because you may make a mistake, giving presentations once a year will probably never lead to a reduction in your fear. On the other hand, if you practice giving presentations for five or ten days in a row, you will notice a substantial reduction in fear over the course of the practices. Weekly practice works better than practicing once a month. Daily practice works better than once a week. We recommend that you try to practice at least four or five days a week for an extended period each time. Or, if the situation is one that comes up even more frequently, try to practice whenever you have the opportunity.

Expect to Feel Uncomfortable

Don't measure the success of an exposure practice by whether you feel uncomfortable. Rather, a successful exposure practice is one that you complete, regardless of how you feel. If you chose an appropriately difficult situation, you *should* feel anxious. That's why you are doing the exposure practices in the first place. If you feel anxious during an exposure practice, it's a sign that you need to continue practicing rather than an indication that things are not going well. If you don't feel uncomfortable during a practice, we recommend that you choose a more difficult practice next time.

With repeated practices, your discomfort will decrease. However, that doesn't mean that there will be a decrease in discomfort each time you practice. In fact, some practices may be more difficult than previous ones. This may be because it is a more difficult situation or because you are feeling less prepared (more tired, less confident, more stressed out, and so on). For every few steps forward, there may be a step back. Also, it's possible that on days when you practice exposure, your overall level of stress will be higher. You may even be more irritable with people who are close to you. As your anxiety decreases, other stress-related feelings such as irritability will decrease as well.

Don't Use Subtle Avoidance Strategies

Subtle avoidance strategies are techniques that you may use to make encountering an anxiety-provoking situation more bearable. These may include distraction, reassurance seeking, checking, and other "tricks" for managing the discomfort. These techniques may help you to manage your discomfort in the short term. However, like more obvious forms of avoidance, they prevent you from learning that your perfectionistic thoughts are exaggerated or untrue. In addition, subtle avoidance techniques can undo the effects of your exposure practices. Therefore, try not to use these techniques if at all possible.

Use Cognitive Strategies to Cope with Discomfort During Practices

What you tell yourself, or how you interpret the situation, can have a big impact on your experience during an exposure practice. Therefore, it will be helpful to use some of the cognitive strategies discussed in chapter 7 to deal with negative thoughts that occur during exposure practices. For example, you may decide to use the process of hypothesis testing as a way of dealing with negative predictions. Using this method, you can treat your exposure practices like small experiments designed to test the validity of your perfectionistic thoughts. Before an exposure practice, identify any negative predictions that you are making. Then, after your exposure practice, take note of whether your feared outcome actually occurred. By treating each exposure practice as an experiment to test out your hypotheses about what might happen, you will learn that many of your feared outcomes don't come true. There are a few other specific strategies that can be helpful for dealing with anxiety or discomfort experienced during your exposure practices. If you are purposely entering situations where you fear that you may behave imperfectly or incorrectly, make a decision to allow yourself to be imperfect. Ask yourself the question, "Can I handle imperfection in this situation?" Also, remember that the anxiety is temporary and will gradually decrease. In most cases, the worst thing that will happen during an exposure practice is that you will feel uncomfortable.

In your journal, keep track of your exposure practices. For each practice, record (1) the date and time of the practice, (2) a description of the practice, including the specific exercise, the duration of the exercise, and other relevant details, (3) your average discomfort level during the practice (using a scale from 0 to 100), and (4) how you challenged any negative thinking that arose during the practice. You should notice a decrease in your discomfort levels as you continue to practice exposure.

Response Prevention

A second strategy for changing perfectionistic behaviors is *response prevention*. Response prevention involves stopping yourself from engaging in problematic perfectionistic behaviors. This strategy is related to exposure, in that it provides an opportunity to test out the accuracy of your negative predictions (in fact, it should be used along with exposure). The main difference is that exposure involves doing something anxiety provoking (such as giving a presentation), and response prevention involves preventing the behaviors that you use to protect yourself from feeling uncomfortable or to prevent bad things from happening (for instance, memorizing your presentation beforehand to ensure you don't make any mistakes). By preventing these safety behaviors, you will learn that many of these actions serve no real function other than to decrease your anxiety or discomfort for a short time. For example, if you tend to check your work over and over, preventing the rechecking will teach you that if you stop checking excessively, the quality of your work doesn't suffer as much as you expect it to. Other perfectionistic behaviors for which response prevention can be helpful include correcting or checking the behavior of other people, looking at your watch or clock often (to make sure that you are on time), checking your weight or physical appearance, arguing with teachers or professors to have a point or two added to your course grade, excessively washing or cleaning, or participating in any other repetitive behavior that you use to make sure that your standards are met or to reduce your anxiety about not meeting your standards.

It is important to do what you can to prevent these behaviors. At first, you may find that your anxiety or discomfort increases significantly when you prevent the behaviors. You may worry about the consequences of not checking, cleaning, or correcting. However, after a while, the discomfort will probably decrease as you learn that nothing terrible happens when you start to eliminate these behaviors.

The behaviors associated with your perfectionism may be so ingrained and habitual that you are not even aware of them. There are a number of ways to increase your awareness of these behaviors. First, you can record in your journal times when you engage in behaviors such as checking, repeating, correcting, cleaning, counting, or asking for reassurance. Pay special attention to the specific situations, moods, and places that trigger these behaviors, as well as the way you feel after you engage in the behaviors. This exercise should make you more aware of the perfectionistic behaviors that need to be stopped. If you still have trouble identifying these behaviors, ask someone who is close to you to help point them out. With practice, you should eventually become more aware of your perfectionistic rituals.

Communication Training

A third strategy for changing perfectionistic behaviors is communication training. Communication training is useful when perfectionism affects the way you communicate with other people. For example, perfectionism causes some people to communicate in a disapproving or judgmental way with others who do not meet certain perfectionistic standards. If this is a problem for you, it may be important to examine how you communicate your high expectations to other people in your life. Often, perfectionism is associated with an intense drive to change the behavior of other people so it conforms to your high standards. This drive may cause you to constantly nag, correct, or even offend other people with the message that their behavior is not good enough. This message can cause them to feel angry or hurt.

For individuals who are more self-focused in their perfectionism, communication may be affected by a tendency to communicate passively and to have difficulty listening to what other people are saying. A full discussion of how to change communication patterns is beyond the scope of this book. For a more detailed discussion of this topic, there are several books on communication training listed in Further Readings at the end of this book. There are, however, a few general guidelines that we can provide for you, based in part on recommendations from McKay, Davis, and Fanning's book *Messages: The Communication Skills Book* (2009).

Be Assertive

Everyone encounters situations in which the behavior of other people is inconsistent with their own expectations. However, perfectionism can lead people to communicate their disapproval in a way that is not terribly helpful. By understanding how you communicate and by working on your communication skills, you can lessen the risk of alienating others.

There are three general styles of communication. The first style, known as *passive communication*, involves communicating indirectly and putting the needs and rights of others ahead of your own needs. For example, rather than expressing disagreement about a particular topic, a person who communicates passively may be more likely than others to pretend to agree, in order to avoid being criticized. Similarly, a passive communicator may find indirect ways to express his or her needs and desires. Some perfectionists (particularly people who tend to feel depressed or socially anxious) may constantly feel that they are not living up to their own standards. They may be at risk for using passive communication if they believe that other people will find what they have to say to be uninteresting or unimportant. Passive communication is usually not an effective form of communicating. Other people are unlikely to hear your message if it is communicated passively.

A second style of communication is known as *aggressive communication*. Aggressive communication puts your own needs ahead of the needs of other people and may involve putting pressure on other people to do things your way. It may be associated with being hurtful or insulting to those around you and usually leads to the other person shutting down and not listening to you or becoming very angry with you. People who have perfectionistic beliefs about how other people should behave may become quite pushy and aggressive in their attempts to have other people conform to their excessively high expectations.

The third and most effective style of communication is called *assertive communication*. Being assertive involves taking into account both your own rights and needs as well as the rights and needs of the other individual. Assertive communication involves three main components: describing the situation in the most objective, nonbiased, and nonjudgmental way possible; describing how the situation affects the way you feel (the emotion that you are experiencing); and describing how you would like the situation to change. Although assertive communication is not guaranteed to work, it tends to be more effective than passive and aggressive communication styles. Following are illustrations of how each of the three communication styles might be used to tell a child that his or her bedroom needs to be cleaned:

Passive: Look into the room, let out a sigh and roll your eyes.

Aggressive: Say to the child, "You are a complete slob. You are never going to amount to anything unless you can learn to be more organized."

Assertive: Say to the child, "Your toys are all over your floor. I feel frustrated when I have to clean your room. I would like you to clean your room before you go out today, please."

Unlike passive communication, assertive communication is likely to be heard and understood by the other individual. Unlike aggressive communication, assertive communication is less likely to lead the other person to automatically disagree or feel hurt.

Listen

An important part of any communication is listening to the other person. Listening involves hearing what the other person has to say and making a genuine attempt to understand his or her point of view. Perfectionism can get in the way of listening. If you are overly critical of the other person, you may tend to focus your attention on mistakes the other person makes rather than on the entire communication. If you are overly critical of yourself, you may miss important aspects of the other person's communication if you are paying too much attention to how you are coming across or are thinking about what you are going to say next while the other person is talking.

A helpful way of making sure that you have heard and understood what the other person has said is to repeat back to the person what you have heard and to ask for clarification if there is a misunderstanding. However, moderation is the key. If you happen to be a person who compulsively asks for reassurance and checks excessively to make sure you understand other people, we recommend that you cut back rather than increase this behavior.

Pay Attention to Nonverbal Communication

The words people say are only a small part of their communication. Nonverbal communication plays an enormous role in how others interpret what you say. Nonverbal communication includes such things as voice quality (things like tone, volume, inflection, rate of speech), facial expressions, and body posture. Even if your words are not critical of the people around you, your perfectionism may lead you to communicate your disapproval in nonverbal ways (frowning, crossing your arms, leaning back, and so on). If you can be aware of your nonverbal communication patterns, you can also take steps to ensure that you are not inflicting your perfectionistic standards on others in nonverbal ways.

Prioritizing

Do you have difficulty getting things done on time? Or, do you spend so much time trying to get everything done that you sacrifice other important areas in your life? A fourth strategy for changing perfectionistic behaviors involves prioritizing. Prioritizing is important for individuals who always feel like they have to get everything done right away. It may also be helpful for people who have problems deciding what to do first (in case they make a "wrong" decision). The process of prioritizing involves three steps.

The first step involves generating lists of tasks that need to be completed. Ideally, this should be done on paper (for example, in your journal). You may include separate lists for things that need to be done today (take out the garbage, finish a report, get a haircut, and so on) and things that need to be done sometime, but not right away (invite neighbors over for dinner, buy a new lamp, get a new passport, take up tennis, and so on).

The second step involves examining the list (or lists) and ranking the items in terms of importance. Just because it feels important that you finish a task doesn't mean that it is important. To assess the importance of the tasks, you need to assess the possible consequences of not completing an item. When you ask the question, "What will happen if I don't finish the task?" you will come to realize that many of the items are not as important as they seemed.

The third step is to begin completing the tasks in order of importance and urgency. You should try to be realistic about what can be done and about the possible consequences of not completing certain tasks. If you have problems deciding which task to do first, it may be because it doesn't matter which one you do first. If that is the case, pick one task (flip a coin) and start with it.

Overcoming Procrastination

The final strategy for changing perfectionistic behaviors is geared toward overcoming procrastination. People procrastinate for a variety of reasons, including not enjoying the particular task or job, not having time to work on the task, being fearful of not being able to complete the task well, and not knowing where to start. In the case of perfectionism, the last two reasons are particularly relevant. If you tend to procrastinate, some of the strategies that we have discussed already (for example, prioritizing, exposure) may be helpful. We recommend that you break up the task into smaller, more manageable pieces. Rather than thinking about how overwhelming the entire job is, try dividing it into smaller tasks that are easily completed. This strategy was essential in helping us write the first edition of this book. Below is a description of how we managed to divide the task of writing a book on perfectionism into smaller, manageable tasks.

Steps for Writing this Book

1. Develop a table of contents

2. Develop a list of main headings for chapter 1

3. For each main heading, generate a list of subheadings for each topic

4. Write a first draft of the information that belongs under the first subheading

5. Repeat step 4 for each subheading in chapter 1

6. Proofread and make revisions to chapter 1

7. Repeat steps 2 through 6 for each of the other chapters

You can use this same strategy for any task. For example, if you are procrastinating about writing a letter, you can break the task into small jobs, such as getting out the paper, addressing the envelope, developing a brief outline, writing the first paragraph, and so on. Each step in isolation is unlikely to be overwhelming. If you come across a particular step that is overwhelming, break it down into even smaller steps.

CHAPTER 9

Accepting Imperfection

THE COSTS OF CONTROL

Napoleon Hill, the American author of the bestselling book, *Think and Grow Rich*, was quoted as saying, "Self-discipline begins with the mastery of your thoughts. If you don't control what you think, you can't control what you do" (1937). In *The Picture of Dorian Gray*, Irish playwright and author Oscar Wilde had a similar view, "I don't want to be at the mercy of my emotions. I want to use them, to enjoy them, and to dominate them (Wilde 2005)." Is it, in fact, true that we need to be in control of our thoughts and emotions? Well, it's certainly true that extreme thoughts and emotions can make life difficult. But is fighting to control your thoughts and feelings the answer?

In some ways, perfectionism reflects an extreme need for control. Perfectionists often strive to control the emotions, thoughts, behaviors, performances, and appearance of themselves and others. However, it's impossible to have control over all aspects of your life. Furthermore, your attempts to have complete control either haven't worked or have come with an unreasonably high cost (for example, impaired relationships), which is why you're reading this book. Sometimes, it is not until we give up our attempts to control our experiences that we actually start to feel more in control.

That is not to say that all attempts to control your behavior or experiences are a problem. Control-oriented strategies are useful when used in moderation. For example, saying no to that fourth piece of cake, going to bed at a reasonable hour when you have to be up early the next day, or taking time to study the week before a big exam are all examples of control-oriented strategies that are potentially helpful. However, there comes a point at which attempts to control your thoughts and feelings begins to make things worse. Efforts to control experiences are a problem when they are extreme, intense, overly rigid, or ineffective. If you are constantly trying to control your own thoughts and feelings, as well as the behavior of others, and your attempts are not working, don't take it as a sign to simply try harder. Rather, it may be a sign that it's time to give up some of your efforts at having complete control over your experiences.

Many of the problematic perfectionistic behaviors discussed in chapter 4 are really just attempts to increase control over your emotions. Examples of these control-oriented behaviors (and a couple of others) include:

- Avoiding feared people, situations, places, activities, thoughts, and emotions

- Escaping from feared situations

- Overcompensating

- Checking and reassurance seeking

- Repeating and correcting

- Excessive organizing and list making

- Putting off decisions

- Distracting yourself from uncomfortable feelings

Take a look through chapter 4 again if you need a reminder of what these behaviors refer to. Though these strategies help to reduce discomfort in the short term, they also maintain your discomfort in the long term. As long as you continue to use the same strategies that you always use, you will continue to have the same results—anxiety, discomfort, depression, anger, and any other feelings that go along with your perfectionism.

We reviewed many of the strategies for reducing these control-oriented behaviors in earlier chapters. In chapter 7, you learned to observe your thoughts from a distance and to view them as just thoughts (rather than facts). You also learned to challenge your thoughts and to consider alternative ways of viewing things. While, on the surface, this process may seem like attempts to control your thoughts, the cognitive strategies in chapter 7 are actually designed to help you think more flexibly and to consider a wide range of possible interpretations. Many of these strategies are designed to help you accept negative outcomes, rather than assuming they would be unmanageable. Similarly, in chapter 8 you learned strategies for reducing control-oriented behaviors. Rather than avoiding situations that make you feel uncomfortable, we encouraged you to confront situations that make you feel uncomfortable, including purposely doing things imperfectly.

In the remainder of this chapter, we discuss some additional strategies that are helpful for fostering an attitude of acceptance, as opposed to control. These approaches are not really alternatives to the strategies discussed earlier in the book. Rather, they should be thought of as complementary techniques to use alongside the others. In addition, space does not allow for a full consideration of these strategies. Indeed, entire books have been written on these approaches. Rather, we provide you with an overview and suggest that you do further reading if you want to learn more about these approaches.

NEW ACCEPTANCE-BASED TREATMENTS

In recent years, a number of new treatments have been developed that teach people to accept their negative feelings and experiences, rather than trying to change them. For example, psychologist Jon Kabat-Zinn has promoted the use of a meditation-based treatment called *mindfulness-based stress reduction* for dealing with chronic pain, stress, anxiety, and other negative experiences (Kabat-Zinn 1990, 1994). This treatment involves learning to be aware of your thoughts and feelings, rather than constantly trying to change them or distract yourself from them. Instead of dwelling on the past or worrying about the future, people are encouraged to focus on their present experience, or the "here and now." A related treatment approach is *acceptance and commitment therapy* (ACT), a treatment developed by psychologist Steven Hayes and his colleagues Kirk Strosahl and Kelly Wilson (Hayes, Strosahl, and Wilson 1999). In this treatment, people are taught to accept their thoughts, feelings, and other experiences and to make a commitment to changing behaviors so that they are acting in ways that are consistent with what matters most to them.

In this chapter, we provide an overview of mindfulness and acceptance-based approaches, including mindfulness-based stress reduction and ACT. Mindfulness-based treatments and ACT have been adapted for use with a wide range of problems associated with perfectionism, including eating disorders (Heffner and Eifert 2004), anxiety problems (Forsyth and Eifert 2007), depression (Williams et al. 2007), and anger (Eifert, McKay, and Forsyth 2005). In addition, although the research on these treatments is relatively new, preliminary studies suggest that these approaches are useful for preventing relapse in depression (Teasdale et al. 2000), for reducing anxiety (Dalrymple and Herbert 2007; Roemer and Orsillo 2007), and for improving various other problems (Hayes, Follette, and Linehan 2004).

Mindfulness

You may assume that meditation and other mindfulness-based strategies are necessarily weird, "new age," spiritual, or religious in nature. In fact, mindfulness is not necessarily about spirituality or about getting in touch with a higher power, and there is nothing weird or strange about it. Rather, mindfulness is simply a specific kind of attending. Kabat-Zinn (1994, 4) defines mindfulness as "paying attention, in a particular way: on purpose, in the present moment, nonjudgmentally." Bishop et al. recently proposed a similar definition in which two components were highlighted: (1) awareness of one's immediate experience in the present moment, and (2) allowing one's attention to be accepting, non-judging, and compassionate (2004). Although mindfulness meditation can be traced back 2,500 years, to the earliest forms of Buddhist philosophy, it has recently been adapted for use in mainstream modern life. There is nothing about mindfulness that requires people to give up or change their spiritual beliefs, values, or anything else. However, mindfulness may help people to reduce stress and manage negative feelings of anxiety and depression that are often associated with perfectionism.

Mindfulness is difficult to describe in a single chapter, let alone a brief section of a chapter like this. If you are interested in additional general information about this approach, the books cited earlier by Kabat-Zinn are a good place to start. Kabat-Zinn has also produced several excellent audio CD programs to guide you through mindfulness practices (see www.mindfulnesscds.com). Finally, you may be able to access mindfulness classes near where you live. Some of these classes may have a more spiritual focus than others, so you may want to shop around until you find a class that is comfortable for you.

Becoming More Mindful

As we go through our day, most of us spend much of our time on "automatic pilot," doing things in an almost mechanical way and not really taking the time to experience fully what we are doing. For example, when you eat dinner, you may worry about all the work that you need to do after dinner or daydream about a future vacation, rather than allowing yourself to experience your food. At the same time, many of our experiences are associated with evaluation and judgment. Pay attention to your normal stream of consciousness and you will find that you are continually evaluating and judging yourself, other people, and your experiences. For example, you may think you are too fat or too thin, or that the room is too hot or too cold, or that the movie you are watching is exciting or boring. Many of the perfectionistic beliefs that you identified in chapter 3 are also examples of evaluative or judgmental thoughts. On the one hand, it is completely normal to judge and evaluate your experiences. On the other hand, excessive judging and evaluating can feed your perfectionism and lead to high levels of anxiety, depression, and anger.

Normally, we go through life without paying much attention to our most basic experiences and activities, including eating, breathing, and moving. Mindfulness practices are designed to help people to be more aware of their experiences. There are many different exercises that can help to facilitate mindfulness. All of these exercises are designed to help us to slow down, focus our attention, and experience life in a nonjudging, accepting and nonstriving way. The term *nonjudging* refers to experiencing without evaluating. For example, if you start to feel anxious during practice and notice yourself thinking, "I shouldn't be feeling nervous right now—I need to fight this feeling," try to shift toward a less judgmental stance (for example, "I am feeling nervous right now. I will simply let myself feel whatever I am feeling"). *Acceptance* refers to letting whatever happens happen. Nothing specific needs to happen during a mindfulness session. You're not supposed to think any specific thoughts, and you aren't supposed to feel any specific feelings. As with the cognitive strategies described in chapter 7, the process of mindfulness encourages you to view your thoughts as just thoughts (rather than facts). If you notice a negative thought, accept it as just a thought and let it go. The same thing applies with uncomfortable feelings. Notice them and accept them for what they are. *Nonstriving* during mindfulness practices means that you should not be *trying* to achieve anything in particular—not even a state of mindfulness! If you say to yourself, "I must reach a state of mindfulness during this practice," it will undermine the whole process. If you notice your attention wandering, simply be aware of your experiences and gently bring your focus back to the exercise. However, the more preoccupied you are with the need to be mindful, the less mindful you will actually become.

Here are brief descriptions for three different mindfulness exercises. All three of these examples are described in more detail in the book, *Ending the Depression Cycle* (Bieling and Antony 2003), as well as in other sources:

Raisin exercise. In this exercise, you are to eat a raisin slowly and mindfully, without judging the experience. This is often the first practice that people try when learning mindfulness. This exercise is described in more detail below, and we encourage you to try it out for yourself (see exercise 9.1).

Mindful breathing. There are a number of mindfulness exercises that focus on breathing. An example of a simple mindful-breathing exercise is to sit in a comfortable, quiet location and focus on a particular area of the body that is involved in breathing, such as the nostrils or the diaphragm (this is, the muscle located beneath the ribs that is used to fill your lungs with air). In this exercise, you simply focus on your breathing for a period of time. You can start with a brief period, like five minutes. With practice, you can gradually increase the period, if you choose. People often eventually work up to practicing for twenty to thirty minutes at a time, or longer.

Body-scan exercise. The purpose of the body scan is to become more aware of feelings and sensations in your body. Many people have ambivalent relationships with their bodies. You may like aspects of your body and hate other aspects. You may be frustrated with being overweight, think your nose is too big, hate sweating, or suffer with various aches and pains. The body-scan exercise provides an opportunity to be aware of your body without judging. Essentially, this exercise involves focusing on more than twenty parts of your body (toes on the right foot, left thigh, chest, top of head, and so on) one part at a time, while also paying attention to your breathing and maintaining an accepting, nonjudging attitude.

EXERCISE 9.1   The Raisin Exercise

This popular exercise (described briefly above) is often used to introduce people to the process of mindfulness. The exercise requires a few raisins, about a half hour of your time, and a quiet place to sit where you are unlikely to be interrupted. If you can't bear to eat raisins, you can use another food (for example, almonds). The goal of this exercise is to eat a raisin mindfully. First, imagine that you have just arrived on Earth from another planet and have never eaten a raisin before. In fact, imagine you don't even know that the object is called a raisin.

Next, with an object sitting on a table in front of you, focus your attention on it. What does it look like? Notice the color, size, and texture. Does it have a particular fragrance? What does it smell like? Next, spend a couple of minutes with the object in your hand. What does it feel like? Is it hard or soft? What does the texture feel like on your hand? In all likelihood, you will notice things about the object that you have never noticed before. That is the point of the exercise.

Next, press the object against your lips, but don't put it in your mouth just yet. How does the object feel against your lips? Is the scent different than it was when you smelled it earlier, from a distance? Do you notice any changes in how you are feeling? Is your mouth watering? Are you anticipating eating the object? Now, place the object in your mouth, but don't chew it just yet. What does the texture feel like in your mouth? Can you still smell the object? What does it taste like? Do you notice more saliva in your mouth than before? Next, slowly begin to chew the object. How does the flavor change? Is it more intense? Is it sweet, sour, or both? As you chew, be aware of your experiences. You will soon feel the urge to swallow the object, but put off swallowing until after you have been chewing for a few minutes. Just be aware of the experience of chewing the object. After you finally swallow the object, pay attention to any sensations in your mouth and throat, as well as any aftertaste.

Continue this practice with a few additional raisins. When you are done, take a moment to think about the way you normally eat raisins and how the experience of eating raisins mindfully was different than your usual experience. Record your responses to the following questions in your journal. Do you love raisins and normally eat them by the handful? Do you hate raisins and prefer to avoid them? Do you normally snack on them while watching television or working at your computer? Was the experience of eating raisins mindfully different than your previous experience with raisins? What did you learn about raisins or about yourself through this exercise? Were you able to eat the raisins without judging them or without judging the experience? Was the experience the same with each raisin, or did it change over time?

What does eating raisins mindfully have to do with overcoming perfectionism? On the surface, not much. However, exercises like this one can help you to live more in the present moment and encourage you to keep your experiences in perspective, rather than getting caught up in the past or focused on future events over which you have little control. Mindfulness can help you feel more grounded, which in turn can help you deal with day-to-day stresses that arise. If this approach is something you would like to learn more about, check out some of the resources recommended in this chapter, and in Further Readings in the back of this book.

Acceptance and Commitment Therapy (ACT)

As we reviewed earlier, there are two main components to ACT. The first involves learning to accept your thoughts, feelings, and other experiences rather than fighting them or attempting to control them. The second component involves becoming aware of your own values and starting to make life decisions based on these core values, rather than based on your perfectionism and desire to avoid the negative emotions that result from always trying to be perfect.

Accepting Your Experiences

Mindfulness is one approach to achieving a level of acceptance of the thoughts, feelings, and other experiences that currently contribute to your discomfort and distress. However, there are other approaches as well. ACT teaches people to stop struggling against their negative thoughts and feelings; rather, the goal is to accept them. In addition to using mindfulness exercises, this approach also uses stories and metaphors to make key points. Consider the following story as an example:

What Avoiding Pain Cost the Emperor Moth

A man found a cocoon of an emperor moth. He took it home so that he could watch the moth come out of the cocoon.

On the day, a small opening appeared. He sat and watched the moth for several hours, just watching as the moth struggled to force its body through that little hole. Then it seemed to stop making any progress. It appeared to have gotten as far as it could. It just seemed stuck.

Then the man, in his kindness, decided to help the moth. So he took a pair of scissors and snipped off the remaining bit of the cocoon. The moth then emerged easily, but it had a swollen body and small shrivelled wings. The man continued to watch. He expected that, at any moment, the wings would enlarge and open out to be able to support the body. Neither happened! The little moth spent the rest of its life crawling around with a swollen body and shrivelled wings. It never was able to fly.

What the man, in his kindness and haste, didn't understand was this: in order for the moth to fly, it needed to experience the restricting cocoon and the painful struggle as it emerged through the tiny opening. This was a necessary part of a process to force fluid from the body and into the wings so that the moth would be ready for flight once it achieved freedom from the cocoon. Freedom and flight would only come after allowing painful struggle. By depriving the moth of struggle, the man deprived the moth of health.

Reprinted with permission from Forsyth, J. P. and G. H. Eifert, 2007.

This story makes the point that avoiding discomfort and pain in the short term can lead to problems later on. It teaches us that sometimes a struggle is necessary to move forward. Though you may be inclined to do everything you can to avoid the discomfort you experience when your standards are not met, it's possible that allowing yourself to feel discomfort may be more helpful to you over the long term. However, that is not to say that suffering and discomfort should be your goal. From an acceptance perspective, it can be useful to avoid judging your feelings (such as discomfort) in either a positive direction or negative direction. Acceptance doesn't mean seeing suffering as something noble. Discomfort, in and of itself, is neither a terrible thing to be avoided nor something necessarily to be sought out. Rather, discomfort and suffering are just experiences that arise as a result of being human, and sometimes avoiding discomfort makes sense (for example, taking an alternate route when traffic is backed up on the highway).

The Emperor Moth story is just one example of many different stories and metaphors that are used in ACT to help individuals learn that avoiding discomfort and trying to control one's emotions and thoughts are not always the best option over the long term.

Making a Commitment to Change

The second component of ACT involves thinking about what really matters to you and making a commitment to change your behaviors so they are more consistent with your most deeply held personal values. One strategy for identifying your core values is to think about how you want to be remembered after you're gone. Although it can be uncomfortable to think about, death is something that we will all face eventually. Thinking about how you are likely to be remembered after you die versus how you would like to be remembered can be a useful exercise. There is a good chance that you will discover that at least some of your behaviors are inconsistent with how you want to be remembered or with the values you see as most important in life.

EXERCISE 9.2   Writing Your Epitaph

This exercise is based on a practice described by Forsyth and Eifert (2007). Your task is to write your own epitaph (the inscription on your gravestone). However, we would like you to write two versions of your epitaph. The first is your *perfectionist epitaph*—perhaps one that would be written about you if you were to die today. Here is an example of such an epitaph for Tom, a man who always strove to be perfect:

Tom's Perfectionist Epitaph

Here Lies Tom—A Man who Sought Perfection at All Costs

Tom's goal in life was to do everything as perfectly as possible and to make sure that others also lived up to his high standards. He spent much of his life correcting the behavior of his friends, family, and coworkers. Although his two marriages both ended in painful divorce and his children found him difficult to be around, Tom could take comfort in the fact that he did everything he could to help others think about things in the same way he did. Tom was also very devoted to his job in retail management. He put in many long hours and never settled for anything less than perfection in his work or the work of his staff. He always checked and double checked everything to make sure there were no errors. For Tom, work always came before vacations, spending time with friends and family, exercising, and eating well. His goal was to make the world a more perfect place, though he left this earth feeling alone and unfulfilled.

The second epitaph should be your *valued-life epitaph*—a version that might be written if your perfectionism was no longer a problem and you were living your life according to the core values that are most important to you. Your valued-life epitaph should be the one that you would most like to see on your headstone. In your journal, write your perfectionism epitaph, followed by your valued-life epitaph. How are they different? Are you currently living your life in a way that is consistent with how you want to be remembered? If not, what must you change in order to live more consistently with your core values?

The epitaph practice is just one example of an exercise that can help you to identify your personal values. As you work on changing your perfectionism, notice the ways in which your behaviors are inconsistent with your core values and begin to make changes. If you are working at a job that you hate, why not start looking for a new job this week? If you have been meaning to call an old friend, why not do it today? If it is important to you to become more physically fit, start eating healthier and exercising regularly.

It is helpful to think about values as a process rather than a goal. For example, if you are single and want to be in an intimate relationship, behaving according to your values doesn't mean focusing all of your energy on meeting a new life partner. Rather, it means acting in accordance with your values on a day-to-day basis, across situations. For example, you might think about what it is about being in this kind of relationship this is important to you (for example, it may be the opportunity to open up to someone, to allow yourself to be vulnerable, to express love and care, and so on) and make an effort to live according to these values with the people who are in your life now. Even saying hello and smiling at someone else on an elevator might be a step toward beginning to act in accordance with these values.

ACCEPTANCE AND PERFECTIONISM

In summary, acceptance-based strategies for perfectionism have two goals. The first is to become more accepting of your own thoughts, feelings, and experiences, as well as becoming more accepting of others. The second is to begin to recognize that although your perfectionism may tell you that things need to be a certain way, there are many situations in which you have a choice about how to behave. You can choose to behave in a way that is consistent with your most deeply held core values, or you can continue to behave like a perfectionist. Now is as good a time as any to start living the life you want to be living.

PART 3

Working with Specific Problems and Perfectionism

CHAPTER 10

Perfectionism and Depression

THE NATURE OF DEPRESSION

You have probably experienced a period of sadness or depression following a significant loss in your life. Perhaps it was following the breakup of a relationship, death of someone close to you, loss of a job, or inability to achieve some goal. For most people, losses such as these tend to trigger periods of sadness, depression, or grieving. Most people also experience sadness from time to time, even in the absence of a significant loss. They may feel overwhelmed with work, hurt by the behavior of a significant person in their lives, or lonely for no particular reason. Sadness and depression are universal emotions.

Although sadness is a normal experience for all people, sometimes feelings of depression can be so intense or chronic that they begin to interfere with a person's ability to enjoy life or function in his or her environment. The severity of depression (for example, the intensity, frequency, and impact of feeling sad) is on a continuum from very mild to very severe. Although this chapter is written for people who experience a level of depression that interferes with their lives, people who experience depression at mild levels may still find the information helpful, particularly if their depressed feelings are related in part to not meeting their own expectations for themselves or for other people.

Normal Feelings of Sadness

Psychologist Sidney Blatt and his colleagues have identified three components of normal depressed mood: dependency, self-criticism, and inefficacy (Blatt, D'Afflitti, and Quinlan 1976). Although these components are present in normal depressed mood, they also tend to be present in clinical depression, often at a much greater intensity.

Dependency

Dependency is the perception of needing help and support from other people. When people are feeling sad, they tend to want to be around other people. So, after doing poorly on an exam or receiving a poor evaluation at work, you may feel inclined to go out with friends or to spend a quiet evening at home with your family or your partner. Or, when feeling sad, you may be inclined to phone a close friend just to talk. Of course, not everyone responds this way when feeling down. Some people may isolate themselves when feeling sad, particularly if the depression is more severe. Even so, there still may be a perception of helplessness and a desire for support from other people.

Self-Criticism

Self-criticism is a tendency to exaggerate one's faults. A number of researchers have demonstrated a phenomenon known as *state-dependent memory*. In general, when people are in a particular emotional state (for example, feeling sad), they are more likely to recall previous periods when they felt the same way, as well as past events that are consistent with their low mood. For example, if you are feeling sad following the breakup of a relationship, you may tend to remember all of the problems with your previous relationships. You may also exaggerate all of your own shortcomings that you believe contributed to the breakup. Similarly, if you're feeling sad about doing poorly on a task at work, you may dwell on all the ways that you don't measure up to your coworkers' performances or to your own standards.

Inefficacy

Inefficacy is a sense that important events are independent of your actions. In other words, you may believe at times that no matter what you do, you cannot influence the outcome of events (for example, being rejected by other people, losing close people in your life, doing poorly in school, having financial problems, or experiencing other significant life stresses). This feeling of helplessness or a lack of control often goes along with feeling sad or depressed.

Although sadness is a normal part of life for everyone, some people experience levels of depression that interfere with their ability to function properly at work, at home, or in their relationships. When depression is severe enough to cause significant impairment, it is often referred to as *clinical depression.*

Clinical Depression

Researchers and clinicians in the mental health field have identified a number of specific problems (collectively known as *mood disorders)* that are defined in part by the presence of depression. In this chapter, we limit our discussion to two of these disorders that are most often associated with perfectionism. These are major depressive disorder and dysthymic disorder.

Major Depressive Disorder

Major depressive disorder is a mood disorder in which an individual has experienced one or more major depressive episodes. A *major depressive episode* is a period lasting at least two weeks in which a person consistently experiences depressed mood or a loss of interest in almost all of his or her normal activities. In addition, the person experiences several additional symptoms, which may include changes in weight or appetite, changes in sleep, feeling very restless or very slowed down, loss of energy, feelings of worthlessness or excessive guilt, poor concentration or difficulty making decisions, and thoughts about death or suicide (American Psychiatric Association 2000).

Although major depressive episodes are defined as lasting at least two weeks, they more typically last up to several months. The average age at which major depressive disorder begins is in the mid-twenties, although the problem can begin at any age, including during childhood. Some people experience only a single episode of major depression, perhaps triggered by a stressful life event. For others, depression may be long lasting or may be associated with a series of briefer episodes. For people who experience more than one major depressive episode, mood may return back to normal between episodes, or there may still be some minor symptoms of depression left over after the full-blown episode has improved.

Dysthymic Disorder

People with *dysthymic disorder* experience sadness and depression over a longer period, and usually at a milder level relative to people with major depressive disorder. Technically, to receive a diagnosis of dysthymic disorder, a person must experience a period of two years or longer in which he or she feels sad or depressed most of the day, on most days. Although the minimum duration is two years, people with dysthymic disorder often report having felt down and blue for many years. In addition to the low mood, people with dysthymic disorder must experience at least two additional symptoms, which may include changes in appetite, changes in sleep, low energy, poor self-esteem, poor concentration or difficulty making decisions, and feelings of hopelessness.

As you can see, major depressive disorder and dysthymic disorder share many features. Nevertheless, there are important differences. Major depressive disorder is typically associated with discrete episodes, whereas dysthymic disorder is generally more long lasting. Second, a major depressive episode must be associated with depressed mood or loss of interest (in addition to the other associated symptoms) day after day for the required period of two weeks or longer. In contrast, people with dysthymic disorder do not necessarily feel down every day—just most days. Finally, the intensity of the depression tends to be much worse in major depressive disorder than in dysthymic disorder.

CAUSES OF DEPRESSION

If you have had significant problems with depression, you may have had one professional or another tell you that your depression is caused by a chemical imbalance in your brain, problems in the way your parents brought you up, genetics, or any number of other factors. Despite the many different theories that have been proposed to explain depression, we don't really know *the* cause of depression. In fact, it now seems that depression is caused by many different factors and that different people may experience depression for different reasons. Although researchers are beginning to get a clearer understanding about the variables that contribute to depression, they still cannot determine the cause of depression for any one person. However, the problem does seem to be due to a complex interaction of both biological and psychological processes.

Biological Factors

Depression is very much influenced by our biology, including our genetic makeup, brain chemistry, and other factors. We'll discuss the role of biology in depression in this section.

Genetics

A number of studies have demonstrated that depression runs in families (Sullivan, Neale, and Kendler 2000). For example, averaging across studies, a person is up to three times more likely to suffer from major depressive disorder if he or she has a parent who suffers from the problem than if there is no depression in the immediate family. Of course, the fact that depression runs in families does not, in and of itself, mean that depression is inherited genetically. It could be that depression is learned from growing up in a home with other people who are depressed. To demonstrate a genetic basis for a problem such as depression, scientists must turn to twin studies, adoption studies, and studies that directly measure the presence and absence of genes that are believed to be related to depression. In general, there is some evidence, particularly from twin studies, that depression is in part genetically based (Sullivan, Neale, and Kendler 2000). However, the evidence from other genetic research methods has been mixed. Although genetics may be important in the development of depression for some individuals, it should be pointed out that depression is not inherited in the same way as traits (for instance, eye color). Genetics may predispose people to develop depression, but it is no guarantee. Even in pairs of identical twins (who are genetically identical), it is not unusual for one twin to experience depression and the other one to be free of it.

Neurotransmitters

Many studies have examined the relationship between neurotransmitter levels and depression (Stahl 2008). *Neurotransmitters* are chemicals in the brain that are responsible for sending messages from one nerve cell to another. In general, the neurotransmitter model of depression that has obtained the most support suggests that depression is associated with low levels of *serotonin* and/or *norepinephrine*. Neurotransmitter models of depression are based in part on the fact that medications that raise levels of these substances seem to improve depression. In addition, there is other evidence supporting a role for these transmitters in depression. However, the relationship between neurotransmitters and depression is complex, and doctors cannot simply measure how much serotonin or norepinephrine there is in the brain to see if there is an imbalance.

Other Biological Factors

Numerous other biological processes are thought to be involved with depression in some people (Thase, forthcoming). Hormonal levels probably play a role in some types of depression. In addition, abuse of alcohol and other drugs can increase a person's likelihood of developing depression. Finally, factors such as the amount of exposure to sunlight and even sleep patterns may have an effect on depressed mood.

Psychological Factors

Many studies have shown that psychological factors are important in the development and maintenance of depression. For example, various life stresses (for example, physical or sexual abuse, divorce, unemployment) may put certain people at risk for depression. Also, a person's style of thinking can increase his or her chances of feeling depressed. One of the most influential psychological theories of depression describes how thinking contributes to feeling depressed. This model, proposed by Dr. Aaron Beck and colleagues (1979), is known as the *cognitive theory of depression*. Beck proposed that depression is associated with a tendency to think negatively about the *self* (for instance, "I never seem to achieve anything I set out to do"), the *world* (for example, "Nobody cares about me"), and the future (thoughts such as, "Things will never improve"). In addition to these three types of thinking, Beck also emphasized the role of other negative beliefs (for example, "I have to be perfect") and tendencies to interpret situations in a negatively biased way.

There are other psychological theories of depression as well, several of which overlap considerably with Beck's approach, in that they propose that thoughts and interpretations play an important role in maintaining depression. You may wish to review chapter 3 regarding the role of thoughts in perfectionism. Many of the thoughts and beliefs that contribute to perfectionism are relevant to depression as well.

PERFECTIONISM AND DEPRESSION

Recall from chapter 1 the three types of perfectionism: self-oriented perfectionism (a tendency to set unreasonably high standards for one's own behavior), other-oriented perfectionism (a tendency to demand that others meet your unrealistically high standards), and socially prescribed perfectionism (the belief that others have impossible standards, and that you must meet these standards in order to win their approval).

Researchers have examined the relationship between these types of perfectionism and the symptoms of depression and have reported a number of interesting findings:

- People with high levels of perfectionism (particularly self-oriented perfectionism and socially prescribed perfectionism) are at a greater risk of experiencing depression than nonperfectionists, especially during periods of stress (for example, at school, work, and in their relationships) and after experiencing failure (Hewitt and Flett 1990; 1993). For example, people who operate with a high level of perfectionism may be susceptible to depression at a time when they have a lot of tests at school, especially if they don't do as well on some of these tests as they would have liked.

■ Self-oriented perfectionism increases the risk that a depressed individual will continue to feel depressed a year later if the person is under high levels of stress related to his or her work or school, but not if stress is more focused on his or her relationships (Enns and Cox 2005).

■ Socially prescribed perfectionism is associated with feelings of helplessness and hopelessness, both of which have been shown to be components of depression (Hewitt and Flett 1993).

■ Perfectionism appears to be related to other specific aspects of depression, such as tendencies to think negatively about oneself (Flett et al. 2003; Rudolph, Flett, and Hewitt 2007) and to believe that important events are independent of one's actions (Hewitt and Flett 1993).

■ Although it is normal for depression to improve over time (even without treatment), perfectionism tends to remain stable over time (Cox and Enns 2003).

In these ways, perfectionism can put people at risk for developing depression, particularly if the person has experienced certain life stresses or failures. The relationship between perfectionism and depression is not surprising. Perfectionism is the tendency to set unrealistically high standards. Because these standards are unlikely to be met, a person who holds such high standards is bound to fall short of meeting them. Frequent experiences of failure can make a person feel helpless and inadequate and may eventually make a person feel hopeless about things ever improving. Therefore, if perfectionism and depression are both problems for you, you may find that learning to accept lower standards helps you to feel less depressed.

TREATMENTS FOR DEPRESSION THAT ARE SUPPORTED BY RESEARCH

Depression can be effectively treated using a number of approaches. In this section, we discuss three of these, including cognitive behavioral therapy, interpersonal psychotherapy, and medications.

Cognitive Behavioral Therapy

Chapters 7 and 8 discuss many of the components of cognitive behavioral therapy (CBT) in detail, so we will only provide a brief recap here. Basically, the "cognitive" part of CBT refers to techniques used to help people change their negative and unrealistic beliefs, attitudes, and expectations. These techniques include teaching people to identify their negative beliefs, examine the evidence supporting and refuting their beliefs, and engage in small experiments to test out the validity of their beliefs. Behavioral strategies are designed to change behaviors that maintain negative feelings and thoughts. These may include exposure to situations that are anxiety provoking, role playing or practicing difficult interactions that are likely to come up in the future, and learning to communicate more effectively.

Interpersonal Psychotherapy for Depression (IPT)

Interpersonal psychotherapy for depression (IPT) is one of the few psychological treatments other than CBT that has consistently been shown to be effective for depression (Weissman, Markowitz, and Klerman 2000). This approach to treatment is based on the premise that depression stems from problems in interpersonal relationships. Treatment usually lasts fifteen to twenty sessions and tends to be focused on one or more of the following areas of interpersonal functioning: *interpersonal role disputes* (for example, problems adjusting to the demands of a particular social role, such as being a father, employee, daughter, and so on), *interpersonal losses* (such as the loss of a close friend or relative), *interpersonal deficits* (for example, difficulty communicating effectively with your spouse), and *interpersonal role transitions* (things like difficulty coping with life changes such as graduation, divorce, retirement, and so on). In studies comparing IPT to medication and CBT, IPT appears to be as effective as these other approaches (Craighead et al. 2007).

Antidepressant Medications

Below is a partial list of medications that have been shown to be useful for treating clinical depression. As you can see, the list is quite long. These drugs are organized with respect to their effects on particular neurotransmitter (brain chemical) systems that are believed to be involved in depression, such as the ones that involve serotonin, norepinephrine, and dopamine. We have included both the generic name as well as the brand name (in parentheses) for each medication.

Antidepressant Medications

Selective Serotonin Reuptake Inhibitors (SSRIs)
Citalopram (Celexa)
Escitalopram (Lexapro, Cipralex)
Fluoxetine (Prozac)
Fluvoxamine (Luvox)
Paroxetine (Paxil)
Sertraline (Zoloft)

Selective Dopamine Reuptake Inhibitors (SDRI)
Bupropion (Wellbutrin)

Selective Serotonin-Norepinephrine Reuptake Inhibitors (SNRIs)
Duloxetine (Cymbalta)
Venlafaxine (Effexor)

Noradrenergic/Specific Serotonergic Antidepressant (NaSSA)
Mirtazapine (Remeron)

Nonselective Cyclic Antidepressants (Sometimes called tricyclic and heterocyclic antidepressants) Amitriptyline (Elavil) Clomipramine (Anafranil) Desipramine (Norpramin) Imipramine (Tofranil) Nortriptyline (Aventyl or Pamelor) Trazodone (Desyrel)
Monoamine Oxidase Inhibitors (MAOIs) Phenelzine (Nardil) Tranylcypromine (Parnate)
Reversable Inhibitors of Monoamine Oxidase-A (RIMA) Moclobemide (Manerix) [not available in the United States]

All of the medications listed in the table are associated with side effects, which may include such symptoms as dry mouth, headache, dizziness, upset stomach, sexual difficulties, weight gain, insomnia, or other symptoms, depending on the medication. Some antidepressant medications may interact with other prescription medications, over-the-counter medications, alcohol, illegal and recreational drugs, or even certain foods (in the case of MAOI antidepressants). We recommend that you discuss possible side effects and drug interactions with your doctor if you are interested in trying an antidepressant (or any medication, for that matter). Although side effects are relatively common, many people are able to tolerate antidepressant treatment with no side effects. Furthermore, when side effects do occur, they are often mild and tend to improve with time or adjustment of the dosage. Nevertheless, in rare cases, some medications may be associated with more severe side effects. Ask your doctor about the side effects of any specific medication that he or she recommends.

With such a long list of available antidepressants, how does one choose one antidepressant over another? There are several factors that come into play. The first is effectiveness. Your doctor should recommend a medication that has been shown to be effective for your pattern of symptoms. Second, your doctor should take into account the side-effect profile of the medication as well as possible effects on medical conditions that you may have. Third, your doctor should consider possible interactions with other medications that you may be taking, as well as interactions with alcohol and other drugs that you may use occasionally. Fourth, the cost of the pills varies from medication to medication. If cost is an issue (for example, if you don't have a drug plan), you should mention it to your doctor. Finally, the decision of which medication to use should be influenced by your past responses to particular medications. If one medication was effective and well-tolerated in the past, it might make sense to try it again. If you have a history of not responding to an adequate dosage of a medication in the past, perhaps this time you should try a different medication.

If a particular medication does not work for you, don't give up. First, you should make sure you are on an adequate dosage. Doctors are often concerned that patients will be unable to tolerate the specific medication, so the initial recommend dosages are often too low to be effective. If you are able to tolerate the medication, the dose will usually be increased over the first few weeks of use to a dose likely to be effective. If you're not sure whether you are on an adequate dosage, obtain a second opinion from another family doctor or psychiatrist. Second, antidepressants take a few weeks to work. It's not uncommon for people to take these medications for up to six or even eight weeks before noticing any benefit. Third, if a particular medication does not work for you, there are other options. There may be another medication that is effective for you, or you may benefit from a psychological treatment such as CBT or IPT. Finally, it is possible to boost the effects of some antidepressants using other medications such as lithium carbonate. Lithium is normally used to treat bipolar disorder or manic depression (a problem in which people experience both extreme highs and lows in mood). However, when used in conjunction with an antidepressant, lithium has been shown for some people to improve upon the benefits achieved by an antidepressant alone (Thase et al. 2007).

Electroconvulsive Therapy

Electroconvulsive therapy (ECT) is often administered after all other treatments for depression have been attempted and failed, unless the person is very seriously ill, in which case it may be recommended as an initial treatment. ECT is still very controversial and is often discussed in a negative light by the media. Today, ECT is very different than the way it has been portrayed in movies such as *One Flew Over the Cuckoo's Nest*. The procedure is done under anesthetic and involves inducing stimulation of the brain by delivering a shock to the brain lasting less than a second. The seizures that used to be triggered during ECT are now suppressed by the use of muscle relaxants. The main side effect of ECT is confusion and loss of short-term memory that lasts for about a week or two. Despite these side effects, many individuals who do not respond to medications may find ECT to be effective for depression (Mathew, Amiel, and Sackeim 2005).

A more recent development is Transcranial Magnetic Stimulation, which uses magnetic waves to stimulate the brain while the person remains fully conscious. This treatment is done as an outpatient procedure, as is ECT, and people go home or on to their workplace after the session.

HOW TO CHANGE PERFECTIONISTIC THINKING AND BEHAVIOR IN DEPRESSION

For a detailed review of all the strategies for overcoming perfectionism, see chapters 7 through 9. In this section, we will highlight some of the techniques that may be helpful for you if you suffer from depressed mood or if you tend to feel down when your expectations are not met.

Changing Perfectionistic Thoughts that Contribute to Depression

You may recall from chapter 7 that we recommend following five steps for changing perfectionistic thoughts: identifying perfectionistic thoughts, listing more reasonable alternative thoughts, reassessing the advantages and disadvantages of the original thoughts and the alternative thoughts, and choosing a more realistic or helpful way of viewing situations. In addition, we suggest a variety of specific techniques that can be helpful for changing perfectionistic thoughts. Several of these will be particularly helpful for individuals who tend to feel sad or depressed. These include: examining the evidence, taking another perspective, compromising with yourself, hypothesis testing, changing your social comparison habits, and looking at the big picture. Others may be helpful as well, so it is worth looking over the material in chapter 7 for further possibilities.

In the case of depression, you should pay particular attention to depressive beliefs about yourself, such as beliefs that you are worthless, incompetent, or generally deficient in some way. If you hold these beliefs, you may find it helpful to think carefully about what these labels mean. Sometimes, attempting to define labels such as "worthless" and "incompetent" will lead you to realize that these words do not really capture who you are (or who anyone is, for that matter). Consider the following therapy vignette. In this vignette, the therapist uses the strategy of taking another perspective to help Jonathon to evaluate his own worth using the same criteria that he uses to judge other people.

Jonathon: Most days, I feel completely worthless. I just sit around the house and nothing seems to get done.

Therapist: Let's look at the word "worthless." Exactly what does that word mean to you?

Jonathon: Well, I suppose that a worthless person is someone who doesn't contribute to society and doesn't do anything—someone like me.

Therapist: Can you think of anyone else who you would describe as worthless?

Jonathon: Actually, no. I can't.

Therapist: If you were to meet someone else who is worthless, how would you know it?

Jonathon: I don't really think of other people as being worthless.

Therapist: What if you met a person who, like yourself, was unemployed and not spending time with friends? Would you consider that person to be worthless?

Jonathon: Not at all. If anything, I would feel for that person.

Therapist: It seems that you have different standards for yourself than you do for other people. Is it possible to change your view of yourself to match the view that you might have of another person who is similar to you?

Jonathon: I guess it's possible that I'm not worthless, although I still believe that there are lots of things in my life that need to change.

Here is another therapy vignette that illustrates how a therapist helps Andrea to change social-comparison strategies that may contribute to her depressed feelings:

Andrea: My daughter's report card just arrived, and it was just average. To make things worse, my nephew is doing very well in school. I know my brother is going to tell me about my nephew's report card, and I'm going to feel terrible.

Therapist: Why will you feel terrible?

Andrea: My daughter should be doing at least as well as my nephew. I feel that her report card reflects badly on me.

Therapist: How do your nephew's grades compare to everyone else's in the class?

Andrea: He is always at the top of the class. That just makes it worse.

Therapist: What effect does it have to compare your daughter's report card to that of the top student in the class?

Andrea: It makes me feel miserable.

Therapist: People can be measured in many different dimensions, including physical appearance, intelligence, artistic talent, physical fitness, aptitude for sports, knowledge of particular topics, physical health, income, school performance—and the list goes on and on. In fact, each of these dimensions can be subdivided into other dimensions. For example, physical appearance includes such things as height, weight, hair color, complexion, and so on. Each of us performs well in some of these dimensions. In other dimensions, we may perform poorly, compared to most people. However, in most dimensions, we tend to be somewhere in between—in other words, average.

Andrea: Now that you mention it, there are lots of ways in which my daughter really outshines my nephew. He just studies all the time, but my daughter has lots of outside interests and is quite good at sports.

In addition to changing negative thoughts about yourself, you should also examine your negative thoughts and absolutes about the world (for instance, "People should always be interested in what I have to say") and about the future (for example, "I will never find a relationship that makes me happy"). Not only are thoughts such as these usually untrue, but they also contribute to feelings of depression.

CHANGING PERFECTIONISTIC BEHAVIORS THAT CONTRIBUTE TO DEPRESSION

A number of strategies may be helpful for dealing with perfectionistic behaviors that are associated with depression. Exposure exercises designed to disprove perfectionistic beliefs can reduce the intensity of these beliefs. Exposure can help reduce depression in other ways as well. Often, when people are feeling depressed, they tend to become socially withdrawn and uninterested in their usual hobbies and activities. Therefore, they begin to avoid doing things because they believe that they are unlikely to enjoy themselves. The net result of the avoidance, however, is to decrease the person's enjoyment of life, thereby contributing to the depression and the lack of motivation to do things. Exposure can have the effect of breaking that cycle. By forcing yourself to do things that normally are interesting to you, chances are that you may enjoy them more than you might expect. Going places and doing things, despite not having the energy or interest in being active, may help to increase your interest in doing things over time. For more details on how to conduct exposure practices, see chapter 8.

In addition to exposure, several of the other behavioral strategies discussed in chapter 8 may be helpful. For example, if you tend to have difficulty communicating directly and assertively when you're feeling down, you may find some of the suggestions regarding assertive communication helpful. In addition, procrastination can often be a problem for people who are feeling depressed. Check out chapter 8 for methods of overcoming procrastination.

CHAPTER 11

Perfectionism and Anger

Like sadness and fear, anger is a universal emotion that is experienced by everyone. Despite the fact that all people feel anger from time to time, most people don't enjoy feeling angry, and they may even feel embarrassed about expressing anger in front of others. The experience of anger is often associated with other feelings, such as irritation, disappointment, rage, or a feeling of hatred and dislike toward another person, a situation, or even yourself.

When feeling angry, you may also experience a desire to be aggressive or destructive, or you may feel the urge to seek revenge toward another person who has let you down. Usually, anger is associated with a sense of blame. That is, when you feel angry, you are probably assigning blame to another individual or yourself for behaving in an unacceptable way. Also, anger is typically associated with strong beliefs about the way a situation *should* be.

Although anger can increase the likelihood of aggression, there is little evidence to support a strong relationship between anger and aggression in general. Anger prepares you to be aggressive if the need arises, but it does not cause aggression directly. Most people, across situations, are able to control their anger and prevent it from leading to verbal or physical attacks on others. Furthermore, even when a person is aggressive, it is often not related to anger but rather to a need for dominance or control. For example, people who injure their victims during a robbery have probably not been provoked in any way and probably aren't angry at the victim. Similarly, when children tease or hurt other children in the school yard, it probably has little to do with anger and more to do with a desire to dominate the other person or look strong in front of peers.

People differ with respect to their threshold for feeling anger. An experience that might cause anger for one person may not have the same effect on another individual. Although some drivers become very angry when other drivers make mistakes—such as cutting off another car, tailgating, driving too slowly, or going through a red light (this anger toward other drivers is often referred to as "road rage" in the media)—other drivers tolerate these situations without much reaction.

As we discussed in previous chapters, perfectionism puts people at risk for becoming angry more easily. If you tend to have high standards that are rigid and inflexible, you are at risk for not having your standards and expectations met. Not being able to achieve a goal is one of several common triggers for anger.

COMMON TRIGGERS FOR ANGER

Psychologist Carroll Izard identified three common triggers for anger: restraint, interruption of goal-oriented behavior, and aversive stimulation (1991). We will consider each of these in turn.

Restraint

Restraint involves some force blocking your desired actions in a particular situation. Restraint can be physical or psychological in nature. Physical restraint involves actually holding a person down in order to prevent him or her from doing something or going somewhere. Studies show that even infants as young as four months old respond with anger when their arms are restrained (Sternberg and Campos 1990). Psychological restraint involves being prevented from doing something by some social or psychological force (for example, having to follow particular rules or regulations to avoid getting in trouble). You probably recognize the experience of becoming angry when you are restrained or prevented from doing something that you want to do. As a teenager, you may have become angry when your parents prevented you from going out with friends. As an adult, you may become angry when you get into your car, only to realize that the tire is flat and you are going to be late for an appointment.

Interruption of Goal-Oriented Behavior

Interruption of goal-oriented behavior is very similar to restraint, in that a person is prevented from reaching a particular goal. An example is feeling angry when you are interrupted while concentrating on a task, such as reading a book, watching a good movie, or filling out your income-tax forms. Although most people enjoy breaks from time to time, uninvited interruptions may be less welcome for some people, especially when there is a perceived pressure to finish a task by a certain time. Because perfectionism can often be associated with high standards for performance or a drive to finish jobs quickly, being interrupted is more likely to be a trigger for anger among perfectionistic people.

Aversive Stimulation

Aversive stimulation involves being exposed to an unpleasant stimulus, such as extreme cold or heat, intense pain, a loud noise, a nasty odor, or a morally offensive comment. For example, if you are shopping in a crowded shopping mall, you may become irritable following several hours of exposure to noise, crowds, and uncomfortable stuffiness (especially if you're wearing warm clothing).

Other Triggers for Anger

There are many other possible triggers for anger. For example, most people feel angry when they have been deceived, treated poorly, or hurt by another person. In addition, you probably have had times when disapproval from others has led you to feel angry. You may also feel anger toward others even when their behavior is not directed at you (for instance, feeling angry at your best friend's boss when you find out that your best friend was unjustly fired; feeling angry at a politician for making a decision that you don't agree with).

Anger can be directed at yourself as well. If you make a mistake on an important job at work, you may feel angry for not doing the perfect job that you had anticipated. You may even feel angry about feeling angry. It is not unusual for people to experience anger toward themselves if they lose control when feeling angry toward another person.

WHEN IS ANGER A PROBLEM?

Chronic problems with anger can contribute to high blood pressure, heart disease, excess stomach acid, and other physical problems. Interpersonally, anger can lead to less intimate relationships, as friends, coworkers, and family members learn to avoid talking about certain issues in order to prevent themselves from being the victims of your anger. In extreme cases, people may avoid you completely, leading to complete social isolation. Finally, continual displays of anger can affect your self-esteem by making you feel guilty, embarrassed, out of control, or inadequate.

Although anger is a normal emotion that everyone experiences, it can be problematic when it happens too frequently, when it happens too intensely, when it leads to physical or psychological aggression, when it leads to relationship difficulties, and when it leads to any other types of significant impairment in a person's life (for example, individuals who are so angry that they cannot work on their term paper that is due the next day; people who get fired for telling their boss what they really think of him or her).

THE DEVELOPMENT OF ANGER

The experience and expression of anger is mediated by a complex interaction among various biological and psychological factors. As we mentioned earlier, there is evidence that the capacity to express anger is present from infancy. In addition, many animals are capable of expressing anger, often in ways that are very similar to the expression of anger in humans. From a biological perspective, the limbic system (including the hypothalamus and amygdala) has been implicated in the expression of anger.

In addition, your learning experiences during childhood probably have a large impact on how you express anger. There is evidence that parents are more tolerant of anger in boys than in girls. Researchers have found that parents of boys tend to respond to anger with attention, which may strengthen the angry behavior. In contrast, parents are more likely to tell their daughters that their anger is inappropriate and instruct them to stop being angry (Radke-Yarrow and Kochanska 1990). This pattern seems to continue in adults. Men who express anger in the workplace are generally viewed more positively than men who express sadness, and their anger is often assumed to be related to external circumstances (for example, "He is angry because of something that happened to him"). In contrast, women who express anger in the workplace are viewed (by both men and women) more negatively, and their anger is more likely to be attributed to internal factors (for instance, "She is an angry person").

Other research has lent further support to the view that behavior by parents contributes to the expression of anger in children. For example, one study found that toddlers are more likely to express anger frequently if their parents respond to their problem behaviors with anger (Crockenberg 1985). In contrast, parents who respond to toddlers with other emotions, such as fear or sadness, are more likely to have children with fewer behavioral problems and a well-developed capacity to empathize with other people. It should be noted that behavior by parents is not the only social influence on the way a person expresses anger. There is also evidence that a child's peer group has an impact on the development and maintenance of anger and anger-related behavior (Lemerise and Dodge 2008; Snyder et al. 2007).

Because anger is a universal emotion influenced by such factors as brain functioning and childhood learning experiences, you may be tempted to assume that there is nothing you can do to change your angry behavior. Nothing could be further from the truth. More than fifty studies have investigated the effectiveness of cognitive and behavioral treatments for anger, and overall this approach to treating anger has been shown to be quite effective (DiGiuseppe and Tafrate 2007; Feindler 2006; Gorenstein et al. 2007). Learning to change the thoughts and behaviors that help to maintain your difficulties with anger is the best way to overcome the problem.

The Role of Thoughts in Anger

When you respond with anger, it is not the situation or event that leads you to react, but rather your interpretation of the situation or event. For example, imagine that your child arrives home from school and hands you a midterm report card. Upon examining the report card, you notice failing grades in math and science. How would you respond to this situation? What emotions would you be feeling? What thoughts might you be having? Now, imagine how other people you know might respond to this situation. Think about specific people, such as your partner, family members, coworkers, and so on. Would any of them respond differently to this situation than you? Can you imagine another parent feeling differently when confronted with this situation? There are many different ways that a parent might respond. Furthermore, the specific reaction is likely to be influenced by the person's beliefs about the situation. The table below provides examples of thoughts that might be associated with particular emotional reactions in response to a child's disappointing report card.

Emotions and Thoughts Table

Emotion	Thoughts
Angry	My child did not study hard enough. My child should have performed better. My child is making me look bad by not doing well in school.
Sad	If I were a better parent, my child would be doing better in school. My child will never amount to anything.
Concerned	My child must be feeling terrible about this. What if my child cannot pull up these grades by the end of the year?
Neutral	There is still time for these grades to improve. Perhaps a tutor could help my child raise the math and science grades. I had some poor grades when I was in high school. A couple of poor grades won't matter much in the long run.

In this example, you can see how the specific beliefs that you hold affect your emotional response to the situation. By examining the accuracy of your angry beliefs and trying to change them to be more realistic and moderate, you will find it easier to control your anger.

PERFECTIONISM AND ANGER

Perfectionism can lead to anger when you apply your unreasonably high expectations and standards to other people. You may also become angry at yourself when you do not meet your own specific goals or expectations. Any belief that you have about how you or other people *should* be puts you at risk for feeling angry if these expectations are not met. Beware of statements or thoughts that include words such as "should" and "must," especially when they are accompanied by words such as "always" and "never." Examples of perfectionistic expectations that may lead to anger when they are not met include the following:

- I should never be late for appointments.

- My doctor should be able to diagnose and treat any symptom I have.

- My children should always dress the way I want them to.

- People should never tell lies—even white lies.

- Nice people never talk about others behind their backs.

- I should lose five pounds.

- My children must never swear.

- People should never eat with their hands.

- People should always do exactly what they say they will do.

CHANGING PERFECTIONISTIC THOUGHTS AND BEHAVIORS THAT CONTRIBUTE TO ANGER

Chapters 7, 8, and 9 contain many different strategies that are useful for combating the thoughts and behaviors that are associated with perfectionism, including those that contribute to anger. You may wish to review these chapters. The remaining sections of this chapter highlight a number of strategies that are especially helpful for dealing with anger.

Become Aware of Your Anger Before It Becomes Intense

People are often unaware of their anger, especially when it is at low levels. Therefore, the first step to reducing your anger is to increase your ability to detect anger before it gets out of hand. Be aware of subtle signs that you may be feeling angry. These may include a tendency to use sarcastic comments or put-downs, a feeling of tension in your body, being grouchy or irritable, or being overly sensitive to comments from other people. If you are in a situation where things are not going your way, be aware of whether you are becoming angry and take steps to keep the anger from getting the best of you (some possible strategies are described throughout the rest of this chapter). When anger is very intense, it may be hard to think clearly, so catching it early can be helpful.

In fact, you can even deal with the anger before it happens. If you anticipate being angry in a situation, try to challenge your angry thoughts before they occur. For example, if you are expecting a negative performance appraisal in an upcoming meeting with your boss, plan how to deal with the situation before it happens. Before the meeting, brainstorm possible ways of dealing with the situation that are unlikely to be damaging to you or your situation at work.

Challenge Your Perfectionistic Thoughts

Rather than accepting your angry thoughts as facts, test out their validity by using the strategies discussed in chapter 7. Examine the evidence supporting your angry beliefs. Search for other ways of interpreting the situation. The following therapy vignette illustrates how to make your standards more flexible in order to become more tolerant and decrease your angry feelings.

Beth: My daughter just came home from college with a lip ring, and I'm absolutely furious.

Therapist:	What bothers you about the piercing?
Beth:	It looks repulsive. Also, I'm worried that when other people see it, it will cause problems for her. Nobody will ever find her attractive with that thing.
Therapist:	The thought that you just mentioned is a "worry" thought. What "anger" thoughts are you having? For example, do you believe that you've somehow been hurt by your daughter getting her lip pierced?
Beth:	Well, she knows that I don't approve of it, and she did it anyway. We've talked about it in the past, and I let her know how I feel. She has completely disregarded my feelings, and I believe that she has no respect for my opinions.
Therapist:	So, you interpret the lip piercing as evidence that your daughter doesn't respect your opinions. Are there other possible interpretations?
Beth:	Not that I can think of.
Therapist:	Would you say that any time a person decides to purchase a piece of clothing or adopt a new hairstyle that another person does not find attractive, it is a sign of disrespect?
Beth:	Of course not, but this is different. This is such a radical change.
Therapist:	Can you think of anything that you may have done in the past that your own parents thought was radical or inappropriate?
Beth:	Actually, when I got my ears pierced, my parents didn't talk to me for a week.
Therapist:	Today, the role of body piercing is not very different from that of ear piercing forty years ago. If you look around the city, there are many people your daughter's age who have a piercing in one place or another.

Beth: What if she can't find a job after graduation because of her lip ring? It's possible that employers out there will see it the way I do!

Therapist: Let me throw the question back at you. What if she can't get a job because of the lip ring?

Beth: I guess she will take out the lip ring or find a place to work where it doesn't matter. I can see what you're getting at. Even though I don't like it, it's not as bad as I thought at first.

In general, asking yourself some of the following questions may help you to challenge the perfectionistic thoughts that contribute to your anger:

- Is this situation really as important as it feels?

- What if this situation doesn't go my way? Does it really matter?

- Do I need to control this situation?

- Is my way the only way to view this situation?

- Would another person necessarily see this situation the same way as I do?

- What if things don't work out the way I want them to?

- Do I know for sure that things will turn out badly if I don't get my way?

- Will getting angry result in the outcome that I want?

Allow People to Be Different than You

People like to be around other people who share important beliefs, attitudes, and values. People who are overly perfectionistic, however, may insist that other people conform to their way of thinking and doing things, even for matters that aren't terribly important. To be less of a perfectionist, you will need to allow other people to be themselves, even if it means that you don't agree with their choices in clothing, hairstyle, career, relationships, and so on.

This doesn't mean that anything goes. In all relationships, there are limitations to what people find acceptable. Most people don't tolerate being lied to or stolen from by friends or coworkers. Similarly, parents generally don't allow their children to do things that are very dangerous. The goal should not be to have no standards, but rather to have more flexible standards. If you can distinguish between standards that are appropriate and others that are unrealistic or excessively high, you will run less of a risk of experiencing unwarranted anger toward other people.

Avoid Using Angry Language

Angry language can help fuel angry feelings. For example, labeling other people as jerks, idiots, incompetent, irresponsible, and so on can make it difficult to change the way you think about them. If you are tempted to label another person, try labeling his or her behavior instead. For example, if your housemate has not taken out the garbage in a few weeks, rather than saying, "My housemate is lazy and inconsiderate," try saying, "My housemate has not taken out the garbage in a few weeks."

In addition to avoiding labeling, it can be helpful to make it a habit to think before you speak, particularly when you're angry. Before saying what's on your mind, imagine hearing the words that you are about to say. Would you find the words helpful if someone said them to you? If not, keep your thoughts to yourself. You don't have to say everything you're thinking.

Assume Responsibility for Your Actions

As we discussed earlier, anger is often caused by blaming another person for a problem or holding on to rigid beliefs about how something *should* be. To overcome a problem with excessive anger, it's important to understand all the different factors that contribute to a situation, including your own role. Situations are often complex, and rarely is a particular person entirely responsible for a problem or situation.

Imagine that you confided in your friend Tom that you didn't like his friend Alison. If Tom told Alison how you felt about her, you might feel angry and betrayed because Tom has talked about you behind your back. Although it's true that Tom may have made a mistake in this situation, it would be important for you to assume some responsibility for what happened as well. By telling Tom about your feelings toward Alison, you would also be guilty of gossiping. Also, you would be in part responsible for the information getting back to Alison.

Similarly, arguments and disagreements are rarely the fault of any one person. Rather, they are usually determined by a complex interaction of many different factors, including the specific situation that two people are arguing about, the manner in which each person is discussing the topic (tone and volume of voice, body language, use of sarcastic comments and insults, and so on), the personal state of each person (fatigue, hunger, anxious or depressed mood, previous stresses during the day, and so on), and possible miscommunication. During a disagreement, it is easy to notice all the ways in which the other person has contributed to the argument. It's much more difficult to take responsibility for your own behaviors that may have helped fuel the disagreement.

Admit When You Are Wrong

People often believe that it is important, above all else, to be consistent. You may fear that if you back down on a particular issue or if you change your mind, you will appear uncertain, others will not take you as seriously, and your opinion will be less respected in the future. There are situations in which this may be true. For example, a politician who makes a commitment (for example, "No new taxes") during an election campaign and then breaks the promise after being elected may be perceived as dishonest, manipulative, or indecisive. However, in most cases, people respect other people who are able to change in the face of new information or after realizing that they have made a mistake. If you realize that your expectations have been unreasonable, people will appreciate you admitting that you were wrong. People generally appreciate an apology when it is sincere.

Practice Exposure Exercises

If you tend to overreact to other people doing things differently than you, structured exposure to the situation may help you to be more tolerant. For example, if it upsets you to have your partner clean up after dinner (because it is never done to your high standards), arrange for your partner to clean up every day for a couple of weeks (of course, this will depend on your partner's agreeing to participate). During the practices, your job will be to refrain from making any comments or criticisms. Over the course of the practices, you will probably become more tolerant of your partner's cleaning standards.

Before beginning any exposure practices, we recommend that you review the relevant parts of chapter 8 to make sure that the exercises are structured in a way that maximizes their effectiveness.

Take Some Time Out

Time out involves physically or mentally taking a break from a situation. For example, you might lie down, take a walk, phone a friend, watch TV, or get involved in some other activity that gets you out of the situation. Sometimes, you won't have the opportunity to physically get away from a situation. In these cases, just taking the time to count to ten may be enough of a break to prevent you from saying something that you might regret later. Your anger is likely to decrease if you get away from the triggers that remind you of why you are angry. After a break, you are likely to see the situation in a more realistic light. Often, by the time you return to the situation, the anger will have subsided. Time out is especially helpful when your anger is too intense to make use of some of the other anger-management strategies, such as challenging your angry thoughts.

There are helpful and unhelpful ways of taking time out. It's best to never storm out of a room or hang up the telephone on another person. Even though this may make you feel better, the other person is likely to become more angry or hurt, and the problem will escalate. If you need to take a break, explain to the other individual that you are feeling angry and that you want some time to think about things. Be specific about how much time you need ("I'll be back in an hour" or "I'll phone you tomorrow"). If the other person wants to continue the conversation, make an appointment to talk at a later time when your anger is likely to have decreased—and make sure you keep the appointment.

Try Physical Exercise

Physical exercise (for example, running, walking, cycling, swimming, aerobics, sports, and so on) is a good way to blow off steam. With regular exercise, you may also feel more energetic and healthy, which in turn will make it easier for you to tolerate situations that otherwise might be annoying or frustrating (Hassmén, Koivula, and Uutela 2000).

Practice Relaxation and Meditation

Research has shown that relaxation training and mindfulness meditation can be effective ways to manage anger (Deffenbacher, Oetting, and DiGiuseppe 2002; Polizzi 2008). There are many different methods that can be used to induce a state of relaxation or mindfulness. Progressive muscle relaxation involves learning to relax the muscles of the body to decrease feelings of tension, stress, and anxiety. Imagery, another method that is sometimes helpful, involves learning to imagine particular scenes that are relaxing. Meditation and mindfulness training can help you deal with anger and other negative emotions. Finally, learning to breathe slowly and smoothly can help you relax. A full description of each of these methods is beyond the scope of this book. However, there are a number of places where you can learn more about relaxation and meditation if you are interested. Check out the Further Readings at the end of this book, as well as some of the ideas suggested in chapter 9. Also, you may have access near your home to classes for relaxation training, meditation, yoga, or some other activity that includes a relaxation or mindfulness component.

Use Problem-Solving Strategies

When you are faced with a conflict or problem, use the following steps to solve the problem, rather than losing your temper or stewing in anger:

1. Define the problem. Until you understand exactly what the problem is, you will not be able to solve it.

2. If the problem is complex, break it down into smaller problems. Then choose one problem to work on at a time.

3. Brainstorm all possible solutions to the problem—even solutions that aren't likely to work.

4. Evaluate each solution by listing the potential costs and benefits.

5. Choose the best solution(s) to the problem.

6. Develop a plan for implementing the solutions (for instance, decide what steps need to be taken to make the plan work).

7. Solve the problem by carrying out the solution you have chosen.

8. Evaluate the effectiveness of the solution. If the solution was not effective, repeat the problem-solving steps until you find a solution that works.

Consider the following example. Imagine you are a manager in an office where you supervise several members of the clerical staff. One of your staff members has a tendency to arrive ten or fifteen minutes late for work almost every day. As the supervisor, you believe that lateness is unacceptable and are determined to address this problem. Start by defining the problem. In this case, the problem is that one of your staff is late every day and that lateness makes you angry. Note that the problem has two parts to it—the fact that the employee is late (and the effects of the lateness on his or her work) and your reaction to the person being late. In this example, the lateness is only a problem because it bothers you.

Step 2 involves breaking down the problem into smaller problems, if necessary. However, in this case, the problem is relatively simple and doesn't need to be broken down any further. Step 3 involves brainstorming possible solutions. For example, possible solutions include: fire the employee, only pay the employee for the time spent at work, ask the employee to make up the time later, completely relax your rules regarding lateness (in other words, decide that all lateness is okay), relax your rules somewhat regarding lateness (for example, decide that being up to ten minutes late for work is acceptable), or simply ignore the problem.

Next, evaluate the costs and benefits of each solution. For example, one benefit of firing the employee is that you would no longer have to be angered by the situation. On the other hand, firing the employee might lead to a wrongful dismissal lawsuit, as well as making you feel very guilty and making your other staff members unhappy. Conversely, choosing the solution of somewhat relaxing the rules may work well. This solution will accommodate the employee's morning schedule without really affecting productivity in any way. If the employee believes that you are flexible, he or she may be more inclined to work harder. A potential cost of this solution is that other staff may start to arrive late as well. Or perhaps if you give staff members permission to arrive ten minutes late, they will start arriving thirty minutes late.

Once you evaluate the costs and benefits of each solution, you may find that none of the solutions is perfect. In the end, however, you will need to choose the best solution. If no solution seems potentially useful, take a break from the problem and come back to it later. Perhaps involving another individual in the problem-solving process will help. Another person may be able to generate solutions that were not obvious to you.

Once you are able to choose one or more solutions that are likely to be effective, begin to develop a plan for implementing them. For example, if you decide to relax the rules regarding lateness so that being ten minutes late is acceptable, how will you implement the rule? Will you make an announcement to all staff about the new rule? Or will you wait until someone is more than ten minutes late to tell him or her about the new rule for acceptable and unacceptable lateness? When you have chosen a plan for action, carry it out as soon as possible. The longer you wait to solve the problem, the harder it may be to make the changes.

CHAPTER 12

Perfectionism and Social Anxiety

THE NATURE OF SOCIAL ANXIETY

If you've ever felt uncomfortable in the presence of another person or nervous about making a negative impression on other people, you've experienced social anxiety. Most people experience anxiety or fear in certain social situations, at least some of the time. Perhaps you have felt uneasy in a situation where you were the center of attention (for example, getting married, acting in a play, or giving a formal presentation at work). Or perhaps you have felt uneasy at a big job interview or meeting your partner's parents for the first time. Like any situation that triggers anxiety and fear, social situations can be uncomfortable when they are perceived as threatening or dangerous in some way. In other words, you're more likely to be anxious when you believe that you have something to lose if you say the wrong thing, behave inappropriately, or seem uncomfortable.

Social anxiety exists on a continuum. Some people may appear to never experience anxiety in any social situations, whereas other people avoid all social contact, including going to work and spending time with their family. Most people are in between these two extremes. You may be tempted to avoid social situations that make you uncomfortable. If you don't avoid these situations, you may rely on certain coping strategies to help get you through the situation. For example, a client seen in our clinic was a university professor who had an extreme fear of public speaking—including teaching her classes. Although she was unable to avoid teaching, she found subtle ways to get through her classes. For example, she always taught her students in the dark, using overhead transparencies, so they wouldn't notice her anxiety symptoms. Also, she always wore turtleneck sweaters so that the blushing on her neck wouldn't be visible.

Most social situations that trigger anxiety can be categorized into two main types: performance situations and social-interaction situations. Performance situations are situations in which you are likely to be observed while performing some task. Social-interaction situations involve speaking or interacting with another person. Below are some examples of each:

Performance Situations that Sometimes Trigger Anxiety

- Public speaking (for instance, formal presentations)
- Participating in meetings at work, answering questions in class, and so on
- Singing, acting, dancing, or reading aloud
- Using a public restroom with someone else in the room
- Doing aerobics or playing sports
- Writing with other people watching
- Eating or drinking with other people watching
- Going out in public without dressing "nicely"
- Being sexually intimate

Social-Interaction Situations that Sometimes Trigger Anxiety

- Going to parties (especially when the other guests are strangers)
- Being introduced to new people

- Talking with people in positions of authority (for example, a boss or teacher)

- Being assertive

- Initiating casual conversations

- Maintaining casual conversations

- Going out on a date

- Going to job interviews

- Sharing private details about your life with another person

- Talking on the telephone

- Confronting another person about a problem

In anxiety-provoking social situations, people are typically apprehensive about two different aspects of the situation. First, they have anxiety-provoking thoughts about the situation itself. For example, they may worry that others will find them to be incompetent, unattractive, unintelligent, or boring, despite the fact that they are actually unlikely to be judged negatively in the situation. Second, they have anxiety-provoking thoughts about looking nervous in front of other people. For example, they may worry that other people will notice specific anxiety symptoms (for instance, shaky hands or a sweaty forehead). People who are socially anxious often see their anxiety as a sign of weakness and take great pains to make sure that other people don't notice the symptoms.

Because people who are socially anxious often avoid social situations, they may lack certain skills to perform well in these situations. For example, a person who is uncomfortable talking to other people may lack certain conversational skills that others take for granted (for example, how to make appropriate eye contact, how to ask questions of the other person, and so on). Similarly, people who completely avoid sports or dancing are unlikely to be extremely accomplished at either of these activities until they have opportunities to practice and develop their skills.

Like other emotional states, social anxiety may be thought of as having three main components: the physical, the cognitive, and the behavioral. The *physical component* includes all the physical symptoms that people experience when anxious, including racing heart, irregular breathing, dizziness, shaking, sweating, blushing, or an unsteady voice.

The *cognitive component* includes the beliefs, interpretations, and predictions that contribute to the anxiety (for instance, "This person will think I'm an idiot"). This component also includes a tendency to pay too much attention to information that confirms the anxiety-provoking beliefs. For example, if you are nervous while giving a presentation, you are more likely to notice the people in the audience who seem bored or unhappy than the people who seem interested in your talk. Also, when confronted with an ambiguous situation (something like a person who seems uninterested in what you're saying), you are more likely to interpret the situation in a way that is consistent with your anxiety (for example, "This person finds me boring") than with a more neutral interpretation (such as, "This person seems very distracted").

The *behavioral component* of social anxiety usually involves avoidance of the feared situation. This may include complete avoidance (such as not going to a party), or more subtle forms of avoidance (for example, going to a party but only talking to certain "safe" people). In addition, social anxiety may be associated with other behaviors, such as checking your appearance in the mirror and constantly trying to figure out whether people are reacting negatively to your behavior.

SOCIAL ANXIETY DISORDER

Social anxiety disorder (also called *social phobia*) is a term used to describe social anxiety that is extreme enough to greatly bother a person or cause significant interference in the person's life. The criteria that professionals use to define social anxiety disorder include the following (American Psychiatric Association 2000):

- The person experiences an intense fear of one or more social or performance situations in which the person fears that he or she will do something embarrassing or show signs of anxiety.

- The person becomes very anxious or panicky when exposed to a feared social situation.

- The person recognizes that the fear is out of proportion to the real danger.

- The person avoids the situation or endures it with intense discomfort.

- The social anxiety bothers the person or leads to significant interference in functioning.

- If the person is under eighteen years old, the problem has lasted at least six months.

- The social anxiety is not due to another problem (for example, the person is not avoiding social situations simply because he or she is feeling depressed and is uninterested in socializing).

Note that social anxiety disorder may involve many different situations or as few as one situation (for example, public speaking). The main difference between social anxiety disorder and normal levels of social anxiety and shyness are that in social anxiety disorder, the anxiety usually occurs more frequently and more intensely, and the anxiety causes problems for the person by interfering with work, relationships, or other activities. In many cases, a fear of public speaking would not meet criteria for social anxiety disorder because such fears often don't impact on people's lives in any meaningful way, because many people only rarely have to speak in public. However, for a person who has to make frequent presentations for work, a fear of public speaking may well meet criteria for social anxiety disorder.

Recent epidemiological studies have estimated that up to 13 percent of the general population meets the clinical criteria for social anxiety disorder at some time in their life (Kessler et al. 2005). In addition, social anxiety disorder is often associated with other problems, including depression, eating disorders, and substance abuse. Fortunately, social anxiety disorder often responds quite well to treatment. We will review the treatment options for this problem later in this chapter.

CAUSES OF SOCIAL ANXIETY AND SOCIAL ANXIETY DISORDER

Social anxiety disorder seems to run in families. People who have an immediate family member with social anxiety disorder are two to three times more likely to develop social anxiety disorder compared to people without social anxiety disorder in the family. The fact that social anxiety disorder runs in families is probably related to both the genetic heritability of social anxiety, as well as the process of learning anxious behaviors from parents or other family members. In fact, evidence is now pointing to the fact that social anxiety disorder probably stems from an interaction of both biological and psychological processes.

Biological Factors

Twin studies that have attempted to separate out the effects of learning and genetics have yielded inconsistent results, with some studies showing that genetics plays a moderate role in the development of social anxiety disorder and other studies finding a relatively small genetic contribution. Nevertheless, two personality traits that are associated with social anxiety have been shown to be highly heritable. These include neuroticism—a tendency to feel anxious, tense, and worried, as well as to react emotionally to a variety of stresses—and introversion—a tendency to be relatively quiet and socially withdrawn compared to other people (Birley et al. 2006; Jang, Livesley, and Vernon 1996). Although research on the biological basis of social anxiety is still in its infancy, we are beginning to learn about the role of the brain in social anxiety. For example, a part of the brain known as the amygdala may be involved in social anxiety (as well as other anxiety-based problems). Studies examining patterns of blood flow in the brain have found that people with elevated levels of social anxiety show more activity in their amygdala and that treatment with either medication or cognitive behavioral therapy tends to decrease this activity. In addition, there is evidence that certain brain neurotransmitters (in particular, serotonin) are involved in social anxiety (Stein and Stein 2008).

Psychological Factors

Although a person's biology plays a role in the development and maintenance of social anxiety, psychological factors are also very important. A psychologist by the name of S. Rachman (1976) identified three different pathways to developing fear: *traumatic conditioning*, which involves experiencing some negative event that triggers the fear (for example, being teased after a class presentation may induce a fear of public speaking); *observational learning*, which involves developing a fear by watching someone else behave fearfully in the situation (for instance, developing social anxiety by growing up in a family of shy parents and siblings); and *informational learning*, which involves developing a fear by being told that a particular situation is dangerous (such as being told to "watch your back" when around other people).

A number of research studies support the view that these methods of learning can influence the development of social anxiety (for a review, see Bruch 1989). Compared to people who are comfortable in social situations, people with social anxiety disorder are more likely to grow up in homes where other family members are socially anxious (an example of observational learning), parents use shame as a means of discipline (traumatic conditioning), family members place great importance on the opinions of other people (informational learning), and children are discouraged from socializing (informational learning).

In addition, many researchers believe that people's beliefs play an enormous role in whether they feel anxious in social situations (Clark and McManus 2002). Common beliefs held by people who are socially anxious include (notice that many of these beliefs reflect perfectionistic standards and beliefs):

- I should not appear anxious in front of other people.

- I should always appear to be brilliant.

- I should always be entertaining when I'm talking to other people.

- It is awful to blush, shake, or sweat in front of others.

- People can tell when I am anxious.

- I will not be able to speak if I am too anxious.

- People find me unattractive.

- I will look incompetent if I speak to my boss.

- People will become angry with me if I make a mistake.

PERFECTIONISM AND SOCIAL ANXIETY

Compared to all other types of anxiety and fear, social anxiety may be the most closely linked to perfectionism. Research from our clinic and elsewhere has found that people who are socially anxious are more likely than other people to be overly concerned about making mistakes, particularly in social situations (Antony et al. 1998). For example, they may hold the belief that if they make a mistake or fall short of their standards, they are complete failures. In addition, social anxiety is associated with a tendency to doubt one's abilities in social situations, including one's ability to make a good impression on other people.

If you have a tendency to set overly high standards for yourself, it is likely that you will be unable to meet your strict expectations. If you can't accept the possibility of another person finding you boring, unattractive, or incompetent, you put yourself at risk for feeling anxious when interacting with other people who you perceive as threatening. In addition, if your perfectionism causes you to avoid certain social situations, you prevent yourself from ever finding out whether your anxious predictions are correct.

EFFECTIVE TREATMENTS FOR SOCIAL ANXIETY

Although professionals may use many different treatments to help people overcome social anxiety, only two main types of strategies have been tested out in controlled research studies. These include medication treatments and a variety of different cognitive and behavioral techniques (Antony and Rowa 2008; Rodebaugh, Holaway, and Heimberg 2004).

In the few studies that have compared these two general approaches, both seem to work equally well in the short term. However, there is evidence that cognitive and behavioral treatments have longer-lasting effects compared to medications, once treatment has ended. Studies on combining medications and psychological treatments have generally found little benefit of combined treatments over medication or psychological treatment alone.

Cognitive Behavioral Therapy

Many studies have now established that cognitive behavioral therapy (CBT) is effective for helping people overcome social anxiety disorder (Antony and Rowa 2008). These treatments include three main approaches: using cognitive techniques to identify and change anxious thoughts and predictions regarding social situations, using behavioral techniques (primarily exposure) to help a person confront feared situations until they are no longer frightening, and using social-skills training to teach individuals the skills needed to perform effectively in social situations. Some of the skills that may be taught during social-skills training include how to be more assertive, effectively using eye contact and nonverbal communication, and learning to get close to new people. Cognitive and behavioral methods for dealing with perfectionism are described in chapters 7 and 8 in detail.

Treatments Using Medication

Following is a list of medications that have been shown in controlled studies to be effective for treating social anxiety disorder. Medications for which results have been mixed are not included. We have included both the generic name as well as the brand name (in parentheses) for each medication. Generally, the SSRIs and venlafaxine XR are recommended as the first medications to try for social anxiety disorder (based on effectiveness, side effects, and other factors).

Medications That Have Been Shown to Be Effective for Social Anxiety Disorder

Selective Serotonin Norepinephrine Reuptake Inhibitors (SNRIs) Venlafaxine XR (Effexor XR)
Selective Serotonin Reuptake Inhibitors (SSRI antidepressants) Citalopram (Celexa) Escitalopram (Lexapro, Cipralex) Fluvoxamine (Luvox) Paroxetine (Paxil) Sertraline (Zoloft)
Benzodiazepines (anti-anxiety medications) Clonazepam (Klonopin, Rivotril) Alprazolam (Xanax)
Anticonvulsants Gabapentin (Neurontin) Pregabalin (Lyrica)
Monoamine Oxidase Inhibitors (MAOI antidepressants) Phenelzine (Nardil)

You may notice that many of the medications that have been shown to be effective for social anxiety disorder are actually antidepressants. Antidepressant drugs appear to be helpful for most types of clinical anxiety, even in people who do not feel depressed. Chapter 10 discusses various issues related to taking antidepressant medications (how to choose from the various options, side effects, and so on).

Many of the medication-related issues discussed in chapter 10 are also relevant to the anti-anxiety medications (for example, clonazepam, alprazolam), although there are a few important differences between antidepressants and anti-anxiety medications. First, anti-anxiety medications typically start working within a half hour or so after taking the pill, whereas antidepressants usually take up to four weeks before they start having an effect. In addition, the side effects of anti-anxiety medications are typically different than those for antidepressants. For anti-anxiety medications, the most common side effect is fatigue, which usually improves during the course of treatment. Finally, compared to most antidepressants, anti-anxiety medications are often more difficult to stop taking because they tend to be associated with withdrawal symptoms, particularly when stopped too quickly. Withdrawal symptoms typically include symptoms of increased anxiety and arousal (for instance, racing heart and dizziness). These symptoms can be minimized by decreasing the dosage gradually.

CHANGING PERFECTIONISTIC THOUGHTS AND BEHAVIORS IN SOCIAL ANXIETY

In this section, we discuss strategies for challenging anxiety-provoking thoughts and changing anxiety behaviors associated with social anxiety. For a more detailed discussion of strategies for overcoming social anxiety, check out our *Shyness and Social Anxiety Workbook* (Antony and Swinson 2008).

Challenging Perfectionistic Thoughts

Rather than assuming that your perfectionistic thoughts are true, it is important to treat your beliefs as possibilities or guesses. Unless you are able to accept the possibility that your standards for performance are too high, it will be difficult to shift your expectations to be more realistic. Chapter 7 describes methods of changing your perfectionistic thoughts. Several of these strategies are likely to be helpful for dealing with your anxiety in social situations, including examining the evidence supporting your thoughts, changing perspectives, hypothesis testing, changing social-comparison habits, and using coping statements. We suggest that you review the techniques described in chapter 7 to help replace your anxious thoughts with more realistic thoughts. The following examples illustrate how to replace anxious thoughts with more neutral, realistic thoughts.

Example 1: I'm nervous about going to the party.

Anxious Thought I really don't want to go to that party tonight. I'm not going to know anyone, and the other guests will think I'm boring.

Realistic Thought Because I don't know these people, I don't know how they are going to react to me. Often, I have a better time at parties than I expect to have. Maybe it will be okay. If some people find me boring to talk to, it doesn't mean that everyone will feel that way. Besides, even if people don't enjoy my company at this party, it doesn't mean I'm boring. Sometimes I'm bored when I talk to another person, but it doesn't mean that the person is boring.

Example 2: I feel intimidated and nervous while on a date.

Anxious Thought I am not smart enough to be dating this person.

Realistic Thought I have no idea whether or not I'm smarter than this person. In fact, there are so many different ways that intelligence can be measured, I'm sure there are some areas in which I'm smarter. Even if this person is smarter than me, that doesn't mean I'm not smart. I will always encounter people who are better than me at one thing or another. In fact, in every relationship one person is usually smarter than the other.

Example 3: A coworker comes by my desk to chat, but I have nothing to say.

Anxious Thought   She's going to think I'm an idiot. She'll see me blushing and think there is something wrong with me.

Realistic Thought   Even if she notices me blush, that doesn't mean that she'll think I'm strange. I certainly don't care when I notice someone else blushing. My sister blushes all the time, and no one seems to even notice. If I have nothing to say, she may think I'm nervous—but she may not. Instead, she may think that I'm busy or preoccupied. Even if she suspects that I'm a bit nervous, it doesn't mean that she will care a whole lot, and she probably won't think any less of me. Besides, it's not my responsibility to entertain people all the time. It's okay if someone thinks I'm strange once in a while.

Example 4: I'm having friends over for dinner.

Anxious Thought   They will hate my cooking, and the evening will be ruined.

Realistic Thought   I've cooked for people in the past, and usually people enjoy my cooking. Even if they don't like what I've prepared, it doesn't mean that the evening will be ruined. There are many times that I have had dinner at another person's home and not enjoyed my food. I'm still able to enjoy the evening, and I certainly don't think less of my host if the meal is not to my liking.

Changing Perfectionistic Behaviors

Chapter 8 includes a number of strategies for changing perfection-istic behaviors. In the case of social anxiety, communication training may be a useful method for improving important interpersonal skills. However, the most important strategy for decreasing social anxiety is exposure to feared situations. Repeated exposure to anxiety-provoking social situations will eventually lead to a decrease in anxiety. Exposure practices should be frequent (at least several times per week) and should last long enough to experience a decrease in anxiety or to learn that your feared predictions don't come true.

You may need to be creative to come up with appropriate situations in which you can practice. For example, if you are fearful of giving pre-sentations, there are a number of different places where you can conduct exposure exercises. You can join an organization called Toastmasters, which gives members opportunities to improve their public-speaking skills (check out www.toastmasters.org). Or, you can take a public-speaking course or an acting class. Another possibility is volunteering to speak about your career in front of a group of students in a high school or college. You can even ask a group of friends or family members to be your audience.

If a situation is too frightening, you can begin by conducting *role-play simulations*. A role-play simulation is essentially a "rehearsal" expo-sure in which you practice a social interaction in a safer context, rather than in the real situation. For example, if you are frightened of going to a job interview, you can practice simulated interviews with a friend or family member. You can even ask your "interviewer" to purposely be difficult so that the real interview will seem like a piece of cake in comparison. After practicing in simulated interview situations, you can work your way up to interviewing for jobs that don't interest you espe-cially. These practices will help you be more comfortable in interview situations, so that when the interview for the job you really want comes up, you'll be ready.

If you are afraid of drawing attention to yourself, practice doing just that during your exposure practices. For example, if you are anxious about having your hands shake while you are holding a drink or writing, let your hands shake on purpose. Let your glass shake until you spill your water. Or, when you are filling out a comment card in a restaurant, let your hand shake enough that the card is unreadable and has to be rewritten. If you are afraid that other people will see you sweat when you're feeling anxious, purposely wear warm clothes so that you are more likely to perspire. The goal of exposure is to learn that the situations that you fear are not dangerous. Even if someone sees you shake or sweat, there are no long-term consequences.

Taking Frequent Risks in Social Situations

People who are fearful of social situations often fear rejection from other people. If you are fearful of rejection, one of the best things you can do is take social risks more frequently. You may end up being rejected from time to time, but you will learn not to care about the rejection as much.

For example, if you tend to fear rejection when applying for a job or asking someone out on a date, you may find that it takes you months or years to get up the courage to do these things. You may fear that the person you ask out or the employer who reads your application will find you unappealing or unacceptable. When you finally do find the courage to take the risk, you may end up feeling very discouraged if you are rejected. You may take this as evidence that your anxious beliefs were true. The experience may "prove" that you are not good enough, just as you believed.

There is a problem with this logic. The truth is that most dates do not lead to long-term relationships and most job applications do not lead to jobs. Most people occasionally have the experience of being rejected in social situations such as these. To have the experience of not being rejected, a person has to take risks frequently. For example, if the probability of getting a job is one in twenty (for every twenty jobs that you apply for, you get one job offer), it will take you years to get an offer if you only apply for a job every few months. On the other hand, if you apply for several jobs per week, it probably won't be long before you have an offer.

More frequent social risks will lead to more frequent rejection. However, frequent risks will also lead to things working out from time to time. Remember, if you are looking for a job, you only need one offer.

The number of rejections is not important in the long run. The same is true of dating. Therefore, we recommend that you expose yourself to anxiety-provoking social situations as often as possible. It won't always go smoothly. However, over time the situations will become easier, you will become more skilled at dealing with people in these situations, and your chances of success will increase.

CHAPTER 13

Perfectionism and Worry

Everyone worries from time to time, particularly about events over which they have little control. We all endure daily stresses that affect our jobs, school performance, relationships, and other areas of our lives. In these circumstances, it's common to worry about possible negative outcomes. Just like sadness, anger, and other emotional states, worry is a normal part of life. However, worry can become a problem when it interferes with functioning (for example, making it difficult to concentrate or sleep), causes a lot of distress, or continues even in situations where there is no realistic reason to be worried.

This chapter is written primarily for people who find that they worry often, for long periods of time, and with such intensity that they experience problems such as appetite loss, headaches, or sleeplessness as a result. The information here may also be of value to people who find themselves getting overly tense, irritable, and restless when they are faced with real problems to solve.

WHAT IS WORRY?

Worry involves running over some possible future event in your mind over and over again. Worry is a natural response to feeling anxiety, apprehension, foreboding, or uneasiness. Normally, people worry when there is a reason to be concerned about the outcome of some situation or problem. Most people deal with this sort of worry by assessing the problem they face, getting advice if they need it, and solving the problem if they can. If the problem can't be solved right away, they can usually put the problem out of their minds, at least temporarily, while they go about their business. They may say to themselves, "I will worry about that later; there's nothing I can do about it right now." This type of self-talk can be helpful and is one strategy that many people use to deal with normal, day-to-day worries.

GENERALIZED ANXIETY DISORDER

Although most people are able to put their worries aside when necessary, some people have difficulty turning their worries off. In a condition called *generalized anxiety disorder* (GAD), worry is experienced as difficult to control, and it occurs at an intensity and frequency that leads to significant interference in people's lives. Among people with GAD, worry is excessive, unrealistic, or out of proportion to the actual threat. In addition, the worry is present most days and lasts for an extended period of time. In fact, many people with GAD report that their worry has been a problem for as long as they can remember. Along with the worry, people with GAD experience a range of other symptoms, including feeling restless, keyed up, or on edge; being easily fatigued; having difficulty concentrating or having their mind go blank; experiencing irritability; having muscle tension; and experiencing sleep problems (including trouble falling asleep, problems staying asleep, or not feeling rested in the morning). Often, it's the physical complaints, such as insomnia, muscle pain, and headaches that bring people with GAD to seek help from their doctor or another professional.

GAD affects about 5 to 6 percent of the general population and is slightly more common among women than men (Kessler et al., 2005; Wittchen and Hoyer 2001). It often has a gradual onset, beginning quite early in life. However, for some people, the problem begins after some significant life stress, such as a death in the family or the loss of a job. The intensity of the worry may fluctuate over time. As you might expect, the worry is often worse during times of stress or when there is some realistic threat. Paradoxically, however, some people with GAD describe themselves as very calm and capable during actual emergencies or when there is a real threat to be confronted.

WHAT DO PEOPLE WORRY ABOUT?

Most worriers tend to be anxious across different areas of their life, rather than worrying about just one or two topics. In fact, when asked what they worry about, people with GAD often report that they worry about "everything." Common worry topics for people who are prone to worry include:

- Work or school performance (for example, worries about getting fired, failing exams, and so on)

- Household chores (for instance, excessive worry about not being able to get everything done)

- Money and finances (for example, anxiety about going bankrupt or not being able to pay the bills)

- Health and safety of self (for instance, fear of contracting an illness)

- Health and safety of family and friends (for example, worry about the children's health)

- Relationships (for instance, unnecessary anxiety about spouse being unfaithful)

- Other minor matters (for example, worry about finding a parking spot when driving to work)

THE NATURE OF WORRY

We now know that worry is something that people do in order to *reduce* their anxiety. There is evidence that people worry to distract themselves from physical feelings associated with anxiety, as well as from mental imagery that they find frightening (for instance, the image of one's family dying in a car accident). In fact, a significant number of people who worry excessively believe that worry is a good thing. They may believe that being a worrier prepares them for possible danger, helps them to prevent bad things from happening, and makes them a caring person. Of course, there is no evidence that worry prevents negative events or that worriers are more caring people than those who don't worry excessively.

In addition, research has consistently shown that people who worry excessively pay more attention to threat-related information than people who are less prone to worry (Mogg and Bradley 2005). In other words, if you are a worrier, chances are that you frequently look out for possible cues that something is about to go wrong. This tendency to be on guard for threat contributes to other problems that are associated with worry, including difficulty concentrating or thinking clearly and difficulty falling asleep at night. For a perfectionist, there may be the added demand of having to scan the environment well enough to catch *each and every* indicator of possible threat or danger.

Where does this tendency to always be on guard come from? There is evidence that a history of unpredictable negative events may play a role. Several studies demonstrated that the ability to predict the onset of stressful events affects whether an organism will experience chronic arousal later on (Kandel 1983). In this series of classic experiments, two different groups of sea slugs were exposed to mild electric shocks. In one group, the sea slugs were exposed to shock only when a light was turned on, but not when the light was off (the presence of the light made the shock predictable). In the second group of sea slugs, shocks were administered randomly, regardless of whether the light was on or off (the shock was unpredictable). The purpose of the study was to evaluate the effects of predictable versus unpredictable shock on arousal.

After experiencing the predictable shocks, the first group of sea slugs developed a pattern of arousal that was linked to whether the light was on or off. When the light was on, they showed signs of arousal; when the light was off, they were in their normal resting state. In contrast, after only a few shocks, the sea slugs that received unpredictable shocks became aroused constantly, regardless of whether the light was turned on or off. This group also showed measurable nervous-system changes (sea slugs have neurotransmitters too!) that were not present in the sea slugs that received predictable shocks. The chronic arousal seen in the "unpredictable shock" group is analogous to the chronic arousal reported in people suffering from GAD. Muscle tension is an indirect indicator of arousal and is perhaps the most characteristic physical symptom among chronic worriers. Instead of having peaks and valleys of muscle tension, people with GAD have heightened tension that tends to change relatively little over time.

The implication of Kandel's research for humans is that a history of predictable stressful events may make it easier to turn off worry when the danger or threat has passed. In contrast, for people who experience a series of unpredictable stressful events, there may be increased risk for developing problems with chronic anxiety and worry. Although it may seem like a bit of a leap to generalize from sea slugs to humans, there is also evidence from research on people showing that unpredictable and uncontrollable negative events are a risk factor for developing problems with anxiety (Barlow 2002).

PERFECTIONISM AND WORRY

Frequently, the basis for excessive worry is a need to completely predict and control negative events combined with a belief that failing to control events will lead to some disaster that might otherwise have been avoided. People who worry excessively also have difficulty tolerating uncertainty. If they don't know exactly what is going to happen in an uncertain situation, they often assume the worst. Because perfectionism is associated with standards and expectations that are impossible to meet, people who are perfectionistic are at risk for having events not turn out as desired. For example, if you believe that everyone should always be fifteen minutes early for every appointment, it may be difficult for you to deal with a partner or child who is always running five minutes late. The more intolerant you are of lateness, the more likely you are to be disappointed by other people, and the more likely you are to have a perceived reason to worry.

Procrastination and Worry

Worriers have difficulty sorting out real problems from a background of possible problems that might come along. As a consequence, they may procrastinate and avoid solving problems that arise. It is hard to settle down to sort out one difficulty if you are predicting that there will be other problems that will demand your attention. In fact, you may believe that your attempt to solve one problem will lead to several new problems that will just make things worse. For example, a perfectionistic student may be frightened to ask for help with an assignment, fearing that this request will result in the teacher thinking he or she is lazy or incompetent. The student may therefore avoid working on the assignment completely, and in the end create even more problems as a result. In this example, perfectionistic worry is associated with the belief that "It is better to do nothing than to take a risk and fail."

Avoidance and procrastination are often reinforced or rewarded, especially in the short term. By avoiding an anxiety-provoking situation, you may temporarily feel relief from not having had to deal with the problem. You may be rewarded further if the person who had asked you to do the job forgets to check that the work was completed or changes his or her mind about needing it done. Nevertheless, despite the short-term benefits, procrastination may well lead to negative consequences down the line. For example, you may be left with having to complete your work in a much shorter time than was originally available and under a lot more pressure. In these circumstances, it is unlikely that you will do your best work, and you will probably feel dissatisfied in the end. The need to feel perfectly in control over the outcome and the tendency to avoid taking certain risks may actually make it harder to do a good job.

Overcompensation and Worry

Overcompensating involves taking steps above and beyond those that most people might take to prevent some dreaded event from occurring (see chapter 4 for a more detailed description). For example, parents who are constantly worried about the health of their children may insist on checking their child's temperature at the first sign of any physical symptoms and may even take the child out of school whenever another child in the class is ill. Consider the following case examples.

Joan had two female friends who were both diagnosed with breast cancer several years ago. Although both friends were successfully treated for the illness, Joan subsequently developed intense worry about the possibility of developing cancer herself or of a family member becoming seriously ill. She began to ask for constant reassurance from her husband

and children. She was married to a physician, who initially agreed to examine her and their children as often as Joan requested in an effort to reassure her that they did not have cancer. Eventually, Joan's husband lost patience with her daily requests for reassurance. Her children also refused to answer her continual questions about their health. Joan began to worry that her husband's refusal to examine her was because he had found something wrong with her health and was hiding it from her. Joan avoided seeing her family physician for fear that the doctor might confirm her fear that she was seriously ill. As a result of Joan's constant requests for reassurance, there was considerable strain in the family and she worried that her husband was losing interest in their marriage.

Randall was the father of two daughters in their late teens, both of whom were very successful students. Randall had always worried about how well they did in school and kept very close tabs on their homework. He was also concerned about their safety when they were walking home after school (a total of two blocks). When they were accepted into college, they both decided to move to a city on the other side of the country. Randall tried to get a transfer in his company to be near his children, but his wife didn't want to interrupt her career. She also felt that their daughters should have the freedom to spend some time away. When they left home, Randall found he could not stop worrying about their safety and became very distracted at work. He tried to cope with his anxiety by calling his children as many as three times a day, though his frequent phone calls irritated his daughters and didn't really help to reduce his anxiety for more than a few minutes.

TREATMENTS FOR WORRY, GAD, AND PERFECTIONISM

A number of treatment approaches have been successfully used to treat GAD and excessive worry, including medications, relaxation training, challenging anxiety-provoking thoughts, exposure to feared imagery, preventing safety behaviors, acceptance and mindfulness-based strategies, and problem-solving training. If your perfectionism appears to be related to GAD and excessive worry, you may find these strategies useful.

Treatments Using Medication

The earliest medications shown to be effective for treating GAD were the benzodiazepines (also known as tranquilizers), which are also used sometimes as muscle relaxants or sleep medications (Roy-Byrne and Cowley 2007). The benzodiazepines include such drugs as diazepam, lorazepam, alprazolam, clonazepam, and others. These drugs work very quickly and tend to be quite effective in the short term. Although some people find that these drugs are useful for long-term treatment, their effectiveness may decrease as time goes on unless the dosage is increased. Increasing the dosage of these medications puts people at risk for marked side effects, including drowsiness. In addition, because the withdrawal symptoms for these drugs can include intense anxiety, many people have difficulty discontinuing benzodiazepines. Today, physicians often avoid prescribing these drugs for more than a few weeks at a time.

Another type of anti-anxiety medication is a drug called buspirone. This medication is derived from a completely different family than the older tranquilizers and does not produce drowsiness or dependence. It takes a few weeks to have an effect and therefore is not used for acute anxiety. It is as effective as the benzodiazepines and may work better for people who have not previously used traditional anti-anxiety medications.

Finally, as is the case for other anxiety problems, antidepressants are an effective treatment for GAD and chronic worry. In fact, they are often the treatment of choice for this problem. People who are anxious are often very sensitive to the side effects of antidepressants and can become very agitated with the first few doses. Therefore, these medications should be started at very small doses which then are slowly increased. Treatment should continue for at least several months, and there is a strong risk of relapse after stopping the medication. See chapter 10 for additional information on antidepressant medications. The table below provides a summary of medications that have been shown to be effective for treating GAD. Brand names are in parentheses.

Medications that Have Been Shown to Be Effective for Generalized Anxiety Disorder

Selective Serotonin Norepinephrine Reuptake Inhibitors (SNRIs) Venlafaxine XR (Effexor XR) Duloxetine (Cymbalta)
Selective Serotonin Reuptake Inhibitors (SSRI antidepressants) Escitalopram (Lexapro; Cipralex) Paroxetine (Paxil) Sertraline (Zoloft)
Benzodiazepines and Other Anti-anxiety Medications Alprazolam (Xanax) Diazepam (Valium) Lorazepam (Ativan) Buspirone (Buspar)
Anticonvulsants Pregabalin (Lyrica)

Relaxation Training

Chronic worry can be lessened by learning to relax. Several relaxation methods are available. *Progressive muscle relaxation* involves learning to relax the muscles of the body to decrease feelings of tension, stress, and anxiety. A second method, known as *imagery*, involves learning to imagine particular scenes that are soothing. Finally, learning to breathe slowly and smoothly can help a person to relax. For more information on relaxation training, check out Further Readings at the end of this book.

The main difficulty with relaxation training is that people often forget to practice. Scheduling regular periods to practice at the same time each day will increase the chances of benefiting from this approach. For example, you could try scheduling the practices just before or after other activities that commonly happen throughout your day (for instance, having a drink of water, going to the bathroom, traveling to and from work, and so on). Even taking a few minutes two or three times a day to breathe slowly from the abdomen is a very useful way of breaking up the seemingly never-ending stream of tension and anxiety.

Challenging Anxiety-Provoking Thoughts

One way of combating anxiety is to challenge the thoughts, beliefs, and predictions that contribute to your anxiety. Chapter 7 provides a detailed description of these strategies, and in this section we describe how to apply these strategies to GAD and excessive worry.

Examining the Evidence

Worry is usually associated with two main types of thoughts. The first type of thought is a tendency to overestimate the probability of some unlikely event. In the case examples we presented earlier in this chapter, Joan overestimated the likelihood of developing a serious illness. Randall overestimated the likelihood of something bad happening to his children.

The second common style of thinking involves overestimating just how bad it would be if a negative event were to occur. An example of such a thought is, "It would be an absolute disaster if I arrive at the movie theater and there is nowhere to park." In reality, this situation would probably be manageable if it actually occurred.

In order to combat negative thinking that contributes to worry, it can be helpful to examine the accuracy of your beliefs. This process involves asking yourself a series of questions that help you to assess the situation in a more realistic way. Following are some anxious thoughts and some questions that you might ask yourself to challenge anxious thoughts:

Anxiety-Provoking Thoughts

- I am going to fail the exam.
- I haven't studied enough for this exam.
- I don't know the material for this test.

- If I fail the test, I will never get into graduate school, and I will never amount to anything in life.

Questions for Examining the Evidence

- Do I know for sure that I will fail the exam?

- Have I done well on past exams, even when I thought I would fail?

- Did I study less than I usually do for similar exams?

- What is really likely to happen if I fail the exam?

- Are the results of a single exam likely to have a huge impact on my overall average?

- Is it possible for a person to fail a single exam and still do well in life?

Attempting to answer questions such as these is a powerful method for challenging the perfectionistic beliefs that contribute to your worry. Following is an illustration of how Zack's therapist helped him to use this method for challenging anxious thoughts about money and finances:

Zack: I am constantly worried about not having enough money to pay the bills. It drives my wife crazy, because I'm always trying to control the way she spends her money.

Therapist: Specifically, what are you predicting will happen?

Zack: I'm afraid that I won't have enough money to pay the rent or to make my car payment. I also worry about my credit-card bills getting out of hand. Sometimes I even think that I will go bankrupt. I worry that the whole family will end up living on the street.

Therapist: Do you have any evidence to support these predictions?

Zack: No, not really. In fact, I pay off my credit-card balance each month. I'm even two payments ahead on my car loan.

Therapist: Can you think of any evidence that contradicts your worries about money?

Zack:	To start, I have never been in debt before. Also, I've never missed a bill payment in the past, even though I worry about it all the time.
Therapist:	What if you were short for several of your bills on a particular month?
Zack:	That would be terrible.
Therapist:	What would actually happen?
Zack:	I imagine that my debts would start to double and triple. I might never get out of debt.
Therapist:	Do you know anyone who once missed a bill payment?
Zack:	My brother misses payments from time to time.
Therapist:	What happens when he misses a payment?
Zack:	Nothing seems to happen. He usually just makes it up the next month.
Therapist:	Do you know anyone who has declared bankruptcy?
Zack:	Someone I work with declared bankruptcy about a year ago.
Therapist:	Did this coworker end up living on the street?
Zack:	No. In fact, she was under much less stress after the bankruptcy than before. (pause) I guess even if I had a temporary financial setback, I could manage it.

Shifting Perspectives

It is often easier to solve another person's worries than your own. Therefore, a helpful strategy for dealing with your own worries is to imagine that you are giving suggestions to a close friend or relative who has similar worries. Consider the following dialogue as an example:

Emily:	I am terrified to go to sleep at the end of the day. I lie in bed worrying that a stranger is going to come into my

home in the middle of the night. It's even worse when my partner and children are away.

Therapist: When you get into bed, how likely do you think it is that someone will break into your home?

Emily: Realistically, I know the chances are low. It's never happened before. But, when I'm lying there, trying to fall asleep, it feels much more likely. Maybe 50 percent likely.

Therapist: Do you worry that people might break into your friends' and neighbors' homes?

Emily: No, not really. It feels like it's more likely to happen in my home, although I know that doesn't make any sense.

Therapist: What would you say to neighbors who were fearful of having someone break into their house?

Emily: I would probably say that it is unlikely. I would remind them that they have lived there for several years, and there has never been a break-in before.

Therapist: Can you apply that same logic for your own situation?

Tolerating Uncertainty and Ambiguity

Learning to tolerate uncertainty can combat your tendency to worry about unpredictable and uncontrollable situations. There are many situations that you can't predict or control. Fortunately, however, it's not terribly important that you be able to control most situations. A helpful way of tolerating unpredictable events is to generate a list of possible outcomes and to consider ways of dealing with each outcome. For example, if you are stuck in traffic and are late for a job interview, you have two options. You can worry about how terrible it is that you are late, or you can accept the fact that you are late, even though you don't know what the outcome will be. Perhaps the interviewer will be understanding and squeeze you in at a later time. Perhaps the interviewer will reschedule the appointment for another day. Perhaps the interviewer will confront you about being late and send you home without the opportunity to interview again. Regardless of what happens, chances are that the outcome will be manageable.

Hypothesis Testing

If you tend to make unrealistic predictions about negative things that might happen, testing the validity of your predictions using mini-experiments can be a helpful way of challenging your anxious thoughts. Before conducting the experiment, make one or more explicit predictions regarding the outcome. Then, conduct the experiment and evaluate the outcome. Did your predictions come true? If so, was it as bad as you expected? For example, if you are worried about an airline losing your luggage on your next trip, check your luggage at the gate and see what happens. If your luggage doesn't get lost, you will have gained valuable information about the likelihood of losing your luggage. If your luggage does get lost, you may learn that the situation is not as bad as you feared it would be (lost luggage is often found a few hours later).

Exposure to Feared Imagery

As we mentioned earlier, worry is often used as a strategy to avoid experiencing frightening mental imagery. You learned in chapter 8 that one of the most effective ways of overcoming fear is to expose oneself to feared objects and situations. For examples, if you fear heights, your fear will gradually decrease as you begin to spend more time in high places. People who worry excessively often fear experiencing certain images and feelings. Therefore, treatments for GAD have begun to include exposure to these images and feelings as a component of therapy.

Imagery exposure involves a few steps. First, it is important to come up with an image that is disturbing to you. For example, if you are anxious about an upcoming exam, you might imagine being in the exam and not knowing the answers to any of the questions. It's helpful to write out an imagery script describing all the details. As you develop your script, be sure to describe the situation in as much detail as possible. Continuing with the example of an upcoming exam, your script might include a description of the room, the color of the exam paper, who else is in the room, where the teacher or professor is standing, and so on. You should include details related to all senses. In addition to describing what you *see* in the room, your script should include a description of what you *hear*, *smell*, and *feel*. For example, is the room warm or cold?

Can you hear the buzz of the lights? Also, be sure to include a description of your own responses in the script, including any thoughts running through your head and any physical feelings you are experiencing in the imagined situation.

Often, people read their script into a recorder and then listen to it repeatedly for about thirty minutes per day, until it no longer arouses anxiety. A detailed description of how you can use imagery exposure to combat anxiety is described elsewhere (Antony and Norton 2009).

Preventing Safety Behaviors

Try to ride out your worry without engaging in perfectionistic behaviors such as checking or seeking reassurance. As discussed in chapter 4, these behaviors block you from learning that your anxious thoughts are unrealistic. By preventing these behaviors, you will learn to tolerate uncertainty and imperfection. For more details on prevention of safety behaviors, see chapter 8. Antony and Norton also discuss this strategy in more detail (2009).

Acceptance and Mindfulness-Based Strategies

As we reviewed in chapter 9, the more you try to control your anxiety, the worse it's likely to get. Learning to be aware of your experiences without judging them and learning to accept your thoughts and feelings will likely make it easier to manage your anxiety. Strategies such as mindfulness meditation and those used in acceptance and commitment therapy have been found to be helpful for GAD. Chapter 9 describes these strategies. For an even more detailed description, check out the *Mindfulness and Acceptance Workbook for Anxiety* (Forsyth and Eifert 2007).

Problem-Solving Training

In chapter 11, we discussed how learning to solve problems effectively can help to combat feelings of anger. Problem-solving training is also sometimes useful for dealing with excessive worry and GAD. We recommend that you check out the section on problem solving in chapter 11.

CHAPTER 14

Perfectionism and Obsessive-Compulsive Behavior

There are two psychological problems that include obsessive-compulsive behavior as a core feature. The first is *obsessive-compulsive disorder* (OCD), which is an anxiety disorder associated with persistent disturbing thoughts (obsessions) and repetitive behaviors aimed at decreasing the discomfort caused by these thoughts (compulsions). Many people diagnosed with OCD have perfectionistic standards for certain activities. The second problem, called *obsessive-compulsive personality disorder* (OCPD), is characterized by a tendency to be overly perfectionistic, orderly, and inflexible. Although these are two different conditions, they overlap to some extent, and it is not unusual for a person to experience features from both disorders. Even if you don't have all of the symptoms of either disorder, you may still experience some symptoms from one or both of these problems.

OBSESSIVE-COMPULSIVE DISORDER

Obsessions and compulsions, the core features of OCD, may not be what you think they are. In this section, we start by defining each of these terms.

What Is an Obsession?

To most people, the word "obsession" refers to any persistent thought, desire, or drive that controls a person's behavior. Die-hard fans of a music group or celebrity are often said to be obsessed with their idols. A doctor who works around the clock to discover a cure for a serious disease may be considered obsessed with his or her work. Even people who love a particular food so much that they eat little else are often said to be obsessed with that food. In contrast to this common use of the word "obsession," mental health professionals have a very specific meaning for this term that is somewhat different.

An *obsession* is defined as a recurrent and persistent thought, image, or impulse that is experienced as intrusive and inappropriate and causes significant anxiety or distress. In other words, people who have obsessions (according to this psychological definition of the word) are very distressed by these thoughts and do not want to have them. In this way, obsessions are different than other types of repetitive thoughts that a person may have (for examples, fantasies). To be considered a true obsession, the thought cannot simply be an exaggerated worry about everyday problems in such realms as job performance, money, or relationships. The person must also try to make the disturbing thoughts go away by ignoring them, pushing them out of consciousness, or undoing their effects by some other thought or action.

Obsessive thoughts are very common in the general population. In fact, up to 90 percent of people experience intrusive obsessive thoughts from time to time. Common themes for these thoughts include concerns about having things organized in a particular way (for example, urges to organize books, CDs, and DVDs in alphabetical order), worries about becoming contaminated by some object or substance (for instance, germs, cleaning products, bodily fluids), urges to do something aggressive or hurt another person (for example, stabbing a close relative, shouting obscenities at someone in public), thoughts about accidentally harming another person, disturbing religious thoughts, disturbing sexual ideas, and repetitive doubts about whether a task has been completed correctly (for instance, whether the stove has been turned off, whether a mistake was made in a report or term paper). Typically, people who experience obsessions usually realize that the thoughts are not realistic. Also, even though the person may fear acting on the obsession, obsessive urges are almost never actually acted upon. For example, it would be highly unusual for a person with aggressive obsessions to actually carry out the thought, unlike a person who actually has problems with aggressive behavior.

What Is a Compulsion?

Compulsions are behaviors that are repeated over and over again in response to an obsession or according to rigidly applied rules. Compulsions are aimed at preventing harm from occurring or at decreasing anxiety or distress. They may include physical behaviors, such as washing, or mental behaviors, such as silently repeating words in your head. Like obsessions, compulsions are very common in the general population. Most people engage in compulsive behaviors from time to time.

The types of compulsions that people have are often closely related to the content of their obsessive thoughts. For example, people who have obsessions about contamination or cleanliness typically engage in compulsions to prevent themselves from becoming contaminated or dirty. These may include frequent hand washing and cleaning, as well as avoiding situations or locations where contamination may occur, such as public restrooms. Other common compulsions include checking (for example, appliances, locks, accuracy of work), counting, repeating actions, putting things in order, asking for reassurance, praying when you don't really want to, repeating certain words, explaining or confessing, and hoarding.

What Is OCD?

For most people in the general population, intrusive thoughts and compulsive behaviors don't cause significant problems. For example, you may avoid certain situations because of concerns about contamination (for example, eating a candy that has fallen on the floor, sitting on a public toilet seat) or you may check your locks and appliances a couple of times. Or perhaps you have distressing thoughts that come and go occasionally. Most people experience these symptoms from time to time with little distress or interference in their life.

In contrast, people with OCD experience obsessions and compulsions more frequently and more intensely than the average person. They are also bothered more by their obsessions and take greater pains to resist or suppress their upsetting thoughts. To be diagnosed with OCD, the obsessions or compulsions must be bothersome, time consuming (for instance, they take up more than an hour per day), or interfere with a person's life. For example, it's not unusual for a person with OCD to experience obsessions throughout the day. For some people, compulsive behaviors such as washing or checking can take up so much time that the person is unable to work, socialize, or be involved in other important activities. OCD affects between 1 and 3 percent of the general population and appears to be about equally prevalent in men and women. Although the problem tends to begin in early adulthood, it is not unusual for people with OCD to have the problem begin in childhood.

OCD and Perfectionism

Perfectionism is often a feature of OCD. For example, Amanda had contamination fears related to eating foods that may have gone bad. She was afraid that if she ate something that was contaminated, she might become ill. As a result, she had strict standards for what she was willing to eat. There were many different foods that she avoided eating completely (including all foods containing meat, certain fruits and vegetables, and certain dairy products). In addition, if an item looked anything less than perfect (for example, if there was a small spot on a piece of fruit), she refused to eat it. Her fear was worse when eating in restaurants than at home, because she could not be sure about the quality of the food or of the chef's standards for cleanliness. She realized that her fears were excessive and unreasonable, and yet she had difficulty putting them aside. Her approach to food was perfectionistic, in that she had inflexible rules about which foods she could and could not eat and she refused to eat anything that didn't meet her strict standards.

Juan was worried that other people might misunderstand what he told them and that something terrible might happen as a result. For example, when making plans with friends, he was fearful that either he or his friends would show up at the wrong location or time. As a result of his fear, he needed to repeat things several times when he spoke to other people. Also, he tended to check that the other person understood everything properly. After speaking to someone, he often phoned them back several times to ensure that all the details from their conversations were clear. Whereas most people are able to tolerate the possibility that a mistake may have occurred during a conversation, for Juan, mistakes were unacceptable. His perfectionistic beliefs were manifested in his unwillingness to risk making an error or being misunderstood.

Causes of OCD

As is the case for all psychological problems, the causes of OCD are complex and involve both biological and psychological processes.

Biological Factors

Three different lines of research support a role for biological factors in the cause and maintenance of OCD. First, there is indirect evidence of altered functioning in the brain neurotransmitter called serotonin. For example, medications that increase levels of serotonin in the brain appear to be effective for many people who suffer from OCD, whereas most medications that affect other brain neurotransmitters don't have much of an impact on OCD symptoms (Stewart, Jenike, and Jenike 2009). Second, there is evidence that genes inherited from parents play a role in OCD (van Grootheest et al. 2005). Finally, there appear to be differences in brain functioning in people with OCD compared to people without OCD (Britton and Rauch 2009).

Studies using *positron-emission tomography* (PET) and *functional magnetic resonance imaging* (fMRI) (methods of measuring brain activity) show that OCD is associated with increased blood flow in the brain areas known as the prefrontal cortex and basal ganglia. Medications that increase levels of serotonin appear to reverse this abnormality. Interestingly, psychological treatments (including cognitive behavioral therapy) also seem to cause the blood flow in brains of people with OCD to return to normal. Thus, it may be the case that the abnormal brain activity that shows up in PET and fMRI studies is a result of the disorder rather than a cause.

Psychological Factors

A person's learning experiences and beliefs also influence the onset and course of OCD. From a cognitive perspective, OCD is not so much a problem with obsessions as it is with people's interpretation of their obsessions. Remember that most people experience thoughts that are obsessional in nature from time to time. The difference between people who experience the occasional obsessional thought without being bothered by it and those who become very distressed by their obsessional thoughts has to do with what people think the obsessional thought means. People who are bothered by obsessional thoughts often have lots of negative beliefs about what the thought means. For example, they may believe that their obsessional thought will come true unless they do something to counter it, or they may believe that their thoughts are morally wrong and that thinking about doing something terrible is as bad as actually doing it. People with OCD also often believe that they should have absolute control over their thoughts (Purdon and Clark 2002).

Beliefs such as these cause people to feel that they must do something about the thought, such as washing, checking, or other such rituals. At the very least, they cause the individual to want to suppress the thought. Behaviors such as compulsions and suppression of frightening thoughts are sometimes helpful in the short term, but over time, they actually serve to increase the frequency of obsessions and subsequent compulsions. When the thought is suppressed, exposure to the thought is terminated. This means that the person doesn't get the chance to get used to the thought, and the thought remains upsetting. In fact, suppressing upsetting thoughts seems to either increase the frequency of the thoughts later, or at least to make the thoughts more upsetting next time they occur (Marcks and Woods 2007; Purdon 2004; Purdon, Rowa, and Antony 2005).

Because behaviors that reduce anxiety are more likely to be repeated, the more a person engages in the compulsion, the more he or she is likely to continue engaging in the compulsion. The sense of relief associated with anxiety reduction can lend credibility to the idea that the ritual is the only thing that keeps the thought from becoming harmful in some way. Finally, by engaging in the ritual, the individual never has the opportunity to learn that the obsessional thought is not, in fact, dangerous. Thus, the thought continues to be upsetting, and the ritual continues to be used as a means of coping with that distress.

Treatment of OCD

Two general treatment approaches have been shown in controlled studies to be effective for helping people who suffer from OCD: medications and cognitive behavioral therapy. Medications that increase serotonin levels in the brain have been shown to decrease OCD symptoms. These include the tricyclic antidepressant clomipramine (Anafranil), the serotonin and norepinephrine reuptake inhibitor (SNRI) venlafaxine XR (Effexor XR), and selective serotonin reuptake inhibitors (SSRIs) such as citalopram (Celexa), fluoxetine (Prozac), fluvoxamine (Luvox), paroxetine (Paxil), and sertraline (Zoloft).

In studies comparing these medications to one another, they appear to be equally effective for treating OCD (Dougherty, Rauch, and Jenike 2007). The decision to choose one medication over another should be based on factors such as side effects, cost, and a history of response or nonresponse to one or more of these medications in the past. Although these medications are all antidepressants, they appear to be effective for people with OCD, even if depression is not a significant problem. For more information on these and other antidepressant medications, see chapter 10.

In addition to medications, cognitive behavioral strategies have been shown to be effective for helping people overcome OCD. Specifically, exposure to feared situations and prevention of compulsive rituals (together known as "exposure and response prevention") seems to be the treatment of choice for this problem. Some researchers have also found that teaching people to challenge their unrealistic thoughts using cognitive techniques (such as those described in chapter 7) is sometimes helpful.

Studies that have compared medication treatments to exposure and response prevention have generally found that both approaches are equally effective in the short term. However, after treatment ends, the effects of exposure and response prevention tend to be longer lasting than those for medication. For more details on how to conduct exposure and response prevention, see chapter 8. In addition, the end of this chapter includes a section on how to apply these strategies to obsessive-compulsive symptoms in particular.

OBSESSIVE-COMPULSIVE PERSONALITY DISORDER

The second type of problem discussed in this chapter is obsessive-compulsive personality disorder, or OCPD. This problem shares a number of features with OCD and can occur in people with OCD. However, OCPD and OCD are viewed as different conditions.

What is OCPD?

The hallmark of OCPD is an excessive concern with order, organization, rules, lists, and trivial details. People with OCPD are often perfectionistic to the point of not getting anything done. For example, they may spend so much time making lists of things that need to get done (and refining their lists), that the tasks on the list don't get completed. Or they may devote so much energy to including every small detail when they tell a story that the main message of the story is lost.

In addition, people with OCPD typically spend excessive amounts of time and energy on their work, often at the expense of other important aspects of their life such as having fun and enjoying time with friends and family. People with OCPD tend to be overly conscientious, rigid about their views, and inflexible about issues related to ethics and morals. They have difficulty delegating jobs to other people for fear that tasks will not be completed correctly. They may also have difficulty throwing things away, just in case they are needed in the future. In many ways, OCPD is the psychological disorder that is most closely related to perfectionism.

Research on OCPD

Compared to OCD, very little research has been conducted with people suffering from OCPD. Therefore, we know very little about the causes of this problem and almost no controlled studies have tested the effects of specific treatments for OCPD. In fact, we do not even have reliable data on the prevalence of this disorder. Despite the lack of adequate research, it is likely that both biological and psychological factors contribute to OCPD. The limited literature available on treatment suggests that the cognitive and behavioral strategies discussed in chapters 7 and 8 are likely to be effective (Bailey 1998; Ng 2005).

OVERCOMING PERFECTIONISM ASSOCIATED WITH OBSESSIVE-COMPULSIVE BEHAVIOR

Strategies for dealing with obsessive-compulsive behavior include response prevention and exposure, each of which is discussed in this section.

Response Prevention

As we mentioned earlier, exposure to feared situations combined with prevention of compulsive rituals is the key to overcoming obsessions and compulsions. This approach is likely to be helpful for OCPD behaviors as well, such as excessive organizing and list making. Recall that rituals have a number of negative effects that serve to maintain the fearfulness of the obsession and are self-perpetuating. Thus, the first step toward decreasing your obsessive-compulsive behavior is to stop all rituals. This is because any rituals that are performed during or following an exposure practice can "undo" the benefits of the exposure. For example, if you are learning to overcome obsessive fears of contamination from germs, touching "contaminated" objects will do you no good if you wash your hands after every exposure practice. To benefit from exposure, you must first cut out all rituals.

Ben had an intense fear that he might lose something or accidentally throw something important away. Over time, his doubts broadened to include thoughts that he might purposely throw something away and then forget that he had done it. As a result of these fears, he engaged in a broad range of checking behaviors, particularly when going from one place to another. Before getting out of his car, he checked throughout the car for items that he may have left in the trunk, under the seats, between the seats, or anywhere else that he could think of. He even checked under the hood, even though he knew rationally that he had not opened the hood. Before entering his home, he checked outside his house and behind the bushes in his front yard. Before leaving his home, he checked in all drawers, cupboards, closets, and garbage cans in each room. In addition to spending many hours per day checking, he also asked people for reassurance. For example, he typically asked his partner whether she had emptied the garbage cans in the house, fearing that some important papers may have been thrown out.

As illustrated in this example, the rituals may be quite complex. Before you can begin to prevent your rituals, you will need to become aware of the specific rituals that you use and the situations and feelings that trigger your rituals. What types of repetitive behaviors do you engage in? These may include checking, cleaning, washing, counting, list making, reassurance seeking, repeating certain behaviors, purposely thinking a particular thought (for example, a prayer, a safe word), or engaging in any other behavior that you feel compelled to do.

Are there particular situations where you are most likely to engage in these rituals? Are they more likely to happen when you are in a particular mood (perhaps feeling anxious, sad, angry, bored)? When you are tired or hungry? When you are in a certain place (like home, work, outside)? When you are with certain people (for instance, strangers, relatives, children, coworkers, alone)? In your journal, keep track of your rituals, as well as the situations that trigger your rituals.

Once you have identified the rituals that you want to stop, the next step is to find ways to prevent the rituals. At first, this task may be very difficult. The urges to do the ritual may be very intense. Over time, however, the urges will gradually decrease. Anything you can do to prevent the rituals in the beginning will pay off in the long run. Remember, the worst thing that is likely to happen if you don't complete a ritual is that you will feel uncomfortable. Below are some strategies that you can use to prevent yourself from engaging in your compulsive rituals. Remember, if you can get through the first few days, resisting the urges should become easier.

Strategies for Resisting Rituals

- You will experience anxiety when you begin resisting your rituals. Remind yourself that the anxiety is unpleasant but not dangerous.

- Do something that makes it impossible for you to perform the ritual. For example, turn off the water from the main source in your basement so you won't be able to wash your hands. Or, mail a letter immediately after writing it so you cannot check what you wrote.

- Remind yourself that your anxiety will decrease eventually, and that the more frequently you resist the ritual, the easier it will be to resist it.

- Remind yourself when you are doing fine and are not experiencing the obsession—or performing the rituals—that this proves that the ritual really doesn't help. By focusing on your successes when you're not performing the rituals, you will be better able to see that your desire to perform the ritual is driven by anxiety rather than by genuine necessity.

- Ask friends and family members to point out when you are performing a ritual or compulsive behavior.

- Ask friends and family members not to participate in your rituals. For example, ask them not to give you reassurance, even when you ask for it, but rather to remind you that performing the ritual is not a good idea.

- If you "slip" and actually perform a ritual, try to undo the effects of the ritual as soon as possible. For example, if you are practicing learning to tolerate having a less organized desk and you give in to your urges and spend four hours organizing your desk, mess it up again as soon as possible and continue your practice.

- If the urge is completely overwhelming and you feel as though you are about to give in and perform the ritual, take yourself out of the situation. Go for a walk, watch TV, or do something else until the urge subsides.

Exposure Exercises

After you have successfully resisted performing your compulsive rituals for a few days, the next step is to begin exposure to situations that you find anxiety provoking or uncomfortable. Exposure may be conducted gradually. That is, you can begin with easier situations and work your way up to more challenging situations.

Chapter 8 is worth reviewing because it discusses in detail exactly how to conduct your exposure practices. However, the main principles to keep in mind include: continue your exposure practice session until your anxiety or discomfort has decreased significantly or you have learned that your feared predictions don't come true (this can take a few minutes to several hours); if your anxiety decreases quickly, move on to a more difficult practice; repeat exposure practices frequently (conduct longer practices at least four to five days per week, as well as mini-practices throughout the day); expect to feel uncomfortable—over time, your discomfort will decrease; and continue to try more and more challenging practices until you can comfortably handle the situations near the top of your hierarchy.

Following is an example of how to use exposure and response prevention for a perfectionistic behavior:

Response-Prevention Example

Problem: You feel compelled to correct anyone who makes a mistake when speaking, such as mispronouncing a word or presenting an inaccurate statement.

Treatment Plan: Tell people who are close to you that you have decided to stop correcting other people. If necessary, ask others to point out when you inadvertently correct them. To start, it is very important to resist all urges to correct others. If the urge is overwhelming, take a break from the situation (for example, excuse yourself to go to the bathroom) until the urge to correct the other person passes. Pay attention to how long it takes for the urge to decrease. Over time, you will notice that it's not so important after all that you correct people about trivial mistakes or disagreements.

After you have successfully resisted the urges to correct other people, try purposely exposing yourself to situations that trigger this urge. For example, spend time with people who make frequent errors when they are talking and people who, in the past, have tended to trigger your urges most strongly. You could even ask some people to purposely make errors on occasion, in order to provide you with opportunities to practice preventing your "correcting" rituals.

Setting Time Limits

Most people have been told at one time or another that they didn't take their time to do a job properly. In general, the more time that is spent on a project, the better the quality of the work. However, there is a point at which the benefits of spending more time on a job become fewer and fewer. For example, spending two minutes brushing your teeth will clean your teeth much more effectively than spending only ten seconds.

However, for every additional minute that you spend brushing beyond the first two minutes, the benefits become smaller and smaller. In fact, if you spend too long brushing, you can destroy the enamel that protects your teeth and actually put yourself at greater risk for developing dental problems.

Another cost of spending too much time on a particular task is that it leaves you too little time to do other things. Taking the time to do very good work is not worth much if you never complete the job or if it interferes with your ability to get other important things done. On the other hand, rushing through a task so that the quality of your work is very poor can also lead to negative consequences. Ideally, you should try to balance the quality of your work with the amount of work that you get done. There may be times when it is better to do a fair job on several different tasks than an outstanding job on only one task. You will need to evaluate your priorities to decide whether it's worth spending less time on certain activities.

Do you tend to spend too much time completing certain tasks, such as washing, cleaning, writing a letter, filling out a form, or even telling a story? If so, setting time limits for specific activities will be very helpful. This can be done in two ways. You can gradually decrease the time that you allow for the activity. For example, if you normally spend an hour in the shower each day, you can reduce the allowed time by ten minutes per day until you reach the point of spending no more than ten minutes in the shower. Alternatively, you can make the change more abruptly by immediately reducing the allowed time to a more typical level (for example, ten minutes for a shower, fifteen minutes to write a short letter, and so on). To help you end tasks at the proper time, set a timer or have a friend let you know when the time has ended. When time is up, stop what you are doing—even if the task feels incomplete. Next time, you will have the opportunity to pace yourself differently if you need to work more quickly. If you are not sure what an appropriate time is for a particular task, ask several people how long they would take.

USING COGNITIVE STRATEGIES TO CHANGE OBSESSIONAL BELIEFS

In chapter 7, we described a number of techniques that are useful for changing perfectionistic thoughts. The techniques that are most likely to be effective for changing thoughts that are associated with OCD and OCPD include: evaluating the evidence for your beliefs, learning to compromise, taking another person's perspective, hypothesis testing, looking at the big picture, using coping statements, and learning to tolerate uncertainty (see chapter 7 for detailed descriptions).

Following is an example of how learning to change thoughts can reduce obsessive-compulsive thinking:

Meg:　　It seems like all of my spare time is spent doing housework.

Therapist:　Why do you spend so much time cleaning?

Meg:　　I grew up in a home where cleanliness was very important. I guess I worry that if the house is not clean, guests will think I'm a slob.

Therapist:　How much cleaning do you actually do?

Meg:　　On weekdays, I clean for about an hour before work and for about three hours after dinner. On weekends, I spend up to six hours a day cleaning. Each day, I try to wash the floors, vacuum my carpets, dust the entire apartment, and clean inside and under the stove and fridge. On weekends, I do bigger jobs like cleaning the windows and cleaning out the fireplace.

Therapist:　Do your friends spend as much time cleaning as you do?

Meg:　　No. In fact, when I visit friends there are often dishes in the sink and sometimes the floors are quite dirty.

Therapist:　What do you think of friends who have homes that are not as clean as your apartment?

Meg: It doesn't really bother me, as long as it's someone else's home.

Therapist: Do you think that other people are offended when they visit your friends and see dishes in the sink?

Meg: Probably not.

Therapist: Then how likely is it that people will be offended or judge you negatively if your floors are not washed daily or if there is a dish or two in your sink?

Meg: I guess it's unlikely. It just doesn't feel right to have people over without spending the day cleaning first.

Therapist: Is it possible that your tendency to be overly clean might make people uncomfortable?

Meg: Actually, several people have commented on how clean my apartment is and how they were fearful of spilling a drink or making a mess. I have several friends who seem less relaxed at my apartment than when we get together at another home.

Therapist: Perhaps you could test out the accuracy of your predictions by inviting several friends over after a few days of not vacuuming, dusting, or cleaning the floors. Leave some dishes in the sink, and leave the couch cushions messy. Seeing how people react to this change will help you to determine whether all your cleaning really makes a difference in what people think of you.

CHAPTER 15

Perfectionism, Dieting, and Body Image

DIETING AND BODY IMAGE CONCERNS IN WESTERN CULTURE

Anyone influenced by Western culture is likely aware that they live in a society that is preoccupied with appearance. Thin is in, and people go to great lengths to attain the thin beauty ideal. This culture equates thinness with beauty, and furthermore, associates thinness with all sorts of positive character traits. The most common way to gain control over one's physical appearance is through dieting. Dieting is a multibillion dollar industry in the United States. According to some estimates, the American public spends more on diet-related products (books, videos, pills, and so on) than the government spends on education, employment, and social services combined (Brownell and Rodin 1994). Dieting can also put people at risk for developing certain problems, including eating disorders.

The drive to be thin appears to be a socio-cultural phenomenon. Variables such as a person's culture and the period in which he or she grew up have an enormous impact on the way they view body shape and dieting. It has been estimated that 39 percent of women and 21 percent of men in the United States are dieting at any one time (Hill 2002). These numbers are considerably higher than the 7 percent of men and 14 percent of women who described themselves as dieters in the year 1950 (Brownell and Rodin 1994).

The prevalence of eating disorders has also increased dramatically over the past few decades. In addition, cultural differences appear to affect the incidence of eating disorders as well. One study assessed the prevalence of eating disorders among Egyptian women studying in Cairo universities and Egyptian women studying in British universities (Nasser 1986). Whereas 12 percent of the women studying in England met criteria for an eating disorder, there were no instances of eating disorders among women in the Egyptian universities. Not surprisingly, there is evidence that the prevalence of eating disorders is increasing in non-Western countries, as their economies become more industrialized and their people become more influenced by Western cultures. In fact, a recent study of women living in Tanzania found that the incidence of eating disorders was directly related to the degree of exposure to Western culture and media (Eddy, Hennessey, and Thompson-Brenner 2007). In addition, a study of people from the Old Order Amish community, who live in the United States but are separated from Western industrial society, found that young Amish did not have the same body image problems as young people in Western industrial society (Platte, Zelten, and Stunkard 2000).

PERFECTIONISM AND THE DRIVE TO BE THIN

People who diet restrict their food intake not only in the hopes of losing weight, but also in order to avoid becoming fat. As much as thinness is viewed as a positive trait in our culture, fatness is viewed as negative and is associated with all sorts of negative character traits. From a young age, children tend to discriminate against overweight children, and this carries into adulthood, where overweight people suffer from prejudices in many areas of life.

These societal standards encourage perfectionism. This perfectionism is often carried out in the way that people eat. Many people engage in black-and-white thinking when they think about food. They consider some foods forbidden (like cookies and ice cream) and others permissible (like salads and fruits). We often hear people remark that they have "been good today" if they have adhered to their diets and consider themselves "failures" if they have eaten some of those forbidden foods. In effect, this perfectionistic style of thinking sets people up for difficulties with eating, and perfectionism is often associated with body image problems and eating disorders (Bardone-Cone et al. 2007)

Psychologists Peter Herman and Janet Polivy devised a boundary model of eating that explains how dieters (people who restrict their food intake in order to prevent weight gain) and nondieters (people who do not engage in such behaviors) eat (1984). Nondieters, on a simple level, eat when they feel hungry and stop when they are full. In other words, satiety (fullness) acts as a boundary, or a "stop-eating" mechanism. Dieters, on the other hand, have set up for themselves a diet boundary. Dieters decide that if they eat a certain amount, they have maintained their diets, but if they eat more than that amount, they have broken their diets. Usually, the diet boundary acts as a stop-eating mechanism, but if the diet is broken, dieters will eat lots of food, often until they are overly full. Herman and Polivy have called this the "what the hell" effect— once the diet is broken, dieters think that they may as well eat with abandon, usually indulging in foods that are considered forbidden.

Biological factors also play a role in causing dieters to break their diets. An important factor in why dieters fail to stay on their diets is the body's powerful drive to meet its basic energy needs. By definition, dieters chronically take in less energy (food) than the body requires to meet its energy needs—with the goal of lowering the overall body weight. The body's natural defense against starvation is to overeat, having endured severe caloric restriction.

A great deal of self-control is required to fight the body's natural drive to feed itself. There are many factors that can undermine this self-control, including experiencing social pressure to eat fattening food, drinking alcohol, and feeling depressed. Dieters also tend to engage in overeating when they feel anxious, particularly when they are made to feel bad about themselves. Researchers have suggested that overeating serves as a way of escaping self-awareness (Polivy and Herman 1993). It is less distressing to focus on food (how it tastes, smells, and so on) than to focus on feeling bad about oneself. However, this strategy is helpful only in the short term. After overeating, dieters tend to feel guilty and even worse about themselves than before they started eating. The failure to maintain the self-control required in dieting and the bad feelings that result from this failure can precipitate episodes of overeating and further bad feelings. Therefore, dieters get caught in a vicious cycle.

In general, dieters are more perfectionistic than nondieters. As we already mentioned, dieters set up a beauty ideal for themselves that they would like to attain. Often, this ideal is unrealistic and based on what they see in the media. Dieters also set up unrealistic standards for eating, often restricting their intake to dangerously low levels. As mentioned earlier, the body's natural defense against starvation is to overeat. For example, in one study conducted by a researcher named Keys, a group of healthy men (with no previous issues around eating or body weight) were put on a severely restricted diet (Keys et al. 1950). Interestingly, these men ended up having episodes of overeating after having endured severe caloric restriction. In addition, the men in this study became preoccupied with food. Their conversations and daydreams often revolved around eating, food, and related topics.

Although a tendency to be overly concerned with body shape can affect anyone, women are especially prone to having unrealistic standards regarding weight (Cohn and Adler 1992). In one study, Killen and colleagues found that one-third of tenth grade girls believed they were overweight, even when they were not (1986).

PERFECTIONISTIC THOUGHTS RELATED TO EATING AND WEIGHT

Researchers have consistently shown that a person's beliefs about dieting and weight have an enormous impact on eating-related problems, including tendencies to be underweight; engage in binge eating; or engage in various purging behaviors such as self-induced vomiting, laxative abuse, and excessive exercise. Following is a list of perfectionistic thoughts that contribute to concerns about eating and weight. As you read the list, pay attention to particular beliefs that you hold:

- Some foods are forbidden; some are permissible.

- If I eat a forbidden food, I have messed up my diet.

- If I eat a bit of a forbidden food, I may as well eat tons of it, since I already broke my diet.

- If I eat a forbidden food, I'll get fat.

- If I start to eat, I'll lose control.

- I can never be too thin.

- I feel fat, therefore I *am* fat.

- If my clothes are too small, it's because I am fat.

- I have to exercise (purge, take laxatives, and so on) after eating, or I'll get fat.

- You can't get anywhere in this world if you're fat.

- I'll never find a boyfriend/girlfriend (or a job, friends, and so on) unless I'm thin.

- I'll only be special and unique if I'm thin.

- If I gain a few pounds, I'll keep going until I'm obese.

- I have to look like _____ (model, actress, and so on).

PERFECTIONISM AND OTHER CONCERNS ABOUT YOUR PHYSICAL APPEARANCE

Although weight and body shape are among the most common sources of body dissatisfaction, people are often unhappy with other aspects of their physical appearance. You may believe that the curve of your nose is unattractive or that your balding head is a turnoff to other people. In fact, people's tendency to be displeased with the way they look helps to fund an entire industry of plastic surgeons, as well as manufacturers of cosmetics and other products designed to help people look their "best." Being unhappy with your physical appearance is often caused by setting unnecessarily high standards regarding how you *should* look, despite the fact that other people are typically much less critical of your appearance than you might think. Following are some physical features that tend to be a source of dissatisfaction for some people:

- Receding hairline or baldness

- Too much hair (on face, chest, back, arms, and so on)

- Unhappy with hair type (for example, curly versus straight hair)

- Wrinkles, graying hair, sagging facial features, and other signs of aging

- Being too short or too tall

- Body parts that are too big or too small (for example, nose, ears, breasts)

- Poor complexion

- Unhappy with face (for example, double chin, small cheekbones, asymmetrical face)

- Unhappy with other body parts (for example, feet, hands, legs)

- Unhappy with other physical features (for example, voice, body odors, posture)

PERFECTIONISTIC BEHAVIORS THAT CONTRIBUTE TO BODY-IMAGE PROBLEMS

Almost everyone likes to look their best. Because it feels good to be complimented on one's physical appearance, most people try to look good. However, people who are overly concerned about their physical appearance tend to rely too often on strategies for improving or masking perceived physical flaws. In addition, they tend to engage in behaviors that maintain their unrealistic standards by preventing them from disproving their perfectionistic beliefs. Chapter 4 describes various behaviors that contribute to perfectionism.

Following is a list of behaviors that are particularly relevant to body-image problems. Most people engage in these behaviors from time to time. However, if you have particularly strong beliefs about the importance of your physical appearance, you may be using these behaviors excessively, to the point that they are costing you in terms of their financial impact (cosmetics, salon services, and cosmetic surgery are expensive), the time they take up (spending several hours a day trying to look perfect doesn't leave much time for other things), their potential threat to your health (being underweight can be dangerous), or their impact on your emotional well-being (for example, withdrawing socially leads to a reduction in the number of pleasurable activities you experience). Some examples of perfectionistic behaviors linked to body image include:

- Frequent checking and measuring (for example, looking in the mirror, weighing self)

- Excessive grooming (constantly fixing hair, fussing with blemishes)

- Wearing clothes that are too small (this can maintain the belief that you are overweight, even if you're not)

- Hiding body parts that you believe are unappealing (for example, wearing large clothes to hide your figure, long pants to hide your legs, a hat to hide a balding head, and so on)

- Avoiding contact with other people (for fear of rejection because of your appearance)

- Excessive weight-loss behaviors (such as dieting, exercise, purging, diet pills, and so on)

- Cosmetic surgery

- Excessive use of cosmetic products and services (like makeup, hair dye, frequent expensive haircuts, electrolysis, tanning salons)

- Reading and information seeking (for example, reading fashion and beauty magazines)

- Comparing your appearance to that of other people

PSYCHOLOGICAL PROBLEMS ASSOCIATED WITH A DISTORTED BODY IMAGE

A number of psychological disorders are associated with distorted attitudes and perceptions regarding body shape and physical appearance. These include the eating disorders anorexia nervosa and bulimia nervosa, as well as body dysmorphic disorder, which is a condition associated with body-image problems unrelated to eating and weight.

Anorexia Nervosa

Anorexia nervosa is diagnosed when a person refuses to maintain a weight that is at least 85 percent of that expected for the individual's height and age (American Psychiatric Association 2000). In addition, people with this condition have an intense fear of becoming fat, even though they are actually underweight. Individuals with anorexia nervosa also have distorted beliefs regarding their body shape, including denial that they are underweight or a tendency for their self-esteem to be almost entirely tied to their weight. To be diagnosed with this disorder, women must have stopped menstruating for at least three months, which is an indicator of starvation. At very low weights, the female body is unable to produce the hormones necessary for menstruation. Of course, this criterion does not apply to males, who make up about 10 percent of the people who suffer from anorexia nervosa (Weltzin et al. 2005).

The most serious problems associated with anorexia nervosa involve complications associated with being severely underweight. These include low blood pressure, lowered levels of potassium and sodium, heart problems, low iron, decreased bone mass, hormonal changes, hair loss, brittle fingernails, dry skin, and in some cases, death. In fact, complications of anorexia nervosa were responsible for the deaths of musician Karen Carpenter and gymnast Christy Henrich, among others. In addition, anorexia nervosa is often associated with other psychological problems, such as depression, obsessive-compulsive disorder, and substance abuse.

Treatment of Anorexia Nervosa

Although findings from treatment studies have been mixed, most experts believe that medications are relatively ineffective for treating anorexia nervosa. Instead, nonmedical treatments are typically used (Wilson and Fairburn 2007). The first stage of treatment involves helping the person to gain weight. If the person is severely underweight, this stage may occur on an inpatient basis so that possible medical complications can be managed.

Weight gain is achieved by structuring all food intake and ensuring that the person eats regular meals and snacks. Helping the patient gain weight is often relatively easy, especially if the person's meals are supervised. Ensuring that the person does not relapse is more difficult. Unless the individual learns to change his or her beliefs about eating and body shape, it is unlikely that the weight will be maintained. Typically, the second stage of treatment involves cognitive behavioral therapy (to change attitudes and problem behaviors) and sometimes family therapy (to improve patterns of family communication that may contribute to the problem).

Bulimia Nervosa

Bulimia nervosa is associated with frequent binge eating combined with behaviors designed to keep weight under control (for example, self-induced vomiting, laxative use, exercise, fasting, diet pills). Binge eating involves eating a very large amount of food in a relatively short period of time, along with a perceived lack of control over eating during the binge. In some cases, a binge can include more food than the average person eats in an entire day. In bulimia nervosa, the binge eating and associated purging behaviors must occur at least twice per week for a period of three months or more. In addition, the person's self-evaluation is tied to body shape and weight (American Psychiatric Association 2000).

People with bulimia nervosa tend to be embarrassed about their episodes of bingeing and purging and go to great trouble to prevent others from finding out about their problem. In addition, bulimia is often associated with other problems including depression, anxiety disorders, substance abuse, and various medical complications (such as electrolyte imbalances, dental problems, gastrointestinal problems, and so on) related to binge eating and purging.

Medications for Bulimia

Treatment with selective serotonin reuptake inhibitors (SSRIs) such as fluoxetine (Prozac) appears to be helpful for decreasing binge eating, purging, and depression among people suffering from bulimia nervosa. Other types of antidepressants, including tricyclic antidepressants and monoamine oxidase inhibitors, also have been shown to be effective for treating the symptoms of bulimia (Wilson and Fairburn 2007).

However, there are several reasons to consider a psychological approach before trying medication for this problem. First, studies comparing treatments involving medication to psychological approaches such as cognitive behavioral therapy have generally shown better outcomes with the psychological treatments or a combination of medication and therapy (Whittal, Agras, and Gould 1999). Second, patients tend to drop out of medication treatments more often than cognitive behavioral therapy. Finally, the relapse rates tend to be higher when bulimic patients stop taking their medications, compared to when they stop cognitive behavioral therapy. For more information on antidepressant medications, see chapter 10.

Psychological Treatments for Bulimia

A number of studies have demonstrated that cognitive behavioral therapy is an effective treatment for bulimia (Wilson and Fairburn 2007). This approach includes educating people about the consequences of restricting their food intake, binge eating, and purging. In addition, patients are taught to set goals to gradually develop healthy eating habits and to challenge their perfectionistic and inaccurate attitudes regarding body image, weight, dieting, and eating. Finally, people are helped to recognize the situations, emotions, and thoughts that trigger their urges to restrict, binge, or purge, and they are encouraged to develop healthier coping skills.

Another psychological treatment that may be effective for treating bulimia is called interpersonal psychotherapy (IPT). This approach (described in chapter 10) focuses on helping people find new ways to manage the ways in which they deal with their relationships with other people (Wilson and Fairburn 2007).

Body Dysmorphic Disorder

Body dysmorphic disorder is a preoccupation with a perceived defect in one's appearance. Sometimes the defect is completely imagined, and other times the perception may be based on a small anomaly (for example, a larger than average nose, a barely noticeable scar, and so on), but the person's preoccupation is very much out of proportion to the nature of the actual defect or body feature. The concern about the perceived defect is bothersome or interferes significantly with the person's ability to function at work, in social situations, or in other important life domains (American Psychiatric Association 2000).

The areas that are most commonly a focus of concern among people with body dysmorphic disorder include various parts of the face and head (for example, hair, nose, eyes, lips), as well as other body parts (such as the waist, legs, breasts, buttocks, or penis). Most people with this problem feel as if more than one area of their body is defective, and some individuals are dissatisfied with their entire body. Although many people with this disorder seek cosmetic surgery to correct the imagined defect, they are often unhappy with the results of the surgery or with the surgeon's advice not to have an operation.

Treatment of Body Dysmorphic Disorder

Researchers have only recently begun to examine medication treatments for body dysmorphic disorder. Preliminary findings from several studies suggest that the SSRI antidepressants are effective for treating this condition (Phillips and Hollander 2008). The SSRIs include fluoxetine (Prozac), fluvoxamine (Luvox), sertraline (Zoloft), paroxetine (Paxil), citalopram (Celexa), and escitalopram (Lexapro, Cipralex). These medications are discussed in more detail in earlier chapters on depression (chapter 10) and obsessive-compulsive behavior (chapter 14). Several studies suggest that cognitive behavioral therapy may also be helpful for people suffering from body dysmorphic disorder (Williams, Hadjistavropoulos, and Sharpe 2006). Cognitive strategies are used to teach the individual to identify unrealistic and distorted beliefs about the perceived defect and learn to replace distorted beliefs with a more realistic view. Behavioral strategies such as exposure and response prevention encourage the person to confront anxiety-provoking situations (for example, socializing with other people) without engaging in various behaviors to hide the perceived physical defect. The patient is also encouraged to stop other compulsive rituals such as checking mirrors, asking for reassurance, and making comparisons to other people.

OVERCOMING PERFECTIONISTIC THINKING AND BEHAVIOR IN BODY-IMAGE PROBLEMS

Chapters 7 through 9 describe a number of strategies that are helpful for changing perfectionistic beliefs and behaviors. In this section, we highlight several of these techniques, as well as a few other ideas for dealing with perfectionism in the context of problems related to being overly concerned with your physical appearance.

Education

Education is an important tool for combating distorted beliefs about dieting, body image, and related topics. Unfortunately, there is a lot of bad information out there. The media constantly presents a distorted view of the ideal body shape. Magazines, television, and movies often suggest new diet and exercise plans, show off underweight models and celebrities, and generally send out the message that it is extremely important to be thin and attractive. To combat this potentially harmful message, it's important that you check out the facts regarding diet, exercise, weight, and health.

For example, there is growing evidence that, to a large extent, body weight is determined by genetics. With healthy eating and moderate physical activity, your body will naturally find its genetically preferred weight. Research increasingly suggests that a healthy lifestyle (especially fitness), rather than body weight, is one of the best predictors of health.

Furthermore, the belief that one should control one's weight is associated with more disturbed eating, body dissatisfaction, and poor self-esteem compared to having the belief that one should live a healthy lifestyle (Laliberte et al. 2007).

Challenging Perfectionistic Beliefs

Rather than assuming that your perfectionistic beliefs are true, it is important to test the validity of your beliefs by examining the evidence. The following therapy vignette illustrates some of the questions that you might ask yourself in order to become more accepting of your physical appearance. In this example, Adam is taught to challenge his perfectionistic beliefs about what it means to be balding:

Therapist: How much time do you spend thinking about that fact that you are balding?

Adam: It's on my mind all the time. I haven't dated in about three years, mostly because I'm afraid of having someone discover my bald head. I wear a toupee, but I still worry that it might fall off sometime. If I could afford a hair transplant, I would do it in a second.

Therapist: Do you recall how you came to be so unhappy about being bald?

Adam: I've always hated it. I'm only thirty-five! I should have more hair than I do. I think baldness is unattractive. I think other people find it unattractive as well.

Therapist: Do you have any evidence that other people find baldness unattractive?

Adam: Before I started wearing the toupee, a few people made comments about my thinning hair. Also, I constantly hear jokes about bald people. For example, on Seinfeld, people are always making fun of the fact that the George Costanza character is bald.

Therapist: Have you ever teased someone about some physical characteristic?

Adam: I used to make fun of my brother because he's shorter than me. But now that I've lost my hair, I don't make fun of anyone about anything.

Therapist: Did the fact that you teased your brother mean that shorter people are unattractive?

Adam: I know that some women prefer men who are taller, but I think there are lots of people who couldn't care less.

Therapist: Turning our attention back to Seinfeld, is George's balding head the only thing that was ever made fun of on the show?

Adam: No. In fact, that show makes fun of everything and everyone.

Therapist: So, it's possible to be teased about almost any physical feature. What does that say about your earlier statement that you knew that your baldness was unattractive because you were teased?

Adam: I guess that just because I was teased doesn't mean that it's ugly.

Therapist: Can you think of any evidence that baldness is attractive?

Adam: Well, there are a number of bald celebrities that I know many people find attractive. People like Bruce Willis, Sean Connery, and Patrick Stewart. Also, lots of people shave their heads. I guess that means that they find baldness attractive.

Therapist: What if someone did find you unattractive because you were bald? Would that mean that everyone would find you unattractive?

Adam: I suppose not. Different people like different things.

Changing Social-Comparison Habits

Perfectionism often leads to the habit of comparing oneself to other people who are seen as better in particular dimensions. For example, if you are overly concerned about being overweight (even though you are at a healthy weight), you may tend to compare yourself to people who are underweight. Or, you may compare your current weight to your weight in the past, at a time when you were strictly dieting and therefore likely below your natural, healthy weight. These types of comparisons serve to maintain your perfectionistic thoughts. If you are overly concerned about your weight, you need only consider the body type you may have inherited from your family (collect information about your parents and extended family—what did they weigh at your age, and what were their eating and exercise habits at the time?). You might also try to determine what your own adult weight has been at times in your life when you were eating a healthy diet and exercising moderately.

Finally, instead of focusing on people whose body type is different than yours (although perhaps what you consider to be more ideal), try to see what is attractive in people whose body type is closer to your own. Comparisons with extremely thin people (such as models) are what lead many women to try dieting. For most women, this means fighting your natural body type. Not surprisingly, 95 to 98 percent of dieters regain the weight they lose within five years. In the meantime, many struggle with binge eating and feelings of failure. Learning to evaluate your lifestyle rather than your weight and learning to compare yourself to those of your body type are extremely important steps in changing unrealistic, perfectionistic thoughts and attitudes about your body.

Similarly, if you are dissatisfied with the size of your nose, it is not helpful to compare yourself to people with smaller noses. If your nose is larger than average, you will find that most people have smaller noses, but that will tell you very little about *your* physical attractiveness. Remember, half of the people you encounter each day also have noses that are bigger than average. It doesn't necessarily mean that you are unattractive. In fact, most people are different than the average person in one feature or another. If you must compare yourself to other people, don't just make comparisons based on your physical features that bother you.

Hypothesis Testing and Exposure

One of the most powerful ways of testing perfectionistic thoughts about your physical appearance is to create small experiments that are likely to disprove your beliefs. For example, if you are fearful that other people won't be attracted to you if you are wearing shorts, try wearing shorts when you are out with other people and see what happens. Chances are that people will treat you no differently than when you're wearing long pants.

If the thought of having other people see some aspect of your physical appearance is terrifying, exposure practices may be helpful. Exposure (described fully in chapter 8) involves entering a feared situation repeatedly for an extended period, until the situation no longer produces anxiety. To deal with distorted perceptions regarding some aspect of your body, practices may include allowing people to see the "defective" feature. For example, practices may involve taking off your hat to expose your bald head or not wearing makeup in order to expose a mole or scar. You may want to start by making a list of avoided situations, rank-ordering them, and trying them out gradually.

Preventing Safety Behaviors

Preventing safety behaviors involves stopping the behaviors that you rely on to reduce your anxiety about your physical appearance. Following are examples of how this strategy can be used for various problems related to distorted body image:

- Avoid weighing yourself more than once per month.

- Do not look in the mirror except when getting ready for work in the morning.

- Comb your hair no more than twice per day.

- Do not wear sunglasses to cover your eyes.

- Stop all dieting and purging.

- Stop going to tanning salons.

PART 4

What Next?

CHAPTER 16

Preventing Perfectionism from Returning

EVALUATING YOUR PROGRESS

At the end of chapter 5, we mentioned that the process of assessing your perfectionism should be an ongoing one. Now that you have worked through this book, the next step is to evaluate the current status of your perfectionism. One way of doing this is to return to the issues raised in the chapter on assessment (chapter 5) and other early chapters and to re-evaluate where you're at currently. In your journal, answer each of the following questions:

EXERCISE 16.1 Re-Evaluating Your Perfectionism

Of the perfectionistic thinking styles described in chapter 3, which are currently a problem? Does your perfectionistic thinking occur less often? Are your thoughts less intense and less upsetting than they were at the beginning of treatment?

Of the perfectionistic behaviors described in chapter 4, which are currently a problem? Do you engage in perfectionistic behaviors less often than before? Which behaviors do you still need to work on?

In chapter 5, you began to complete perfectionism diaries whenever you found yourself behaving in a perfectionistic matter. Have these episodes decreased in terms of how frequent, extreme, or upsetting they are?

Are you more flexible in your thinking now that you have learned new strategies for combating perfectionism? For example, if you discover that a particular standard is impossible to meet, are you able to lower your standards to a more realistic level?

Have you noticed a change in the sorts of situations that trigger your perfectionistic responses? Are there fewer triggers now?

In chapter 5, you identified situations that are impacted by your perfectionism (for example, work, school, relationships, and so on). Are the same situations currently affected by your perfectionism? Are they impacted to the same degree as before?

Has your awareness of your perfectionism changed? Are you more aware of the ways in which perfectionism affects (or used to affect) your life? Are you able to notice your perfectionistic thoughts and behaviors more easily than before?

Have others commented on the ways in which your perfectionism has changed? Does your perfectionism affect others less than it did before?

Have you noticed a change in your moods as a result of working through this book? Are your feelings of depression, anxiety, and irritability less frequent or less intense than before?

How much better is your perfectionism? Is it 20 percent better? 50 percent better? 80 percent better? Choose any number from 0 to 100.

THE NEXT STEPS

The strategies in this book are not a *cure* for perfectionism. Chances are that perfectionism is still an issue for you, even if you have been practicing the techniques you have learned. Though a small number of people may overcome all issues with perfectionism as a result of using the strategies in this book, for most people the gains are likely to be more modest. We hope that you have noticed significant changes, that you have become less of a perfectionist than before, and that your tendency to feel anxious, depressed, or irritable has decreased. However, despite how much better things may be, it is possible that you will continue to struggle with perfectionism from time to time. So what's next? Here are some options for possible next steps.

Continue to Use the Strategies in This Book

If the strategies in this book have been useful, but you still have some remaining perfectionism that you want to work on, you can continue to use the strategies in this book to work on your remaining issues. For example, you can continue to complete perfectionism diaries, to monitor and challenge your perfectionistic thoughts, to confront situations that make you feel uncomfortable, and to practice accepting your uncomfortable feelings rather than fighting them or trying to make them go away.

Seek More Detailed Information

For some readers, a general book on perfectionism like this one may not provide enough detail for the specific problems they are dealing with. For example, if your perfectionism is mostly related to depression, then a treatment focused on depression may be important for you. Similarly, a more specialized program for anger management, social anxiety, worry, body-image issues, or obsessive-compulsive problems may be warranted if any of these are issues for you. Further Readings, at the back of this book, provides recommended readings that focus on these issues in more detail.

Find Professional Help

In some cases, working through these strategies on your own may be difficult. The support of a professional who can either prescribe medications or help you to apply the psychological strategies described in this book may be helpful. If you have tried to use these strategies on your own and have experienced only limited success, this may be a good time to seek professional help. Chapter 6 provides suggestions for how to find a qualified professional. A therapist can help you work on your perfectionism more generally or work on some of the more specific problems that are often associated with perfectionism, such as depression, anxiety disorders, or difficulties in managing anger and aggression.

MAINTAINING YOUR GAINS

Although there is evidence that the strategies in this book often lead to a reduction in perfectionism and associated problems, there is currently no research on the *long-term* benefits of these strategies. In other words, little is known about whether the effects of treatment for perfectionism are long lasting. However, based on what we know about cognitive-behavioral therapy (CBT) for other problems, there is a good chance that your improvements will continue over time. For many readers, the gains made as a result of the strategies in this book will be permanent. For others, there is a risk that some of your perfectionistic behaviors will start to slip back into your day-to-day life. This section discusses factors that may contribute to a return of perfectionism and strategies that you can use to keep your perfectionism away.

What Causes Perfectionism to Return?

Unfortunately, there are no studies that address the question of what causes perfectionism to return once it has been treated. However, there a number of factors that may play a role in whether your perfectionism will worsen in the future:

The Types of Associated Problems You Experience

People who have overcome an episode of depression have a high likelihood of experiencing additional periods of depression in the future, particularly if they have experienced multiple periods of depression in the past. If you have recently overcome an episode of depression, there are a number of strategies that can help to prevent additional episodes of depression, including mindfulness meditation, maintenance CBT, and maintenance medications. The book *Ending the Depression Cycle* (Bieling and Antony 2003) provides detailed advice on how to prevent future episodes of depression. In contrast to depression, problems with anxiety (for example, worry, social anxiety, obsessive-compulsive problems) are less likely to return once they have been successfully treated, particularly with CBT. Nevertheless, a return of symptoms is possible with anxiety-based problems as well.

The Type of Treatment You Received

For many psychological problems, CBT is more likely to lead to long-term gains than medications. Once treatment ends, a return of symptoms is more likely if treatment was with medication rather than CBT.

Stress

Stress puts people at risk for whatever problems they are prone to experience. For example, people who tend to get headaches are more likely to get them during or following periods of stress. People who tend to experience depression, panic attacks, or drinking too much alcohol often report more of these problems when under stress. If you are prone to be a perfectionist, these tendencies are likely to be worse when you are under stress at work, at home, or in other aspects of your life. Fortunately, your level of perfectionism should improve when your level of stress decreases.

Responses from Others in Your Family, at Work, or Elsewhere

If your perfectionism is beneficial to other people, you may find that others prefer for you to continue your perfectionist ways. For example, your partner might miss the old days when you did all the housework so you could make sure it was done to your standards. Similarly, your boss might prefer the time when you worked 80 hours per week to make sure all of your work got done. If you get rewarded for being a perfectionist by those around you, it may be more difficult for you to stick to your new, non-perfectionist standards. Discussing these issues with those who expect you to maintain your perfectionist ways may be useful.

Falling Back into Old Patterns of Thinking and Behaving

If you exercise regularly for a few months and then you suddenly stop, you would expect your muscles to return to their old, weakened state, right? The same is true for perfectionism. If you start to go back to your old ways of thinking about situations and your old ways of behaving, your difficulties will return. It's important to continue challenging your negative thinking, to confront situations that make you anxious, and to emphasize acceptance of your emotional states rather than constantly trying to minimize discomfort.

Keeping Your Perfectionism Away for Good

Based on the above discussion on the factors that affect whether your perfectionism is likely to return, you can probably guess what you need to do to keep it away for good. First, it is important to continue to use the strategies that have been most helpful. Although it may not be necessary to continue to complete perfectionism diaries and the other exercises described throughout this book, it is important to continue to question your perfectionistic thoughts when they occur, to test out the validity of your thoughts by conducting small experiments, and to confront situations directly when you find yourself wanting to avoid them. You need to use the strategies described in chapters 7, 8, and 9 on a regular basis to maintain your gains.

In addition, it's important during times of stress to keep your perfectionism in check. Find ways to manage your stress effectively. For example, make time for yourself. Take a break from whatever is causing you stress to see a movie or go for a walk. Pay attention to your lifestyle habits. Be sure to get enough sleep, to eat properly, and to exercise. Some of the strategies described in this book (for example, relaxation, mindfulness meditation, challenging negative thinking) are useful for managing general stress levels as well.

Coping with a Return of Your Perfectionism

If you notice that your perfectionism gets worse at some point in the future, pull out this book again and start to review the strategies that you found to be most useful the first time. If they worked for you once, chances are that they will work for you again, either on your own or with the support of a professional.

CONCLUSION

We hope this book introduced you to new skills that will help you to deal more effectively with your perfectionism and with the situations where it tends to get triggered. The more you practice these skills, the more improvement you will see. Best of luck as you continue to let go of the rules and standards that have been holding you back until now!

Further Readings

PERFECTIONISM

Self-Help Readings

Burns, D. D. 1980. The perfectionist's script for self-defeat. *Psychology Today* November, 34–57.

Basco, M. R. 1999. *Never Good Enough: How to Use Perfectionism to Your Advantage without Letting It Ruin Your Life.* New York: Touchstone.

Readings for Professionals

Flett, G. L., and P. L. Hewitt, eds. 2002. *Perfectionism: Theory, Research, and Treatment.* Washington, DC: American Psychological Association.

Video Resources

Antony, M. M. 2008. *Cognitive Behavioral Therapy for Perfectionism Over Time.* DVD. Washington, DC: American Psychological Association.

COGNITIVE BEHAVIORAL THERAPY

Self-Help Readings

Burns, D. D. 1999. *The Feeling Good Handbook, Rev. ed.* New York: Plume.

Butler, G. and T. Hope. 2007. *Managing Your Mind: The Mental Fitness Guide.* 2nd ed. New York: Oxford University Press.

Greenberger, D. and C. A. Padesky. 1995. *Mind Over Mood: Change How You Feel by Changing the Way You Think.* New York: Guilford Press.

McKay, M., M. Davis and P. Fanning. 2007. *Thoughts and Feelings: Taking Control of Your Moods and Your Life.* 3rd ed. Oakland, CA: New Harbinger Publications.

Readings for Professionals

Antony, M. M., D. R. Ledley and R. G. Heimberg, eds. 2005. *Improving Outcomes and Preventing Relapse in Cognitive Behavioral Therapy.* New York: Guilford Press.

Barlow, D. H., ed. 2008. *Clinical Handbook of Psychological Disorders.* 4th ed. New York: Guilford Press.

Beck, J. S. 1995. *Cognitive Therapy: Basics and Beyond.* New York: Guilford Press.

Beck, J. S. 2005. *Cognitive Therapy for Challenging Problems: What to Do When the Basics Don't Work.* New York: Guilford Press.

Bieling, P. J., R. E. McCabe and M. M. Antony. 2006. *Cognitive Behavioral Therapy in Groups.* New York: Guilford Press.

O'Donohue, W., J. E. Fisher and S. C. Hayes, eds. 2003. *Cognitive Behavior Therapy: Applying Empirically Supported Techniques in Your Practice.* Hoboken, NJ: Wiley.

Richard, D. C. S. and D. Lauterbach. 2007. *Handbook of Exposure Therapies.* New York: Academic Press.

Wright, J. H., M. R. Basco and M. E. Thase. 2006. *Learning Cognitive-Behavior Therapy: An Illustrated Guide.* Washington, DC: American Psychiatric Press.

COMMUNICATION TRAINING

Self-Help Readings

Christensen, A. & N. S. Jacobson. 2000. *Reconcilable Differences.* New York: Guilford Press.

Davis, M., K. Paleg and P. Fanning. 2004. *The Messages Workbook: Powerful Strategies for Effective Communication at Work and Home.* Oakland, CA: New Harbinger.

Honeychurch, C. and A. Watrous. 2003. *Talk to Me: Conversation Tips for the Small-Talk Challenged.* Oakland, CA: New Harbinger Publications.

MacInnis, J. L. 2006. *The Elements of Great Public Speaking: How to Be Calm, Confident, and Compelling.* Berkeley, CA: 10 Speed Press.

McKay, M., M. Davis and P. Fanning. 2009. *Messages: The Communications Skills Book.* 3rd ed. Oakland, CA: New Harbinger.

McKay, M., P. Fanning and K. Paleg. 2006. *Couple Skills: Making Your Relationship Work.* 2nd ed. Oakland, CA: New Harbinger.

Monarth, H. and L. Kase. 2007. *The Confident Speaker: Beat Your Nerves and Communicate at Your Best in Any Situation.* New York: McGraw-Hill.

Patterson, R. J. 2000. *The Assertiveness Workbook: How to Express Your Ideas and Stand Up for Yourself at Work and in Relationships.* Oakland, CA: New Harbinger Publications.

PROCRASTINATION

Self-Help Readings

Burka, J. B. and L. M. Yuen. 1983. *Procrastination: Why You Do It and What to Do About It.* Reading, MA: Addison-Wesley.

Knauss, W. 2002. *The Procrastination Workbook: Your Personalized Program for Breaking Free of the Patters That Hold You Back.* Oakland, CA: New Harbinger Publications.

DEPRESSION

Self-Help Readings

Addis, M. E. and C. R. Martell. 2004. *Overcoming Depression One Step at a Time: The New Behavioral Activation Approach to Getting Your Life Back.* Oakland, CA: New Harbinger Publications.

Bieling, P. J. and M. M. Antony. 2003. *Ending the Depression Cycle: A Step-by-Step Guide for Preventing Relapse.* Oakland, CA: New Harbinger Publications.

Knauss, W. J. 2006. *The Cognitive Behavioral Workbook for Depression: A Step-by-Step Program.* Oakland, CA: New Harbinger Publications.

Williams, M., J. Teasdale, Z. Segal, and J. Kabat-Zinn. 2007. *The Mindful Way Through Depression: Freeing Yourself from Chronic Unhappiness.* New York: Guilford Press.

Readings for Professionals

Beck, A. T., A. J. Rush, B. F. Shaw, and G. Emery. 1979. *Cognitive Therapy of Depression.* New York: Guilford Press.

Gotlib, I. H. and C. L. Hammen. 2009. *Handbook of Depression,* 2nd ed. New York: Guilford Press.

Persons, J. B., J. Davidson, and M. A. Tompkins. 2001. *Essential Components of Cognitive-Behavioral Therapy for Depression.* Washington, DC: American Psychological Association.

Segal, Z. V., J. M. G. Williams, and J. D. Teasdale. 2002. *Mindfulness-Based Cognitive Therapy for Depression: A New Approach to Preventing Relapse.* New York, NY: Guilford Publications.

Weissman, M. M., J. C. Markowitz, and G. L. Klerman. 2000. *Comprehensive Guide to Interpersonal Psychotherapy.* New York: Basic Books.

Whisman, M. A. 2008. *Adapting Cognitive Therapy for Depression: Managing Complexity and Comorbidity.* New York: Guilford Press.

ANGER

Self-Help Readings

Eifert, G. H., M. McKay, and J. P. Forsyth. 2005. *ACT on Life, Not on Anger: The New Acceptance and Commitment Therapy Guide for Problem Anger.* Oakland, CA: New Harbinger Publications.

McKay, M., P. D. Rogers, and J. McKay. 2003. *When Anger Hurts: Quieting the Storm Within,* 2nd ed. Oakland, CA: New Harbinger Publications.

Nay, W. R. 2004. *Taking Charge of Anger: How to Resolve Conflict, Sustain Relationships, and Express Yourself without Losing Control.* New York: Guilford Press.

Readings for Professionals

DiGiuseppe, R. and R. C. Tafrate. 2007. *Understanding Anger Disorders.* New York: Oxford University Press.

Feindler, E. L. 2006. *Anger-Related Disorders: A Practitioner's Guide to Comparative Treatments.* New York: Springer.

ANXIETY AND WORRY

Self-Help Readings

Antony, M. M. and P. J. Norton. 2009. *The Anti-Anxiety Workbook: Proven Strategies to Overcome Worry, Panic, Phobias, and Obsessions.* New York: Guilford Press.

Davis, M., E. R. Eshelman, and M. McKay. 2008. *The Relaxation and Stress Reduction Workbook.* 6th ed. Oakland, CA: New Harbinger Publications.

Forsyth, J. P. and G. H. Eifert. 2007. *The Mindfulness and Acceptance Workbook for Anxiety: A Guide to Breaking Free from Anxiety, Phobias, and Worry Using Acceptance and Commitment Therapy.* Oakland, CA: New Harbinger Publications.

Gyoerkoe, K. L. and P. S. Wiegartz. 2006. *10 Simple Solutions to Worry: How to Calm Your Mind, Relax Your Body, & Reclaim Your Life.* Oakland, CA: New Harbinger Publications.

Hazlett-Stevens, H. 2005. *Women Who Worry Too Much: How to Stop Worry and Anxiety from Ruining Relationships, Work, & Fun.* Oakland, CA: New Harbinger Publications.

Readings for Professionals

Antony, M. M. and M. B. Stein. 2009. *Oxford Handbook of Anxiety and Related Disorders.* New York: Oxford University Press.

Antony, M. M. and R. P. Swinson. 2000. *Phobic Disorders and Panic in Adults: A Guide to Assessment and Treatment.* Washington, DC: American Psychological Association.

Barlow, D. H. 2002. *Anxiety and Its Disorders: The Nature and Treatment of Anxiety and Panic.* 2nd ed. New York: Guilford Press.

Bernstein, D. A., T. D. Borkovec, and H. Hazlett-Stevens. 2000. *New Directions in Progressive Relaxation Training: A Guidebook for Helping Professionals.* Westport, CT: Praeger.

Davey, G. C. L. and A. Wells, eds. 2006. *Worry and Its Psychological Disorders: Theory, Assessment, and Treatment.* Chichester, UK: Wiley.

Dugas, M. J. and M. Robichaud. 2007. *Cognitive-Behavioral Treatment for Generalized Anxiety Disorder.* New York: Routledge.

Eifert, G. H. and J. P. Forsyth. 2005. *Acceptance and Commitment Therapy for Anxiety Disorders: A Practitioner's Treatment Guide to Using Mindfulness, Acceptance, and Values-Based Behavior Change Strategies.* Oakland, CA: New Harbinger Publications.

Hazlett-Stevens, H. 2008. *Psychological Approaches to Generalized Anxiety Disorder: A Clinician's Guide to Assessment and Treatment*. New York: Springer.

Heimberg, R. G., C. L. Turk, and D. S. Mennin, eds. 2004. *Generalized Anxiety Disorder: Advances in Research and Practice*. New York: Guilford Press.

Rygh, J. L. and W. C. Sanderson. 2004. *Treating Generalized Anxiety Disorder: Evidence-Based Strategies, Tool, and Techniques*. New York: Guilford Press.

SOCIAL AND PERFORMANCE ANXIETY

Self-Help Readings

Antony, M. M. 2004. *10 Simple Solutions to Shyness: How to Overcome Shyness, Social Anxiety, and Fear of Public Speaking*. Oakland, CA: New Harbinger Publications.

Antony, M. M. and R. P. Swinson. 2008. *The Shyness and Social Anxiety Workbook: Proven, Step-by-Step Techniques for Overcoming Your Fear*. 2nd ed. Oakland, CA: New Harbinger Publications.

Hope, D. A., R. G. Heimberg, H. R. Juster, and C. L. Turk. 2000. *Managing Social Anxiety*. New York: Oxford University Press.

Stein, M. B. and J. R. Walker. 2002. *Triumph over Shyness: Conquering Shyness and Social Anxiety*. New York: McGraw-Hill.

Readings for Professionals

Antony, M. M. and K. Rowa. 2008. *Social Anxiety Disorder: Psychological Approaches to Assessment and Treatment*. Göttingen, Germany: Hogrefe.

Beidel, D. C. and S. M. Turner. 2007. *Shy Children, Phobic Adults: Nature and Treatment of Social Anxiety Disorder*, 2nd ed. Washington, DC: American Psychological Association.

Crozier, W. R. and L. E. Alden, eds. 2005. *The Essential Handbook of Social Anxiety for Clinicians*. Hoboken, NJ: Wiley.

Heimberg, R. G. and R. E. Becker. 2002. *Cognitive-Behavioral Group Therapy for Social Phobia: Basic Mechanisms and Clinical Strategies.* New York: Guilford Press.

Hofmann, S. and M. W. Otto. 2008. *Cognitive-Behavior Therapy of Social Phobia: Evidence-Based and Disorder Specific Treatment Techniques.* New York: Routledge.

Hope, D. A., R. G. Heimberg, and C. L. Turk. 2006. *Managing Social Anxiety: A Cognitive Behavioral Therapy Approach Therapist Guide.* New York: Oxford University Press.

Video Resources

Albano, A. M. 2006. *Shyness and Social Phobia.* DVD. Washington, DC: American Psychological Association.

Rapee, R. M. 1999. *I Think They Think: Overcoming Social Phobia.* DVD. New York: Guilford Press.

OBSESSIVE-COMPULSIVE DISORDER

Self-Help Readings

Foa, E. B. and R. Wilson. 2001. *Stop Obsessing! How to Overcome Your Obsessions and Compulsions,* rev ed. New York: Bantam Books.

Grayson, J. 2004. *Freedom from Obsessive-Compulsive Disorder: A Personalized Recovery Program for Living with Uncertainty.* New York: Berkley Publishing Group.

Hyman, B. M. and C. Pedrick. 2005. *The OCD Workbook: Your Guide to Breaking Free from Obsessive-Compulsive Disorder.* 2nd ed. Oakland, CA: New Harbinger Publications.

Purdon, C. and D. A. Clark. 2005. *Overcoming Obsessive Thoughts: How to Gain Control of Your OCD.* Oakland, CA: New Harbinger Publications.

Steketee, G. and R. O. Frost. 2007. *Compulsive Hoarding and Acquiring Workbook.* New York: Oxford University Press.

Tolin, D., R. O. Frost, and G. Steketee. 2007. *Buried in Treasures: Help for Compulsive Acquiring, Saving, and Hoarding.* New York: Oxford University Press.

Readings for Professionals

Abramowitz, J. S. 2006: *Obsessive-Compulsive Disorder.* Cambridge, MA: Hogrefe & Huber.

Abramowitz, J. S. 2006: *Understanding and Treating Obsessive-Compulsive Disorder: A Cognitive Behavioral Approach.* Mahwah, NJ: Erlbaum.

Abramowitz, J. S. and A. C. Houts, eds. 2005. *Obsessive-Compulsive Disorder: Concepts and Controversies.* New York: Springer.

Abramowitz, J. S., D. McKay, and S. Taylor. 2008. *Clinical Handbook of Obsessive-Compulsive Disorder and Related Problems.* Baltimore, MD: Johns Hopkins University Press.

Abramowitz, J. S., D. McKay, and S. Taylor. 2008. *Obsessive-Compulsive Disorder: Subtypes and Spectrum Conditions.* New York: Elsevier.

Antony, M. M., C. Purdon, and L. J. Summerfeldt. 2007. *Psychological Treatment of Obsessive-Compulsive Disorder: Fundamentals and Beyond.* Washington, DC: American Psychological Association.

Clark, D. A. 2004. *Cognitive-Behavioral Therapy for OCD.* New York: Guilford Press.

Rachman, S. 2003. *The Treatment of Obsessions.* New York: Oxford University Press.

Rachman, S. 2006. *Fear of Contamination: Assessment and Treatment.* New York: Oxford University Press.

Steketee, G., and R. O. Frost. 2007. *Compulsive Hoarding and Acquiring Therapist Guide.* New York: Oxford University Press.

Wilhelm, S. and G. S. Steketee. 2006. *Cognitive Therapy for Obsessive-Compulsive Disorder: A Guide for Professionals.* Oakland, CA: New Harbinger Publications.

Video Resources

Antony, M. M. 2007. *Obsessive-Compulsive Behavior.* DVD. Washington, DC: American Psychological Association.

Wilson, R. R. 2005. *Obsessive-Compulsive Disorder.* DVD. Washington, DC: American Psychological Association.

BODY IMAGE AND EATING DISORDERS

Self-Help Readings

Cash. T. F. 2008. *The Body Image Workbook: An 8-Step Program for Learning to Like Your Looks.* 2nd ed. Oakland, CA: New Harbinger Publications.

Claiborn, J. and C. Pedrick. 2002. *The BDD Workbook: Overcome Body Dysmorphic Disorder and End Body Image Obsessions.* Oakland, CA: New Harbinger Publications.

Heffner, M. and G. H. Eifert. 2004. *The Anorexia Workbook: How to Accept Yourself, Heal Your Suffering, and Reclaim Your Life.* Oakland, CA: New Harbinger Publications.

McCabe, R. E., T. L. McFarlane, and M. P. Olmsted. 2004. *The Overcoming Bulimia Workbook: Your Comprehensive, Step-by-Step Guide to Recovery.* Oakland, CA: New Harbinger Publications.

Wilhelm, S. 2006. *Feeling Good About the Way You Look: A Program for Overcoming Body Image Problems.* New York: Guilford Press.

Readings for Professionals

Cash, T. F. and T. Pruzinsky. 2004. *Body Image: A Handbook of Theory, Research, and Clinical Practice.* New York: Guilford Press.

Fairburn, C. G. 2008. *Cognitive Behavior Therapy and Eating Disorders.* New York: Guilford Press.

Fairburn, C. G. and K.D. Brownell. 2002. *Eating Disorders and Obesity: A Comprehensive Handbook.* 2nd ed. New York: Guilford Publications.

References

Ackman, D. 2004. Martha Trial: 'Change the Hold Music—Or Else'. *Forbes,* February 5. http://www.forbes.com/2004/02/05/cx_da_0205martha.html.

American Psychiatric Association. 2000. *Diagnostic and Statistical Manual of Mental Disorders* 4th. ed., text revision. Washington, DC: Author.

Antony, M. M., F. Downie, and R. P. Swinson. 1998. Diagnostic issues and epidemiology in obsessive compulsive disorder. In R. P. Swinson, M. M. Antony, S. Rachman, and M. A. Richter (Eds.). *Obsessive Compulsive Disorder: Theory, Research, and Treatment,* 3–32. New York: Guilford Press.

Antony, M. M., R. E. McCabe, I. Leeuw, N. Sano, and R. P. Swinson. 2001. Effect of distraction and coping style on in vivo exposure for specific phobia of spiders. *Behaviour Research and Therapy* 39:1137-1150.

Antony, M. M. and P. J. Norton. 2009. *The Anti-Anxiety Workbook: Proven Strategies to Overcome Worry, Panic, Phobias, and Obsessions.* New York: Guilford Press.

Antony, M. M., C. L. Purdon, V. Huta, and R. P. Swinson. 1998. Dimensions of perfectionism across the anxiety disorders. *Behaviour Research and Therapy* 36:1143-1154.

Antony, M. M. and K. Rowa. 2008. *Social Anxiety Disorder: Psychological Approaches to Assessment and Treatment.* Göttingen, Germany: Hogrefe.

Antony, M. M. and R. P. Swinson. 2008. *Shyness and Social Anxiety Workbook: Proven, Step-by-Step Techniques for Overcoming Your Fear.* 2nd ed. Oakland, CA: New Harbinger Publications.

Ashbaugh, A., M. M. Antony, A. Liss, L. J. Summerfeldt, R. E. McCabe, and R. P. Swinson. 2007. Changes in perfectionism following cognitive-behavioral treatment for social phobia. *Depression and Anxiety* 24:169-177.

Bailey, Jr., G. R. 1998. Cognitive-behavioral treatment of obsessive-compulsive personality disorder. *Journal of Psychological Practice* 4:51-59.

Bardone-Cone, A. M., S. A. Wonderlich, R. O. Frost, C. M. Bulik, J. E. Mitchell, S. Uppala, and H. Simonich. 2007. Perfectionism and eating disorders: Current status and future directions. *Clinical Psychology Review* 27:384-405.

Barlow, D. H. 2002, *Anxiety and Its Disorders: The Nature and Treatment of Anxiety and Panic* 2nd ed. New York: Guilford Press.

Beck, A. T., A. J. Rush, B. F. Shaw, and G. Emery. 1979. *Cognitive Therapy of Depression.* New York: Guilford Press.

Bieling, P. J. and M. M. Antony. 2003. *Ending the Depression Cycle: A Step-by-Step Guide for Preventing Relapse.* Oakland, CA: New Harbinger Publications.

Birley, A. J., N. A. Gillespie, A. C. Heath, P. F. Sullivan, D. I. Boomsma, and N. G. Martin. 2006. Heritability and nineteen-year stability of long and short EPQ-R Neuroticism scales. *Personality and Individual Differences* 40:737-747.

Bishop, S. R., M. Lau, S. Shapiro, L. Carlson, N. D. Anderson, J. Carmody, Z. V. Segal, S. Abbey, M. Speca, D. Velting, and G. Devins. 2004. Mindfulness: A proposed operational definition. *Clinical Psychology: Science and Practice* 11:230–241.

Blatt, S. J., J. P. D'Afflitti, and D. M. Quinlan. 1976. Experiences of depression in normal young adults. *Journal of Abnormal Psychology* 85:383-389.

Britton, J. C. and S. L. Rauch. 2009. Neuroanatomy and neuroimaging of anxiety disorders. In *Oxford Handbook of Anxiety and Related Disorders*, 97–110. eds. M. M. Antony and M. B. Stein. New York: Oxford University Press.

Brownell, K. D. and J. Rodin. 1994. The dieting maelstrom: Is it possible and advisable to lose weight? *American Psychologist* 49:781–791.

Bruch, M. A. 1989. Familial and developmental antecedents of social phobia: Issues and findings. *Clinical Psychology Review* 9:37–47.

Burns, D. D. 1980. The perfectionist's script for self-defeat. *Psychology Today*, November, 34-57.

Chelminski, R. 2005. *The Perfectionist: Life and Death in Haute Cuisine*. London, UK: Penguin.

Clark, D. M. and F. McManus. 2002. Information processing in social phobia. *Biological Psychiatry* 51:92-100.

Cohn, J. F. and N. E. Adler. 1992. Female and male perceptions of ideal body shapes: Distorted views among Caucasian college students. *Psychology of Women Quarterly* 16:69-79.

Cox, B. J., and M. W. Enns. 2003. Relative stability of dimensions of perfectionism in depression. *Canadian Journal of Behavioural Science* 35:124-132.

Craighead, W. E., E. S. Sheets, A. L. Brosse, and S. S. Ilardi. 2007. Psychosocial treatments for major depressive disorder. In *A Guide to Treatments that Work*. 3rd ed., eds. P. E. Nathan and J. M. Gorman. New York: Oxford University Press.

Cramer, P. and T. Steinwert. 1998. Thin is good, fat is bad: How early does it begin? *Journal of Applied Developmental Psychology* 19:429-451.

Crockenberg, S. 1985. Toddler's reactions to maternal anger. *Merrill-Palmer Quarterly* 31:361–373.

Dalrymple, K. L. and J. D. Herbert. 2007. Acceptance and Commitment Therapy for generalized social anxiety disorder: A pilot study. *Behavior Modification* 31:543-568.

Deffenbacher, J. L., E. R. Oetting, and R. A. DiGiuseppe. 2002. Principles of empirically supported interventions applied to anger management. *Counseling Psychologist* 30:262-280.

DiGiuseppe, R. and R. C. Tafrate. 2007. *Understanding Anger Disorders.* New York: Oxford University Press.

Dougherty, D. D., S. L. Rauch, and M. A. Jenike. 2007. Pharmacological treatments for obsessive-compulsive disorder. In *A Guide to Treatments that Work.* 3rd ed., eds. P. E. Nathan and J. M. Gorman. New York: Oxford University Press.

Eddy, K. T., M. Hennessey, and H. Thompson-Brenner. 2007. Eating pathology in East African women: The role of media exposure and globalization. *Journal of Nervous and Mental Disease* 195:196-202.

Eifert, G. H., M. McKay, and J. P. Forsyth. 2005. *ACT on Life, Not on Anger: The New Acceptance and Commitment Therapy Guide for Problem Anger.* Oakland, CA: New Harbinger Publications.

Enns, M. W. and B. J. Cox. 2005. Perfectionism, stressful life events, and the 1-year outcome of depression. *Cognitive Therapy and Research* 29:541-553.

Feindler, E. L. 2006. *Anger-Related Disorders: A Practitioner's Guide to Comparative Treatments.* New York: Springer.

Flett, G. L., A. Besser, R. A. Davis, and P. L. Hewitt. 2003. Dimensions of perfectionism, unconditional self-acceptance, and depression. *Journal of Rational-Emotive and Cognitive-Behavior Therapy* 21:119-138.

Flett, G. L. and P. L. Hewitt. 2002. Perfectionism and maladjustment: An overview of theoretical, definitional, and treatment issues. In *Perfectionism: Theory, Research, and Treatment,* G. L. Flett and P. L. Hewitt, eds., 5–31. Washington, DC: American Psychological Association.

Forsyth, J. P. and G. H. Eifert. 2007. *The Mindfulness and Acceptance Workbook for Anxiety: A Guide to Breaking Free from Anxiety, Phobias, and Worry Using Acceptance and Commitment Therapy.* Oakland, CA: New Harbinger Publications.

Frost, R. O., P. Marten, C. Lahart, and R. Rosenblate. 1990. The dimensions of perfectionism. *Cognitive Therapy and Research* 14:449-468.

Furmark, T., M. Tillfors, I. Marteinsdottir, H. Fischer, A. Pissiota, B. Långström, and M. Fredrikson. 2002. Common changes in cerebral blood flow in patients with social phobia treated with citalopram or cognitive-behavioral therapy. *Archives of General Psychiatry* 59:425–433.

Gorenstein, E. E., F. A. Tager, P. A. Shapiro, C. Monk, and R. P. Sloan. 2007. Cognitive-behavior therapy for reduction of persistent anger. *Cognitive and Behavioral Practice* 14:168-184.

Hassmén, P., N. Koivula, and A. Uutela. 2000. Physical exercise and psychological well-being: A population study in Finland. *Preventive Medicine: An International Journal Devoted to Practice and Theory* 30:17-25.

Hayes, S. C., V. M. Follette, and M. M. Linehan. 2004. *Mindfulness and Acceptance: Expanding the Cognitive-Behavioral Tradition.* New York: Guilford Press.

Hayes, S. C., K. D. Strosahl, and K. G. Wilson. 1999. *Acceptance and Commitment Therapy: An Experiential Approach to Behavior Change.* New York: Guilford Press.

Heffner, M. and G. H. Eifert. 2004. *The Anorexia Workbook: How to Accept Yourself, Heal Your Suffering, and Reclaim Your Life.* Oakland, CA: New Harbinger Publications.

Herman, C. P. and J. Polivy. 1984. A boundary model for the regulation of eating. In A. J. Stunkard and E. Steller, eds., *Eating and Its Disorders,* 918-927. New York: Raven Press.

Hewitt, P. L. and G. L. Flett. 1990. Perfectionism and depression: A multidimensional analysis. *Journal of Social Behavior and Personality* 5:423-438.

———. 1993. Dimensions of perfectionism, daily stress, and depression: A test of a specific vulnerability hypothesis. *Journal of Abnormal Psychology* 102:58-65.

Hill, A. J. 2002. Prevalence and demographics of dieting. In *Eating Disorders and Obesity: A Comprehensive Handbook*. 2nd ed., eds. C. G. Fairburn and K. D. Brownell, 80-83. New York: Guilford Press.

Hill, N. 1937. *Think and Grow Rich*. Meriden, CT: The Ralston Society.

Hill, R. W., K. McIntire, and V. R. Bacharach. 1997. Perfectionism and the big five factors. *Journal of Social Behavior and Personality* 12:257-270.

Huesmann, L. R. and L. D. Taylor. 2006. The role of media violence in violent behavior. *Annual Review of Public Health* 27:393-415.

Izard, C. E. 1991. *The Psychology of Emotions*. New York: Plenum Press.

Jang, K. L., W. J. Livesley, and P. A. Vernon. 1996. Heritability of the big five personality dimensions and their facets: A twin study. *Journal of Personality*, 64:577-591.

Kabat-Zinn, J. 1990. *Full Catastrophe Living: Using the Wisdom of Your Body and Mind to Face Stress, Pain, and Illness*. New York: Dell Publishing.

———. 1994. *Wherever You Go, There You Are: Mindfulness Meditation in Everyday Life*. New York: Hyperion.

Kain, K. 1995. *Movement Never Lies: An Autobiography*. Toronto: McLelland and Stewart.

Kandel, E. R. 1983. From metapsychology to molecular biology: Explorations into the nature of anxiety. *American Journal of Psychiatry* 140:1277–1293.

Katzmarzky, P. T. and C. Davis. 2001. Thinness and body shape of Playboy centerfolds from 1978 to 1998. *International Journal of Obesity* 25:590-592.

Kessler, R. C., P. Berglund, O. Demler, R. Jin, and E. E. Walters. 2005. Lifetime prevalence and age-of-onset distributions of DSM-IV disorders in the National Comorbidity Survey Replication. *Archives of General Psychiatry* 62:593-602.

Keys, A., J. Brozek, A. Henschel, O. Michelson, and H. L. Taylor. 1950. *The Biology of Human Starvation* Vol. 1. Minneapolis: University of Minnesota Press.

Killen, J. D., C. B. Taylor, M. J. Telch, K. E. Saylor, D. J. Maron, T. N. Robinson. 1986. Self-induced vomiting and laxative and diuretic use among teenagers: Precursors of the binge-purge syndrome. *Journal of the American Medical Association* 25:1447–1449.

Laliberté, M., M. Newton, R. McCabe, and J. S. Mills. 2007. Controlling your weight versus controlling your lifestyle: How beliefs about weight control affect risk for disordered eating, body dissatisfaction, and self-esteem. *Cognitive Therapy and Research.* 31:853-869.

Lemerise, E. A. and K. A. Dodge. 2008. The development of anger and hostile interactions. In M. Lewis, J. M. Haviland and L. F. Barrett, eds., *Handbook of Emotions.* 3rd ed. New York: Guilford Press.

Marcks, B. A. and D. W. Woods. 2007. Role of thought-related beliefs and coping strategies in the escalation of intrusive thoughts: An analog to obsessive-compulsive disorder. *Behaviour Research and Therapy* 45:2640-2651.

Mathew, S. J., J. M. Amiel, and H. A. Sackeim. 2005. Electroconvulsive therapy in treatment-resistant depression. *Primary Psychiatry,* 12:52-56.

McCrae, R. R. and P. T. Costa. 2003. *Personality in adulthood: A five-factor theory perspective.* 2nd ed. New York: Guilford Press.

McKay, M., Davis, M. and P. Fanning. 2009. *Messages: The Communication Skills Book.* 3rd ed. Oakland, CA: New Harbinger Publications.

Merriam-Webster Online Dictionary. 2008. *Perfectionism,* http://www. merriam-webster.com/dictionary/perfectionism. June 26, 2008.

Mogg, K. and B. P. Bradley. 2005. Attentional bias in generalized anxiety disorder versus depressive disorder. *Cognitive Therapy and Research* 29:29-45.

Moscovitch, D. A., M. M. Antony, and R. P. Swinson. 2009. Exposure-based treatments for anxiety disorders: Theory and process. In M. M. Antony and M. B. Stein, eds., *Oxford Handbook of Anxiety and Related Disorders,* 461–475. New York: Oxford University Press.

Nasser, M. 1986. Comparative study of the prevalence of abnormal eating attitudes among Arab female students of both London and Cairo universities. *Psychological Medicine* 16:621–625.

Ng, R. M. K. 2005. Cognitive therapy for obsessive-compulsive personality disorder: A pilot study in Hong Kong Chinese patients. *Hong Kong Journal of Psychiatry* 15:50-53.

Phillips, K. A. and E. Hollander. 2008. Treating body dysmorphic disorder with medication: Evidence, misconceptions, and a suggested approach. *Body Image* 5:13-27.

Platte, P., J. F. Zelten, and A. J. Stunkard. 2000. Body image in the Old World Amish: A people separate from "the world." *International Journal of Eating Disorders* 28:408-414.

Pleva, J. and T. D. Wade. 2007. Guided self-help versus pure self-help for perfectionism: A randomized controlled trial. *Behaviour Research and Therapy* 45:849-861.

Polivy, J. and C. P. Herman. 1993. Etiology of binge eating: Psychological mechanisms. In C. G. Fairburn and G. T. Wilson, eds., *Binge Eating: Nature, Assessment, and Treatment,* 173-205. New York: Guilford Press.

Polizzi, T. N. 2008. An examination of mindfulness-based cognitive therapy for angry drivers. *Dissertation Abstracts International: Section B: The Sciences and Engineering* 68(8-B):5588.

Purdon, C. 2004. Empirical investigations of thought suppression in OCD. *Journal of Behavior Therapy and Experimental Psychiatry,* 35:121-136.

Purdon, C. and D. A. Clark. 2002. The need to control thoughts. In R. O. Frost and G. Steketee, *Cognitive Approaches to Obsessions and Compulsions: Theory, Assessment and Treatment,* 29-43. Amsterdam, Netherlands: Pergamon.

Purdon, C., K. Rowa, and M. M. Antony. 2005. Thought suppression and its effects on thought frequency, appraisal and mood state in individuals with obsessive-compulsive disorder. *Behaviour Research and Therapy* 43:93-108.

Rachman, S. J. 1976. The passing of the two-stage theory of fear and avoidance: Fresh possibilities. *Behaviour Research and Therapy* 14:125-131.

Radke-Yarrow, M. and G. Kochanska. 1990. Anger in young children. In N. L. Stein, B. Levinthal and T. Trabasso, eds., *Psychological and Biological Approaches to Emotion,* 297-310. Hillsdale, NJ: Erlbaum.

Riley, C., M. Lee, Z. Cooper, C. G. Fairburn, and R. Shafran. 2007. A randomized controlled trial of cognitive-behaviour therapy for clinical perfectionism: A preliminary study. *Behaviour Research and Therapy* 45:221-2231.

Rodebaugh, T. L., R. M. Holaway, and R. G. Heimberg. 2004. The treatment of social anxiety disorder. *Clinical Psychology Review* 24:883-908.

Roemer, L. and S. M. Orsillo. 2007. An open trial of an acceptance-based behavior therapy for generalized anxiety disorder. *Behavior Therapy* 38:72–85.

Rowa, K., R. E. McCabe, and M. M. Antony. 2006. Specific phobias. In F. Andrasik, ed., *Comprehensive Handbook of Personality and Psychopathology, Volume 2: Adult psychopathology,* 154-168. Hoboken, NJ: John Wiley and Sons.

Roy-Byrne, P. P. and D. S. Cowley. 2007. Pharmacological treatments for panic disorder, generalized anxiety disorder, specific phobia, and social anxiety disorder. In *A Guide to Treatments that Work,* 3rd ed., eds. P. E. Nathan and J. M. Gorman, 395-430. New York: Oxford University Press.

Rudolph, S. G., G. L. Flett, and P. L. Hewitt. 2007. Perfectionism and deficits in cognitive emotion regulation. *Journal of Rational-Emotive and Cognitive-Behavior Therapy* 25:343-357.

Serretti, A., R. Calati, B. Ferrari, and D. De Ronchi. 2007. Personality and genetics. *Current Psychiatry Reviews* 3:147-159.

Snyder, J., L. Schrepferman, M. Brooker, and M. Stoolmiller. 2007. The roles of anger, conflict with parents and peers, and social reinforcement in the early development of physical aggression. In Cavell,

T.A., and K.T. Malcolm, eds., *Anger, aggression and interventions for interpersonal violence*, 187-214. Mahwah, NJ: Erlbaum.

Stahl, S. M. 2008. *Depression and Bipolar Disorder: Stahl's Essential Psychopharmacology*. 3rd ed. New York: Cambridge University Press.

Stein, M. B. and D. J. Stein. 2008. Social anxiety disorder. *Lancet* 371:1115-1125.

Sternberg, C. R., and J. J. Campos. 1990. The development of anger expressions in infancy. In *Psychological and Biological Approaches to Emotion*, eds. N. L. Stein, B. Leventhal, and T. Trabasso. Mawah, NJ: Erlbaum.

Stewart, E. S., E. Jenike, and M. A. Jenike. 2009. Biological treatment for obsessive-compulsive disorder. In *Oxford Handbook of Anxiety and Related Disorders*, 375–390. eds. M. M. Antony and M. B. Stein. New York: Oxford University Press.

Sullivan, P. F., M. C. Neale, and K. S. Kendler. 2000. Genetic epidemiology of major depression: Review and meta-analysis. *American Journal of Psychiatry* 157:1552-1562.

Teasdale, J. D., Z. V. Segal, J. M. G. Williams, V. Ridgeway, J. Soulsby, and M. Lau. 2000. Prevention of relapse/recurrence in major depression by mindfulness-based cognitive therapy. *Journal of Consulting and Clinical Psychology* 68:615-623.

Thase, M. E. Forthcoming. Neurobiological aspects of depression. In *Handbook of Depression*. 2nd ed., eds. I. H. Gotlib and C. L. Hammen. New York: Guilford Press.

Thase, M. E., J. C. Nelson, G. I. Papakostas, and M. J. Gitlin. 2007. Augmentation strategies in the treatment of major depressive disorder. *CNS Spectrums* 12 (suppl. 22):1–20.

Tozzi, F., S. H. Aggen, B. M. Neale, C. B. Anderson, S. E. Mazzeo, M. C. Neale, and C. M. Bulik. 2004. The structure of perfectionism: A twin study. *Behavior Genetics* 34:483-494.

van Grootheest, D., D. C. Cath, A. T. Beekman, and D. I. Boomsma. 2005. Twin studies on obsessive-compulsive disorder: A review. *Twin Research and Human Genetics* 5:450-458.

Weissman, M. M., J. C. Markowitz, and G. L. Klerman 2000. *Comprehensive Guide to Interpersonal Psychotherapy*. New York: Basic Books.

Weltzin, T. E., N. Weisensel, D. Franczyk, K. Burnett, C. Klitz, and P. Bean. 2005. Eating disorders in men: Update. *Journal of Men's Health and Gender* 2:186-193.

Whittal, M. L., W. S. Agras, and R. A. Gould. 1999. Bulimia nervosa: A meta-analysis of psychosocial and pharmacological treatments. *Behavior Therapy* 30:117-135.

Wilde, O. 2005. *The Picture of Dorian Gray*. In *The Complete Works of Oscar Wilde: Volume III: The Picture of Dorian Gray: The 1890 and 1891 Texts*. New York: Oxford University Press.

Williams, J., T. Hadjistavropoulos, and D. Sharpe. 2006. A meta-analysis of psychological and pharmacological treatments for body dysmorphic disorder. *Behaviour Research and Therapy* 44:99-111.

Williams, M., J. Teasdale, Z. Segal, and J. Kabat-Zinn. 2007. *The Mindful Way Through Depression: Freeing Yourself from Chronic Unhappiness*. New York: Guilford Press.

Wilson, G. T. and C. G. Fairburn. 2007. Treatments for eating disorders. In *A Guide to Treatments That Work*, 3rd ed., eds. P. E. Nathan and J. M. Gorman, 579-609. New York: Oxford University Press.

Winfrey, O. 2000. Oprah's Cut with Martha Stewart. *Oprah Magazine*, September. http://www.oprah.com/omagazine/200008/omag_200008_martha.jhtml.

Wittchen, H. U. and J. Hoyer. 2001. Generalized anxiety disorder: Nature and course. *The Journal of Clinical Psychiatry* 62:15-21.

Martin M. Antony, Ph.D., is professor of psychology at Ryerson University in Toronto, ON, Canada. He is also director of research at the Anxiety Treatment and Research Centre at St. Joseph's Healthcare in Hamilton, ON, Canada, and president-elect of the Canadian Psychological Association. He has published twenty-five books and more than one hundred scientific papers and book chapters in the areas of cognitive behavior therapy and anxiety disorders. He has received early career awards from the Society of Clinical Psychology (American Psychological Association), the Canadian Psychological Association, and the Anxiety Disorders Association of America, and is a fellow of the American and Canadian Psychological Associations. He is past president of the Anxiety Disorders Special Interest Group of the Association for Behavioral and Cognitive Therapies, and has been program chair for the Association for Behavioral and Cognitive Therapies annual conference guide annual convention. He is actively involved in clinical research in the area of anxiety disorders, teaching, and education, and he maintains a private clinical practice. Antony lives in Toronto, ON, Canada. His website is www.martinantony.com.

Richard P. Swinson, MD, is professor emeritus and past chair of the Department of Psychiatry and Behavioural Neurosciences in the Faculty of Health Sciences at McMaster University in Hamilton, ON, Canada. He is also medical director of the Anxiety Treatment and Research Centre and past psychiatrist-in-chief at Joseph's Healthcare, also in Hamilton. He is a fellow of the Royal College of Physicians and Surgeons of Canada, the American Psychiatric Association, and the Royal College of Psychiatrists UK. He was awarded an inaugural fellowship of the Canadian Psychiatric Association in 2006. His research interests lie in the theory, assessment, and treatment of anxiety disorders, particularly obsessive-compulsive disorder and social anxiety disorder. He has published more than 180 peer-reviewed papers, thirty book chapters, and eight books. Dr. Swinson has held numerous research grants since 1966 and has been an invited speaker at many conferences around the world on anxiety disorders and substance abuse disorders. He also chaired the steering committee for the Canadian Anxiety Treatment Guidelines Initiative, leading to the publication of Canadian Clinical Practice Guidelines for the Management of Anxiety Disorders in 2006. He lives in Toronto, ON, Canada.